WHEN GIANTS CONVERGE

WHEN GIANTS CONVERGE

The Role of U.S.— Japan Direct Investment

Dorothy B. Christelow

M.E. Sharpe
Armonk, New York
London, England

Library of Congress Cataloging-in-Publication Data

Christelow, Dorothy B., 1916–
When giants converge : the role of U.S.-Japan direct investment /
by Dorothy B. Christelow.
p.   cm.
Includes bibliographical references and index.
ISBN 1-56324-114-5 (c) — ISBN 1-56324-115-3 (p)
1. Investment, Foreign.
2. Investments, American—Japan.
3. Investments, Japanese—United States.
I. Title.
HG4538.C518   1994
332.6′73—dc20   94-28479
CIP

Printed in the United States of America

The paper used in this publication meets the minimum requirements of
American National Standard for Information Sciences—
Permanence of Paper for Printed Library Materials,
ANSI Z 39.48-1984.

BM (c)   10   9   8   7   6   5   4   3   2   1
BM (p)   10   9   8   7   6   5   4   3   2   1

Contents

List of Tables

Acknowledgments

This book has benefited from many sessions of the Japan Economic Seminar. Two bearing directly on U.S.-Japan direct investment were especially helpful, one session on an earlier paper by the author and another on a paper by Kenneth Froot. Former colleagues at the Federal Reserve Bank of New York—Charles Pigott, Robert McCauley, and Christine Cumming—read an earlier version of the first chapter and provided extremely useful comments. Other chapters received similar treatment from Michael Smitka, Nancy Teeters, and Philip Swan.

At the Department of Commerce, members of the Bureau of Economic Analysis especially Gregory C. Fouch and Patricia C. Walker, were generous in providing information on data revisions and answering numerous questions. Donald Dalton and Phyllis Genther Yoshida, who have worked extensively on Japanese direct investment in U.S. manufacturing, helped enormously by making their database available. At the Japan Economic Institute, Susan MacKnight provided useful interpretation of her own pioneering data collection and wide-ranging analysis, and Douglas Ostrom was helpful in rounding up elusive bits of information.

Any remaining errors and odd opinions are the sole responsibility of the author.

Part I

Overview

1

Changing Roles of the United States and Japan in International Direct Investment

To understand direct investment relations between the United States and Japan since the end of World War II, it is useful to start with an overall view of the two nations' changing roles in international direct investment worldwide. Direct investments by multinationals establishing business operations abroad have made an especially important contribution to global growth and development because of their dual nature—a flow of financial capital and, often, an associated flow of technology. The latter includes product technologies such as a semiconductor performing new functions, and process technologies such as new methods of manufacture or improvements in that semiconductor. The associated technology flows can occur when multinationals invest abroad to exploit their superior technology or to acquire superior technology from others, or possibly both.

During this period, transactions between industrial countries have dominated international direct investment. This investment and associated technology transmission have made a major contribution to the convergence of the technologies and productivity of industrial countries. In global financial direct investment, the United States reversed its role from that of major source in the early postwar years to major absorber in the 1980s, then reverted to a role of modest net investor in the early 1990s. Japan, a minor player in the early years, became the world's largest net investor in the late 1980s and the early 1990s. This transformation of the two countries' financial direct investment roles was related, somewhat loosely, to a reversal of their roles in international capital flows as a whole, and their changing abilities to generate savings in excess of investment.

In related technology flows, the United States was the world's technology leader and largest net exporter of technology in the early postwar period while Japan was the largest net importer. But in more recent years, as technology levels in Japan and other industrial countries pulled closer to those in the United States, the U.S. and Japanese roles became somewhat more balanced but specialized. In product innovation, the United States remained the world leader and a net exporter of product technology, but only by a narrowing margin. Japan approached balance in its global transfers of product technology but remained a net importer from industrial countries. But in process technology—notably manufacturing methods—Japan took the lead and became a net exporter while the United States became a net importer. These changing roles were associated with a convergence of the technology levels of industrial countries.

The first section of this chapter describes the part played by international direct investment in theories of industrial organization and economic growth, and the convergence of the technology levels of industrial countries. The second section describes changing global patterns of financial direct investment flows, the major factors influencing them, and their relation to the balance of payments of major industrial countries. The third section takes a broad first look at the evidence on direct investment–related technology flows and their contribution to the converging technologies of industrial countries.

Direct Investment, Growth, and Converging Technologies

Direct investment differs from other international financial transactions in that the investor acquires part or whole ownership in a business enterprise operating in a foreign country and the investment is frequently associated with the international transfer of what has been variously described as "intangible assets" or "technology." Technology includes not only product innovations but also new methods of management, planning, manufacturing, and sales—what is sometimes called "process technology." The combined financial and technology flows reflect the investing firm's strategy for exploiting its strengths and correcting its weaknesses. These strengths and weaknesses are conditioned by the home country's factor endowments and its stage of economic development—as reflected in levels of education, infrastructure, technology, financial wealth, and savings patterns—relative to the rest of the world.

In the early postwar years, when the United States was both a world leader in technology and a heavy net outward investor, the typical U.S.-based multinational corporation invested abroad to exploit its superior technology, transferring some of that technology, along with financial capital, to foreign countries. Observing this, economists focusing on industrial organization and multinational corporations often described direct investment as a method of exploiting superior technology. In their analysis, technology and capital were bundled together and described as "industry-specific" capital. By the 1970s, when Japan began to make direct investments in industrial countries, Tsurumi (1976) noted that some of these investments were made to acquire technology. Caves (1982) described both lines of analysis in his well-known survey of the literature. As net direct investment flows into the United States gathered force in the 1980s, many U.S. analysts gave more attention to the financial factors influencing direct investment. Some—Reich and Mankin (1986), for example—complained that foreign investors—the Japanese, in particular—were using their access to lower cost capital to acquire U.S. technology that they could then use to compete against U.S. companies.

Direct investment also plays a part in the theory of the growth and convergence of productivity and technology among industrial countries. In the 1950s, a number of writers, beginning with Fabricant (1954), noted that the growth of total output in any economy was not associated solely with increases in the inputs of labor and capital and attributed much of the residual to increases in technology inputs. In the 1960s, others attempted to measure and compare rates of growth in capital and labor inputs and the implied growth of technology. Denison (1962, 1967) was a pioneer in such efforts. Later, Denison and Chung (1976) collaborated to compare sources of growth in Japan with those of other industrial countries in the 1950s and 1960s. Their detailed analysis found technology growth fastest in Japan. Ohkawa and Rosovsky (1973) incorporated a similar approach in their analysis of sources of Japan's strong growth from the Meiji restoration through the 1960s.

In the 1980s, economists' interests shifted to the effect of differing growth rates among countries on convergence of their technologies. Applying the same residual approach, statistical analysis shifted to comparing *levels* of national technologies, labeled "total factor productivity" (TFP) and measured as the ratio of total output to a weighted average of capital and labor inputs. To assure international comparability, outputs and inputs were valued at internationally comparable purchasing power parity prices.

TFP estimates differ considerably with respect to what output and factor inputs are measured. But taken together, they suggest that in the early postwar years, technology levels were far higher in the United States than in other industrial countries, and that technology levels have risen far faster in other industrial countries than in the United States and thus are approaching convergence with U.S. levels. Some of the results from some recent studies will be introduced later in this chapter.

In the 1980s, a number of economists took exception to the possible implications of earlier growth theory that technology was somehow exogenous, an unexplained deus ex machina over which economic players had no control. They noted that technology was created by inputs of both capital and labor (as in expenditures for research and development). Yet despite many useful contributions, a wholly satisfactory reformulation of basic growth theory remained elusive.[1]

One aspect of the endogeneity of technology, that of how it is transmitted from one country to another, has received considerable attention. Early in the postwar period, Vernon (1966) identified multinationals' direct investment in international production of innovative new products as an important means of technology transmission. Others have developed similar lines of analysis. For example, Tilton (1971) described the early dissemination of U.S. semiconductor technology to Europe and Japan, emphasizing the direct investment by U.S. semiconductor companies. More recently, Cantwell (1989) described direct investments in international production by U.S. multinationals and the competitive response by European and Japanese multinationals as part of the technology dissemination process. Baumol (1986) drew attention to the contribution of transfers of technology through direct investment to the postwar convergence of industrial country technologies. Some analysts, for example Scherer (1992) and Grossman and Helpman (1991), have emphasized international trade, noting the competitive challenge posed by exports to importing countries. In practice, the two influences are closely related, since multinationals often start with exports, then proceed to direct investments, which are followed by more related exports. In any case the introduction of direct investment clearly multiplies the ways in which technology can be transmitted— these will be described in detail in later chapters.

As we will see, direct investment flows among industrial countries in the 1980s played a new and somewhat more complex role in the convergence process. The inflow of net direct investment provided one source of capital to the United States, where savings rates had fallen below those in most other industrial countries and below the level required to continue generating innovative technology. At the same time, direct investment flows generated a net flow of product technology from the United States to other countries, including Japan, and a net flow of Japanese process technology to other industrial countries, especially the United States. The continued net outflow of product technology from the United States no doubt contributed to the convergence of the technologies of industrial countries. However, the net flow of financial capital and process technology into the United States probably slowed convergence.

In the following sections we look first at the roles of the United States and Japan in global direct investment flows, the extent to which they financed important changes in the current account balance of payments of both countries, and the financial incentives to which the two flows responded. This is followed by a preliminary look at the two countries' roles in changing direct investment–related technology flows and the convergence of the technologies of industrial countries.

International Direct Investment Flows and Financial Incentives

Since the end of World War II, international direct investment has been primarily a vehicle for redistributing financial capital, ownership, and technology (as broadly defined) among industrial countries rather than transferring them from industrial countries to developing countries. (In this discussion, "industrial countries" refers to those currently so classified by the International Monetary Fund [IMF], which regularly collects and publishes data on international direct investment. They include the United States, Canada, Japan, Australia, New Zealand, Iceland, and the Western European countries.) Industrial countries generated 99 percent of all international direct investment through the 1970s, and nearly as much in the 1980s and early 1990s. Their absorption of direct investment was more variable but averaged over 75 percent of global flows (see Table 1.1).

Changing Roles of Industrial Countries

The patterns of direct investment flows among industrial countries changed enormously during the postwar period. The record for

Table 1.1

The Role of Industrial Countries in International Direct Investment, 1967–93[a]

	1967–69[b]	1970–74	1975–79	1980–84	1985–89	1990–93
Average annual direct investment ($ bil.)[c]						
Investment abroad	−8,662	−17,952	−36,635	−42,745	−130,042	−183,002
Inward investment	5,441	12,111	21,172	36,832	102,290	118,751
Net flows	−3,221	−5,841	−15,463	−5,913	−27,752	−64,251
Percent of global flows[d]						
Investment abroad	99.6	99.4	98.7	97.3	98.3	97.4
Inward investment	73.9	81.6	75.6	69.7	85.2	78.2

Source: IMF (August 1994). Database for international balance of payments statistics.

[a] IMF defines industrial countries as: Australia, Belgium-Luxembourg, Canada, Denmark, Finland, France, Germany, Greece, Iceland, Italy, Japan, Netherlands, New Zealand, Norway, Portugal, Spain, Sweden, Switzerland, United Kingdom, United States. From June 1990, data for Germany includes former German Democratic Republic.

[b] Country coverage is less complete in 1967–69 than in subsequent years.

[c] Increase in assets is minus.

[d] Due to differences in country definitions of direct investment and missing data, global inward and outward direct investment are not equal.

the quarter century for which we have reasonably complete data is summarized in Table 1.2. The table includes shares in industrial country gross domestic product (GDP) to give a better sense of the importance of each country's direct investment flows relative to its size. Since the shares of direct investment and GDP were derived from aggregates expressed in current dollars, some of the decline in the importance of the United States both as a producer and an investor and the corresponding rise in the importance of other countries are attributable to depreciation of the dollar over the period.

In the late 1960s, the United States was the world's principal net investor, with a share in the industrial country total nearly three times as large as its share in industrial country GDP. The United Kingdom was a net investor on a scale similar to its share in GDP, while Japan was a small net investor relative to its size, directing most of its investments to less developed countries. Other rapidly growing continental European countries and resource-rich Australia and probably Canada were the major net absorbers of direct investment among industrial countries. In the 1970s, the United States remained the largest net investor, but on a sharply diminishing scale, as the flow of investments into the United States rose strongly. Japan, Germany, and the Netherlands joined the United Kingdom as significant net investors. Then, in the 1980s, the United States became the world's largest net absorber of direct investment. By the second half of the decade, Japan became the largest net investor by a wide margin, contributing roughly twice as much as the second largest investor, the United Kingdom. By the early 1990s, it appeared that roles were changing once again as the United States became a modest net investor and the United Kingdom and Canada became small net absorbers. Japan, however, remained the world's largest net investor.

The reversal of the United States' role in the 1980s was the net result of a drop in its contribution to industrial countries' investments abroad, from nearly two-thirds in the late 1960s (somewhat high relative to the United States' share in industrial country gross domestic product) to 16 percent in the second half of the 1980s (very low relative to its share in GDP) and a rise in its share of direct investment absorption, from 17 percent to 47 percent over the same period. Its return to the role of net investor in the early 1990s was almost entirely due to a drop in foreign investment in the United States.

Japan's rise to preeminence as a net investor in the late 1980s and early 1990s was very one-sided, based on a strong rise in investments abroad, from 2 percent of the industrial country total (low relative to its share of industrial country output) to 18 percent (roughly in line with its importance as a producer) and abnormally small inward investment, relative to the country's size. The very low foreign investment in Japan was in part due to exceptionally stringent regulation of those investments in the 1950s and 1960s and to institutional barriers in the 1970s and after. These are described in chapter 2. But in addition, Japanese statistics on direct investment exaggerate the one-sidedness of Japan's direct investment relations, since they omit reinvested earnings, an important element of direct investment that is included in the statistics published by most other industrial countries. Japan, being a relatively new investor, relies less on reinvested earnings than do veteran investors from the United States and Europe. U.S. data for U.S.-Japan bilateral direct investments (as seen in Table 2.1) show that, in the 1980s, reinvested earnings averaged over 90 percent of all U.S. direct investment in Japan but less than 5 percent of Japan's direct investment in the United States.

The very large direct investment flows of the 1980s and early 1990s also dramatically altered the net direct investment positions of the two countries. Table 1.3 offers comparisons for 1980, 1990, and 1993. The U.S. position is reported in terms of current costs (net of depreciation), an accounting procedure adopted in 1991 to give due weight to investments in the three preceding decades. The Japanese position is reported in terms of historic costs, thus understating its position relative to that of the United States even though its investments were largest in the 1980s. In the early 1990s, the United States' direct investment position

Table 1.2

Changing Roles of Industrial Countries in International Direct Investment, 1967–93[a]
(percentage of industrial country totals)

	1967–69[b]	1970–74	1975–79	1980–84	1985–89	1990–93
Investment abroad						
United States	61.8	48.3	43.3	20.5	15.7	20.1
Japan	2.1	5.8	5.8	10.0	18.3	15.0
United Kingdom	14.8	16.8	16.9	21.8	20.3	10.8
Netherlands	c	6.3	9.6	10.5	5.8	7.1
Germany	7.2	8.2	9.1	9.6	8.7	11.2
Canada	c	4.7	4.8	8.8	3.9	3.1
Other industrial countries	9.9	9.9	10.5	18.7	27.3	32.8
Investment absorption						
United States	17.0	17.1	28.8	48.8	46.7	21.7
Japan	1.2	1.0	0.6	0.7	0.1	1.3
United Kingdom	19.9	19.1	19.8	14.3	16.0	16.8
Netherlands	9.2	6.3	5.1	4.6	4.1	6.5
Germany	14.5	12.1	6.7	3.2	3.2	4.8
Canada	c	9.4	4.6	0.0	2.0	5.1
Other industrial countries	38.3	35.0	34.4	28.4	28.0	43.9
Net direct investment[d]						
United States	137.5	113.0	63.3	−155.9	−98.6	17.1
Japan	3.7	15.8	13.0	68.0	85.3	40.4
United Kingdom	6.1	11.9	12.8	69.2	36.0	−0.3
Netherlands	c	6.3	15.7	47.3	12.0	8.1
Germany	−5.0	0.2	12.5	49.5	29.0	22.9
Canada	c	−5.2	5.0	63.4	11.2	−0.5
Other industrial countries	−38.1	−42.0	−22.2	−41.4	25.1	12.3

Memorandum: Gross domestic product

United States	49.7	43.0	37.5	40.4	37.6	33.0
Japan	8.3	11.3	14.0	14.5	19.0	19.4
United Kingdom	6.1	5.6	5.4	6.1	5.6	5.9
Netherlands	1.5	1.8	2.2	1.8	1.6	1.7
Germany	7.6	9.7	10.4	8.6	8.2	9.5
Canada	3.9	4.0	3.8	3.8	3.8	3.3
Other industrial countries	22.8	24.5	26.7	24.7	24.4	27.3

Sources: IMF Database for international balance of payments statistics; OECD, *National Accounts Main Aggregates Volume I* (1960–92), pp. 144–45; OECD (1994).

[a] Industrial countries are those so defined by IMF. See footnote a, Table 1.1.

[b] IMF data for 1967–69 are less complete than for subsequent years. This tends to overstate the role of countries for which complete data are available.

[c] No data for all or part of period.

[d] Since industrial countries as a whole were net investors, net investment absorbers' shares were negative.

Table 1.3

International Direct Investment Positions of the United States and Japan, 1980–93 (in billions of dollars)

	1980	1990	1993
United States (current cost)[a]			
Net direct investment position	270.3	183.9	199.5 p[d]
Direct investment abroad	396.2	620.5	716.2 p[d]
Foreign direct investment	125.9	436.6	516.7 p[d]
Japan (historical cost)[b]			
Net direct investment position	16.4	191.5	242.9
Direct investment abroad	20.1	201.4	259.8
Foreign direct investment	3.7	9.9	16.9
(Memo: U.S. direct investment in			
Japan[c])	(6.2)	(22.5)	(31.3)

Sources: Survey of Current Business (June 1994), p. 71; Ministry of Finance (Japan), *Financial Statistics of Japan* (1981, 1991, 1993).

[a] Current cost of reproducing plant, equipment, and other tangible assets, net of depreciation. U.S. data include equity, reinvested earnings, and other intercompany long-term and short-term loans.

[b] Historical cost is approximately equal to the sum of annual direct investment flows. Japanese data include new equity investments and intercompany long-term loans but exclude reinvested earnings and short-term intercompany loans.

[c] U.S. data: historical cost (includes reinvested earnings).

[d] p = preliminary.

abroad was still much larger than Japan's (possibly double, if Japan's position were valued at current costs). But the huge flow of direct investments into the United States in the 1980s reduced the U.S. net position to a level clearly lower than that of Japan.

Direct Investment and the Balance of Payments

The changes in U.S. and Japanese roles in global financial direct investment flows were a part of a transformation of their roles in international capital flows as a whole. The reversal of the larger total was a response to changes in the relation of savings to investment in both countries. In the United States, there was a shift from excess savings to excess investment accompanied by a shift to current account deficit (excess imports of goods and services to meet excess demand) and a net inflow of foreign capital to finance the deficit. Japan moved in the reverse direction from small excess investment and net inflow of foreign capital to large excess savings and net capital outflow. The part played by international direct investment in total capital flows, private and official, and in the balance of payments of the United States and Japan from the 1960s through the early 1990s is shown in Table 1.4.

For the United States, net direct investment flows played a significant part in offsetting U.S. current account surpluses in the early 1960s and in financing U.S. current account deficits throughout the 1980s. But they played a disequilibrating role in the late 1960s, throughout the 1970s, and in the early 1990s. That is, net outward direct investment was far greater than the current account surplus in 1965–69 and 1970–74, and increased in 1975–79 as the current account moved into deficit. It was also mildly outward in 1990–92 when the current account deficit was very large.

For Japan, net direct investment appears to have played no role in financing its brief experience with significant current account deficits in the early 1960s. This was because, in those early years, the Japanese authorities restricted foreigners' direct investment in Japan while permitting Japanese borrowing abroad in sufficient volume to finance the current account deficit.[2] But from the early 1970s onward, net outward direct investment played a significant equilibrating role, offsetting one-third to one-half of Japan's current account surpluses.

Financial Incentives and Direct Investment

The transformation of U.S. and Japanese roles in global international direct investment during the postwar years, even though their relative technology strengths had by no means reversed, has served to direct attention to financial influences likely to have been important. Two influences are often cited. One was the disappearance after 1973 of a longstanding overvaluation of the dollar relative to its purchasing power parity (PPP) exchange

Table 1.4

Net Direct Investment in the Balance of Payments of the United States and Japan, 1960–92

(annual averages, in millions of dollars)

	1960–64	1965–69	1970–74	1975–79	1980–84	1985–89	1990–92
United States							
Current account[a, b]	4,248	2,408	822	–1,490	–29,310	–132,128	–55,053
Net direct investment[a, b]	–2,832	–4,576	–6,600	–9,784	9,220	27,372	–8,377
Other private net capital[a, c]	–3,590	2,164	–7,472	–3,470	17,770	83,920	32,213
Reserves and related items[a]	2,174	6	13,250	14,744	2,320	20,836	31,217
Official reserve assets	966	–44	1,172	–620	–4,072	–4,714	2,483
Liab. const. fgn. auth. reserves	1,208	50	12,078	14,308	6,158	25,550	28,733
Exceptional financing				2,640	1,170		
Japan							
Current account[a, d]	–426	1,028	1,916	4,348	11,340	71,724	75,807
Net direct investment[a, d]	–16	–94	–920	–2,010	–4,018	–23,672	–30,060
Other private net capital[a, c]	552	–604	818	–1,036	–5,794	–36,860	–49,943
Official reserve assets[a]	–110	–330	–1,814	–1,302	–1,528	–11,192	4,197

Sources: IMF, *International Financial Statistics Yearbooks* (1993 and June 1994).

[a] Increase in assets is minus (-).
[b] Includes reinvested earnings.
[c] Includes errors and ommissions, sometimes very large.
[d] Excludes reinvested earnings.

rates with other major industrial countries. (PPP exchange rates for two currencies are those notional rates which would make average prices in the two countries equal to one another.) The other was higher after-tax inflation-adjusted costs of capital in the United States than in other major industrial countries in the late 1970s and 1980s. This implied higher expected returns on business investment in the United States since firms tend to carry investment to the point where the marginal cost of capital equals the expected rate of return on investment.

Turning first to exchange rates, it will be remembered that under the terms of the Bretton Woods Agreement, exchange rates of IMF members were fixed in terms of gold (valued at $35 an ounce) and therefore fixed relative to one another from the late 1940s until 1973. Although changes in valuations of specific currencies were occasionally negotiated among IMF members, such changes were rare. Since 1973, the dollar has been allowed to float relative to the currencies of other major industrial countries although members of the European Community have limited the flexibility of their currencies relative to one another. However, numerous less developed countries peg their currencies to the dollar, other currencies, or a composite of currencies.[3]

The best indication of dollar overvaluation in the early postwar years is the well-known study by Gilbert and Kravis (1954), undertaken for the OECD, estimating 1950 purchasing power parity relationships between the dollar, sterling, the deutsche mark, and the French franc that were relevant for comparing the gross national product of those four countries. They produced two sets of $PPP exchange rates: one based on a comparison of weighted average prices using quantities of GNP components in the United States as weights, and one using average European quantities. Both sets showed undervaluation of the European currencies relative to the dollar. But the undervaluation was far greater when $PPPs were calculated using European quantity weights.

In the 1980s, the OECD itself decided that annual estimates of $PPP exchange rates for all OECD members, based on price comparisons for a single basket of goods and services, would be useful. The basket is derived from benchmark studies, most recently 1990.[4] The OECD estimates and some of the Gilbert-Kravis results are reported in Table 1.5.

While the two sets of estimates are not entirely comparable, they do make clear that the U.S. dollar was overvalued relative to the major European currencies in 1950. Twenty years later, this was still true and also applied to the yen. However, the Canadian dollar was much closer to its $PPP rate. With adjustments in 1971 and 1972 and the abandonment of the fixed exchange rate system in 1973, the major currencies gradually drifted into better alignment with their $PPP rates through the rest of the 1970s and, for the most part, remained so in the 1980s. However, the Japanese yen became quite strongly overvalued relative to the dollar in the second half of the 1980s and remained overvalued in the 1990s, when the European countries joined the trend.

Turning to international differences in the costs of capital and expected returns on business investment, a number of analysts have estimated the costs of capital to nonfinancial business firms in the United States and Japan in the late 1970s and 1980s[5] and a few have extended their research to include other major industrial countries. Table 1.6 is drawn from annual estimates presented by McCauley and Zimmer (1989, 1992) in two recent studies covering the cost of capital for business firms in the United States, Japan, Germany, and the United Kingdom in their domestic markets from 1977 through 1991. Their estimates took separate account of the costs of equity and debt (based on interest rates and equity prices prevailing in domestic markets), the shifting dependence on those two sources of capital in each country, the effect of equity crossholdings by firms in Japan (where that practice is especially important), and depreciation.

They found that the real after-tax costs of capital in the United States were substantially higher than in Germany and Japan and somewhat higher than in the United Kingdom in the late 1970s and early 1980s. But partly reflecting the effects of deregulation

Table 1.5

Undervaluation or Overvaluation of Selected Currencies Relative to GDP Purchasing Power Parity with the Dollar, 1950–93[a] (%)

Year	Japan	U.K.	Germany	France	Italy	Netherlands	Belgium	Sweden	Canada
1950[b]		0.81	0.86	0.89	0.92				
1950[c]		0.61	0.60	0.64	0.52				
1970	0.69	0.68	0.83	0.80	0.67	0.74	0.82	1.09	1.10
1971	0.72	0.72	0.89	0.80	0.68	0.79	0.84	1.12	1.11
1972	0.83	0.76	0.97	0.90	0.74	0.89	0.95	1.22	1.14
1973	0.98	0.75	1.16	1.04	0.78	1.05	1.08	1.34	1.16
1974	1.01	0.75	1.17	0.99	0.77	1.09	1.11	1.33	1.24
1975	0.97	0.82	1.19	1.15	0.82	1.17	1.21	1.48	1.20
1976	0.98	0.72	1.13	1.08	0.71	1.14	1.16	1.49	1.26
1977	1.08	0.75	1.19	1.07	0.75	1.23	1.26	1.49	1.17
1978	1.35	0.85	1.33	1.19	0.82	1.36	1.39	1.51	1.07
1979	1.22	0.99	1.40	1.28	0.89	1.41	1.44	1.58	1.05
1980	1.13	1.19	1.35	1.31	0.95	1.37	1.36	1.63	1.07
1981	1.10	1.04	1.03	1.03	0.78	1.05	1.03	1.36	1.05
1982	0.93	0.92	0.95	0.90	0.72	0.98	0.84	1.12	1.05
1983	0.96	0.81	0.89	0.82	0.71	0.90	0.76	0.97	1.06
1984	0.94	0.71	0.79	0.74	0.66	0.78	0.68	0.93	1.00
1985	0.92	0.70	0.75	0.74	0.64	0.74	0.68	0.92	0.94
1986	1.29	0.81	1.02	0.98	0.86	0.99	0.92	1.16	0.92
1987	1.46	0.92	1.22	1.13	1.02	1.15	1.09	1.33	0.98
1988	1.59	1.02	1.22	1.13	1.04	1.15	1.09	1.41	1.06
1989	1.44	0.97	1.12	1.05	1.00	1.04	1.02	1.39	1.11
1990	1.35	1.07	1.29	1.21	1.19	1.19	1.18	1.58	1.11
1991	1.43	1.12	1.26	1.16	1.18	1.17	1.15	1.65	1.12
1992	1.50	1.10	1.35	1.24	1.21	1.24	1.20	1.72	1.04
1993	1.68	0.93	1.30	1.15	0.96	1.14	1.14	1.22	0.96
Yearly averages									
1970–74	0.85	0.73	1.00	0.91	0.73	0.91	0.96	1.22	1.15
1975–79	1.12	0.83	1.25	1.15	0.80	1.26	1.29	1.51	1.15
1980–84	1.01	0.94	1.00	0.96	0.76	1.02	0.94	1.20	1.04
1985–89	1.34	0.88	1.07	1.00	0.91	1.01	0.96	1.24	1.00
1990–93	1.49	1.06	1.30	1.19	1.13	1.18	1.17	1.54	1.06

Sources: Computed from purchasing power parity exchange rates and actual exchange rates in: Gilbert and Kravis (1954), p. 24; OECD, *National Accounts Main Aggregates Volume I* (1960–1992); *Main Science and Technology Indicators* (1994).

[a] Except for 1970, derived from price comparisons for a single basket of GDP components based on an OECD benchmark study for 1990. This procedure produces more reliable estimates for the 1980s than for the 1970s.

[b] Derived from price comparisons weighted by U.S. quantities of GDP components in 1950.

[c] Derived from price comparisons weighted by European quantities of GDP components.

Table 1.6

Estimated Real After-Tax Costs of Capital for Nonbank Business Firms in Four Industrial Countries[a] (%)

	1977–79	1980–84	1985–89	1990	1991
Equipment, 20-year life					
United States	11.4	11.3	10.4	9.7	8.5
Japan	6.8	9.2	7.6	8.2	7.1
Germany	7.5	7.9	7.1	8.5	6.5
United Kingdom	9.8	10.8	8.7	9.1	8.3

Source: McCauley and Zimmer (1992), Table 2.
[a] Equipment and machinery with life of twenty years.

and ensuing international capital flows, international differences in the costs of capital gradually narrowed in 1990 and 1991.

Most analysts would probably agree that the exchange rate and cost of capital relationships just described made some contribution to the transformation of U.S. and Japanese roles in international direct investment. But there is considerable uncertainty as to how important those influences were. To the extent that U.S. multinationals had better access to dollar financing than foreign multinationals did in the 1950s and 1960s, overvaluation of the dollar made it cheaper for U.S. multinationals than for foreign multinationals to invest abroad and in the United States. This encouraged U.S. direct investment abroad and discouraged foreign investment in the United States. The disappearance of overvaluation in the 1970s eliminated those incentives and disincentives. Similarly, to the extent that Japanese and German multinationals had better access to their domestic markets than U.S. multinationals did in the 1980s, the lower cost of capital in those countries, and the higher expected returns in the United States, encouraged investment by German and Japanese multinationals in the United States and discouraged investments by U.S. multinationals in Germany and Japan.

However, the influence of currency overvaluation and undervaluation and international differences in cost of capital in domestic markets on the direction of international capital flows gradually weakened during the postwar years. From the 1960s onward, foreign multinationals were able to borrow in dollar markets, first in the U.S. markets and, after the U.S. imposition of an interest equalization tax on borrowing by foreigners in 1963, in the newly developing Eurodollar market. In the late 1970s and 1980s, liberalization trends in other countries' foreign exchange and domestic financial markets and the further development of Euromarkets for debt instruments denominated in other currencies gave U.S. multinationals some access to those currencies and lower interest rates. Further, multinationals' affiliates in foreign countries generally had good access to domestic markets in host countries after they had become established members of the business communities in those countries.

Nevertheless, the very fact that cost of capital differences persisted throughout the 1980s suggests that multinationals based in countries with relatively low costs of capital or overvalued currencies continued to enjoy some advantages. Recent studies have produced evidence suggesting that throughout the 1980s, financial institutions such as banks and insurance companies, major sources of funds for multinationals, tended to favor their own nationals more than was required by government regulations.[6] Further, in cases of currency overvaluation, multinationals based in countries with overvalued currencies retain an advantage with respect to that portion of any investment financed with internal funds.[7] Moreover, the ability of multinationals to tap foreign capital markets did not diminish the appeal of countries with higher expected rates of return and/or undervalued currencies as targets for investment by foreign multinationals as well as by their own companies.

Related Technology Flows and Convergence of National Technologies

The distinguishing feature of direct investment is its association with international technology flows and the effect of those flows on economic growth, national technology levels, and their convergence. Advances in technology include both product and process innovations described earlier. These technologies are closely related, since invention of a new product may require new methods to produce it and therefore is likely to spawn subsequent improvements in production methods. Historically, nations striving to catch up with a leader in technology often make their first contributions to new technology by devising improved methods of producing products invented by others. An early example is the invention of the automobile in Europe and the subsequent development of mass production methods of auto assembly in the United States. A more recent example is the invention of the semiconductor in the United States and the development of improved methods of mass producing memory chips in Japan.

While we will be examining technology flows between Japan and the United States in considerable detail in the rest of this book, some general observations about the relation of technology flows in the direct investment relations of the United States and Japan with the rest of the world are in order here.

Technology Intensiveness of Direct Investment

While official direct investment data describe financial flows rather than technology flows, the industry distribution of financial direct investment does tell us something about the kinds of technology flows associated with the two countries' direct investment experience and thus throws some light on their likely importance. Tables 1.7 and 1.8 show the industry distribution of U.S. and Japanese direct investments abroad, and foreign direct investment in those countries. Industries are grouped according to the likely importance of financial capital and technology in motivating those investments. Financial considerations probably motivate investments in banking, other financial institutions, insurance, and real estate. These investments are thus classified as finance-intensive (even though their methods of doing business and the products that they offer have been

Table 1.7

Industry Distribution of U.S. and Japanese Direct Investment Positions Abroad, Selected Years (%)

	United States[a]			Japan[b]		
	1966	1977	1993	1966	1977	1993
Technology-intensive industries	60.9	51.2	42.0	45.8	34.2	33.4
Manufacturing[a]	54.4	48.0	39.8	45.8	34.2	27.7
Transportation, communications, and public utilities[b]	6.5	3.2	2.2	c	c	5.7[d]
Finance-intensive industries	9.1	17.6	33.6	9.8	8.1	35.5
Finance and Insurance	8.8	17.4	33.1	9.8	8.1	19.6
Banking	0.5	3.0	5.2			
Other	8.3	14.4	27.9			
Real estate	0.3	0.2	0.5	c	c	15.9
Mixed	30.0	31.2	24.4	44.4	57.7	31.1
Services[e]	c	2.7	3.3	4.5	3.4	12.1
Trade	11.8	15.2	13.8	12.8	14.2	10.9
Wholesale	10.1	13.3	12.0			
Retail	1.7[f]	1.9[f]	1.8[f]			
Extractive	14.6	12.4	7.2	18.4	25.5	4.8
Mining	7.7	4.1	1.1			
Oil and gas (extraction only)	6.9	8.3	6.1			
Construction	0.7	0.6	0.1	2.6	1.0	0.9
Agriculture, forestry, fishing	0.6	0.4	0.1	2.9	2.7	0.6
Other	2.3	0.0	0.0	3.2	10.9	1.8
Memorandum:						
Direct investment position ($bil.)[g]	51.8	146.0	548.6	0.7	12.7[h]	259.8

Sources: U.S. Department of Commerce (1975, 1981); *Survey of Current Business* (August 1994); Ministry of Finance (Japan); Hyun and Whitmore (1989); *Financial Statistics of Japan* (1994); Krause and Sekiguchi (1976).

[a] While the Department of Commerce reports investment in petroleum extraction, refining, transport, and distribution separately, this table adds them to other investments in those industries. Investment in manufactures includes investment in integrated extraction and refining.

[b] Ministry of Finance (Japan) data on cumulated investment notifications at end of fiscal year ending the following March. Excludes reinvested earnings and disinvestments. In calculating percentages, small investment in branches in unidentified industries is omitted from total.

[c] Included in "Other."

[d] Transportation only.

[e] Includes hotels, etc.; business services; movies and TV, etc.; engineering; health; and other.

[f] Excludes gas stations.

[g] Historical cost, balance of payments basis.

[h] Author's estimate.

greatly affected by the application of computer technology). By contrast, investments in manufacturing, transportation, and telecommunications seem likely to have been associated with significant technology transfers and thus are classified as technology-intensive.

This leaves a number of less clear-cut cases, which we classify as mixed. Investments in services included large U.S. and Japanese investments in hotels, which were probably finance-intensive. But they also included growing U.S. investments in technology-intensive industries such as computer software and management consulting. Investments in trade were often associated with the export of technology-intensive manufactures. But especially in the case of Japanese investments, they also reflected the financial strength of Japanese trading companies. Investments in extractive industries, forestry, and fishing were probably mainly concerned with the desire to assure reliable sources of raw materials, although technological skills and/or financial strength may also have played a part in generating investment.

The distribution of both countries' direct investment positions inward and abroad at various times throughout the postwar period, as shown in Tables 1.7 and 1.8, points to a rising trend in the relative importance of finance-intensive investments in all cases. This probably reflects the liberalization of financial transactions in most industrial countries in the 1970s and 1980s. A decline in the relative importance of U.S. and Japanese investments in extractive industries is also evident.

However, in the manufacturing sector, where technological innovation has been strongest, the United States and Japan present some interesting contrasts. For the United States, this sector's relative importance has been fairly similar for both outward and inward investments—close to half in the 1960s and 1970s and somewhat less thereafter. For Japan, on the other hand, investment in manufacturing accounted for nearly all foreign investments in Japan in the early postwar period and still accounted for over half in 1992. By contrast, the importance of manufacturing in Japan's investments abroad fell continuously, from 46 percent

Table 1.8

Industry Distribution of Foreign Direct Investment Positions in the United States and Japan, Selected Years (%)

	In the United States[a]			In Japan[b]		
	1965	1979	1993	1965	1979	1993
Technology-intensive industries	54.5[c]	52.1	44.4	94.9	78.1	58.2
Manufacturing[d]	54.5[d]	50.5	43.0	94.5	77.7	56.3
Transportation, Communication and public utilities	[e]	1.6	1.4	0.4	0.4	1.9
Transportation	[e]	1.5	0.6			0.8
Communications and public utilities	[e]	0.1	0.8			1.1
Finance-intensive industries	24.7[f]	22.3	29.8	1.8	5.2	13.3
Finance and Insurance		14.8	23.0	1.8[g]	4.4[g]	9.3
Banking		5.7	7.4			
Finance except banking		1.5	6.3			
Insurance		7.6	9.3			
Real estate		7.5	6.8	0.0	0.8[h]	4.0
Mixed	20.8	25.6	27.2	3.7	17.1[c]	12.3
Services	[e]	1.4	8.1	0.0	3.6	8.8
Trade	[e]	19.2	16.9	2.2	12.2	19.4
Wholesale		15.0	14.4			
Retail		4.2	[i]	2.5		
Extractive	[e]	3.4	2.5	[e]	[e]	
Mining	[e]	1.6	2.1			
Oil and gas[d]		1.8	0.4			
Construction	[e]	0.7	0.2	[h]	[h]	0.4
Agriculture, forestry, fishing	[e]	1.0	0.2	[e]	[e]	
Other	18.2	−0.1[j]	−0.7[j]	[g]	[g]	3.5
Memorandum:						
Foreign direct investment position (\$mil.)	8797	64648	419526		3422	15511
(Note: U.S.-reported position in Japan)			675	675	6180	26213

Sources: U.S. Department of Commerce (1983); *Survey of Current Business* (February, 1973, p. 36, and August 1994); Ministry of International Trade and Industry (1994); *JEI Report*, No. 24B, June 24, 1994.

[a] See footnote a, Table 1.7.

[b] Industry distribution is derived from Ministry of Finance (Japan) data for notifications of stock and share transactions through 1986; thereafter also includes parent company loans to affiliates. Cumulated position, end-March in succeeding year. Memorandum item is from Bank of Japan, essentially cumulated balance of payments data.

[c] Includes only industries for which separate data are given.

[d] Petroleum refining estimated.

[e] Not reported separately. If any, included in "other."

[f] Finance, insurance, and real estate reported as a total.

[g] Banking, insurance, and "other" industries are reported together.

[h] Small investment in construction is reported with investment in real estate.

[i] Excludes gasoline service stations.

[j] Residual. Includes items not reported (sometimes negative) and discrepancies due to rounding).

in 1966, when Japan's investments were small and focused on developing countries, to 28 percent in 1993, when its investments were large and focused on industrial countries. At the same time, investment in finance-intensive industries increased sharply. This serves to underline the great importance of financial incentives in driving the surge of Japan's direct investments abroad in the 1980s.

These contrasting industry patterns of investments flowing into and out of the United States and Japan might suggest that the United States' role in technology flows was fairly neutral while Japan's was that of a heavy net absorber of technology-intensive investments. However, the picture changes when one factors in major changes in the volume of both types of direct investment flows during the postwar period. In the early years, when U.S. investments abroad were very much larger than foreign investments, the United States was a strong net investor in technology-intensive industries. But by the latter half of the 1980s, it was a strong net absorber of direct investment in manufacturing, as well as in other sectors, while Japan was a strong net investor.

However, the direction of net investment flows in technology-intensive industries does not imply a similar direction for net technology flows. It is widely recognized that Japan often invests abroad to acquire technology, as well as to exploit its own technology. And as we will see in later chapters, U.S. firms have done the same and have even acquired technology from affiliates overseas when that was not their original reason for investing abroad. So we must look elsewhere to discover the direction of technology flows associated with the direct investment experience of the United States and Japan.

Technology Flows Related to Direct Investment

While direct investment has generated important international transfers of both product and process technology, it is easier to measure the former. Useful but incomplete evidence is available in the form of statistics published by the United States and Japan on their international receipts and payments for royalties and license fees (see Table 1.9). Data for the United States distinguish between parent-affiliate transactions and the rest, allowing us to identify those that are specifically related to direct investment. But the data do not distinguish between payments for new technology transfers and past transfers, and thus are a lagging indicator of technology flows. Japanese data do distinguish between payments for current and past transfers but do not identify those associated with direct investment.

Table 1.9 makes clear that the United States remained a heavy net exporter of product technology throughout the postwar period. Moreover, a large and increasing majority of these transfers were related to direct investment. By contrast, Japan was a net importer of product technology but on a diminishing scale. With respect to new contracts, it was a net exporter as early as the mid-1970s and remained so until the 1990s. However, nearly half of Japan's receipts for technology transfers came from the less developed countries, while virtually all of its payments went to the United States and Europe, leaving Japan a heavy net importer of product technology from these countries.

Although Japan remained a heavy net importer of product technology from industrial countries, innovations in manufacturing process technology of Japanese companies began to pose a competitive threat to producers in other major industrial countries. Rising Japanese exports were met by import restraints in those countries ("voluntary" export restraints negotiated with Japan in the United States' case). This was followed by Japanese direct investment in those industries in the United States and, to a lesser extent, in Europe. The investments were associated with transfers of important process technology to the United States and Europe. The various ways in which the transfers were accomplished are described at some length in succeeding chapters. When one factors in process technology transfers, Japan may have reached balance if not net exporter status in its technology

Table 1.9

International Fees and Royalty Transactions of the United States and Japan, 1960–93 (period averages)

	1960– 64	1965– 69	1970– 74	1975– 79	1980– 84	1985– 89	1990– 93[a]
United States ($ millions)							
Net transactions	954	1,567	2,640	4,536	5,356	8,043	14,609
With affiliated foreigners[b]	738	1,261	2,126	3,781	4,096	6,409	12,010
With unaffiliated foreigners	216	306	514	755	1,259	1,634	2,599
Japan (¥ billions)[c]							
Receipts, all contracts				99.8	207.6	249.9	362.6
Of which, new contracts				36.3	74.8	56.8	62.2
Payments				−193.9	−268.5	−295.8	−393.5
Of which, new contracts				−22.6	−34.2	−45.2	−73.8
Net				−94.1	−60.9	−45.9	−30.9
Of which, new contracts				13.7	40.6	11.6	−11.6

Source: Survey of Current Business (June 1987, September 1992, September 1993, June 1994); Management and Coordination Agency (Japan), as reported in Choy (1991, 1993a, 1994).

[a] 1990–92 for Japan.

[b] From 1960 through 1981, includes some net payments for other direct investment services.

[c] Value of contracts approved, fiscal years ending in March of succeeding year.

transactions with industrial countries in the 1980s. By the same token, the U.S. role in international product and process technology transactions combined clearly moved toward balance, but almost certainly remained that of a strong net exporter.

Converging Technology Levels

This brings us to questions related to the convergence of industrial countries' technology levels. How much convergence has there been since the end of World War II? When did it occur?

And how did technology transfers associated with direct investments flowing into and out of the United States and Japan contribute to that convergence? In this chapter we note some recent studies that attempt to answer the first two questions, and then offer our own preliminary answer to the third question.

As noted earlier in this chapter, total factor productivity (TFP), the weighted average productivity of capital and labor inputs, is generally viewed as the best, but imperfect, indicator of technology levels. TFP refers to both product and process technologies created by preceding expenditures of financial and human capital.

The validity of such measures for purposes of international comparisons depends on the accuracy and international comparability of the measures of output and factor input employed in the calculations.[8] The problems of measuring output in the service industries has long been recognized. But similar problems arise in measuring output in high-technology industries where entirely new products are frequently introduced and the quality of old ones may change exponentially. It is also difficult to capture changes and international difference in the quality of established products, such as steel or automobiles. TFP comparisons for any given year are also complicated by cyclical variability of TFP, since the timing of business cycles differs considerably from country to country.

Table 1.10 presents a sample of the best available evidence on TFP convergence among industrial countries during the postwar period. The evidence suggests that for industrial countries as a group, TFP levels for GDP as a whole continued to converge throughout the postwar period as average TFP levels in other industrial countries continued to pull closer to those in the United States and the coefficient of variation among TFP levels (not shown in the table) continued to fall. By the mid-1980s, average TFP in nine other industrial countries was 91 percent of U.S. levels, and TFP in three of them (Canada, Australia, and Norway) was roughly equal to that of the United States. But for the manufacturing sector, convergence seems to have come to a near halt in the 1970s. From then until the mid-1980s, TFP in other

Table 1.10

Estimates of Total Factor Productivity Levels in Major Industrial Countries Relative to the United States, 1950–90[a] (TFP for United States is 100)

	Gross Domestic Product			Manufacturing	
	Wolff	Dollar-Wolff OECD Database	Dollar-Wolff Own Database	Dollar-Wolff OECD Database	van Ark–Pilat[e]
		Industrial Countries (unweighted average)			
	6 countries[b]	9 countries[c]	8 countries[d]	8 countries[d]	
1950	54				
1960	65				
1967			64		
1970	81	82	75	75	
1973			73		
1975		86			
1979	85	87	71	78	
1982			75		
1985		91		76	

Japan

					Japan
1950	21				30.9
1955	36				40.1
1960	83	77			
1967			74		
1970			92	75	
1973			80		63.7
1975		85	77		
1979	101	90		79	72.4
1982			88		
1985		99		86	82.0
1990					85.1

Sources: Wolff (1991), Table 1; Dollar and Wolff (1993), Tables 4.1 and 5.3; van Ark and Pilat (1993), Table 7 and Figure 4.

[a] TFP levels for GDP are derived by dividing real GDP by a weighted average of real capital and labor inputs. The Wolff estimates for 1950–79 are drawn from his study covering 1970–79. No correction is made for exchange rate over- or undervaluation. The relative importance of labor and capital inputs is assumed to be the same throughout the period for all countries and equal to the average prevailing in the United States and the United Kingdom. In the Dollar-Wolff estimates for GDP, real output is converted to an internationally comparable PPP basis, and factor input weights are based on each country's unadjusted wage share. Their estimates for TFP in manufacturing relate to value added in manufacture. The van Ark–Pilat estimates also relate to value added, and adjustment for international price differences is based on matching prices for identical products for about 30 percent of the total.

[b] Canada, France, Germany, Italy, Japan, and United Kingdom.

[c] Australia, Canada, Denmark, Finland, Germany, Japan, Norway, Sweden, and United Kingdom.

[d] Belgium, Canada, France, Germany, Italy, Japan, Netherlands, and United Kingdom.

[e] Study was confined to Japan-U.S. and Germany-U.S. comparisons.

industrial countries averaged around three-fourths of U.S. levels. The coefficients of variation were little changed after 1970 (OECD database) or 1973 (Dollar-Wolff database). The continued convergence of industrial country TFP levels for GDP as a whole and the arrested convergence in manufactures meant that in other industries the United States had lost technology leadership to others. Dollar and Wolff find that this was the case for agriculture, mining, and a variety of private and government services. However, because of difficulties in measuring output in the service industries, these conclusions are subject to a wide margin of error.

In the case of Japan, however, most of the evidence points to continued convergence of its technology levels with those of the United States in manufacturing, as well as GDP as a whole, throughout the postwar years.[9] (We interpret the spike in manufacturing technology in 1970 in estimates derived from the Dollar-Wolff database as an outlier, since it does not resemble results for surrounding years and disappears when the two scholars apply the same estimating methods to the OECD database.) By 1985, bilateral TFP convergence for GDP as a whole was estimated to have been virtually complete. In the manufacturing sector, Japan's TFP was estimated to have been 86 percent of the U.S. level and higher than that in any other industrial country. This convergence appears to have continued through the remainder of the decade. All of this, combined with what we know about bilateral technology flows and their linkage to direct investment, suggests that the bilateral flows played an especially important role in the convergence of U.S. and Japanese technologies.

Conclusions

During the postwar period, U.S. and Japanese roles in international direct investment flows have undergone some dramatic transformations. The United States, the largest net investor in the first three postwar decades, became the world's largest net absorber in the 1980s but reverted to modest net exporter in the early 1990s. Japan, an insignificant player in the early postwar years, became the world's largest net investor. In the early 1990s, the United States' direct investment position abroad was still the world's largest, but its net investment position was topped by Japan's. Financial incentives—changes in PPP exchange rate relationships and in international differences in costs of capital and expected returns on business investment—played a significant role in producing this transformation. In the 1980s, direct investment helped to finance the United States' current account balances of payments deficit and Japan's surplus, moving excess savings from surplus to deficit countries.

Because the two countries' relative technology strengths did not change as dramatically as their relative financial strengths during the postwar years, the shifts in direct investment–related technology flows were also less dramatic, but still remarkable and important. The United States, whose technology exports had contributed greatly to technology convergence among industrial countries in the postwar period, became less of a net technology exporter as convergence came closer to completion. But it maintained a technology lead based on continued innovation and absorption of technologies from others. Japan became a net technology exporter even though it remained a net importer of product technology from other industrial countries. Its process technology exports were especially helpful to the United States in helping it maintain its technology lead in manufacturing in the 1980s. At the same time, Japan's continued net imports of product technology from industrial countries and its own innovations helped pull Japanese technology closer to U.S. levels.

Notes

1. See the contributions of Paul M. Romer (1994), Gene M. Grossman and Elhanan Helpman (1994), Robert M. Solow (1994), and Howard Pack (1994) to the symposium "New Growth Theory."
2. Krause and Sekiguchi (1976), pp. 440–44.
3. The IMF provides a brief description of Exchange Rate Arrangements

among IMF members in the world tables section of *International Financial Statistics*, published monthly.

4. After each benchmark study the new weighting system is applied to the entire PPP series back to 1970. This procedure makes OECD estimates for early years subject to a wide margin of error than those for recent years.

5. James M. Poterba (1991) surveys other estimates of the costs of capital in the United States and Japan.

6. McCauley and Zimmer (1992) present evidence from several studies.

7. Froot and Stein (1991); McCauley and Zimmer (1992), pp. 10–13.

8. For a recent discussion of these problems, see Griliches (1994).

9. Jorgenson and Kuroda (1992), have also estimated technology levels in Japan relative to the United States. Their conclusion, based on a simple average of relative technology levels in twenty-eight industries of various size, was that there was no convergence between the technologies of the two economies, taken as wholes, after 1970. Their estimates for manufacturing technology included technology levels in raw materials and services entering into the final manufactured product, whereas the estimates for technology in manufacturing reported in Table 1.10 relate only to the value added in manufacturing. For present purposes, the latter seems the preferred measurement.

2

The Changing U.S.-Japan Direct Investment Relationship

The bilateral relations between the United States and Japan reflect the profound changes in their respective roles in global direct investment and related technology transfers during the postwar years, as described in chapter 1. In the first two decades, the United States' direct investments in Japan were of minor importance, compared to its big push into Europe. But they were of enormous importance to Japan, especially for the associated technology transfers which speeded Japan's catch-up with other industrial countries.

By the 1980s, following the reversal of global direct investment flows and the rising importance of Japan as a net investor, both countries found themselves enmeshed in a new relationship important to both of them as net direct investment flows from Japan to the United States came to account for one-third of the United States' net direct investment absorption and one-half of Japan's net investment abroad. While this helped to finance imbalances in both countries' international payments, it also provoked fears that Japan was using its financial strength to gain competitive advantage by buying U.S. technology. In fact, a vigorous two-way flow was supplanting the historically strong technology flow from the United States to Japan. In the newer, rapidly growing high-tech industries, the United States continued to be the larger contributor of leading-edge product technology but benefited from the injection of incremental product improvements and innovations in manufacturing methods from Japan. In mature medium- and low-tech U.S. industries—notably, autos, steel, tires, and machine tools—Japanese investment accompanied by product and process technology proved a revitalizing force.

Financial Flows

As one might expect, given the changing roles of the United States and Japan in global direct investment, net direct investment flows between the two reversed direction in the late 1970s in response to the changing financial incentives described in the first chapter. These flows were gradually transformed from small one-way flows from the United States to Japan in the 1950s and 1960s, to very large and growing net flows from Japan to the United States in the 1980s. Table 2.1 shows this flow reversal as recorded in U.S. balance of payments statistics and also, as a memo item, in Japanese statistics.

The payments records of the two countries differ, because Japan defines direct investment to exclude reinvested earnings and short-term loans between parent and affiliate, whereas the United States—following the usage preferred by the IMF—includes them.[1] It will be noticed that reinvested earnings have long been very important in U.S. direct investment in Japan and became the main element in U.S. investments in the 1980s. In Japan's direct investments in the United States, reinvested earnings were extremely variable. For the 1980s, they averaged less than 5 percent of Japan's direct investment in the United States, and were strongly negative in 1990–93.

The U.S. data show that by the latter half of the 1980s, investments flowing from Japan to the United States were over seventeen times as large as those flowing the other way. Further, valuing the two countries' direct investment positions at historical costs, Japan's position in the United States moved ahead of the U.S. position in Japan in the early 1980s. By 1993 it was $93 billion, roughly three times the U.S. position in Japan.

The asymmetrical nature of the bilateral direct investment relationship—small net flows to Japan in the early postwar years followed by huge flows to the United States, as compared with the more balanced ebb and flow seen in the relationship of the United States with other industrial countries—was mainly the result of the host-country policies of the two countries. In the early postwar years, when financial incentives to U.S. investment in Japan were strong, such investments were severely restrained by Japan's foreign exchange control policies.

Japan initiated regulation of foreigners' direct investments with the enactment of the Law Governing Foreign Investment of 1950. Regulations were at their most stringent between 1950 and 1967. Except for "yen" investments with no right to repatriate income or principal (permitted from 1957 to 1963), all investment requests were subject to case-by-case review. The only investments permitted were those deemed not injurious to any Japanese company and likely to contribute to improvement in balance of payments. With a few notable exceptions, described in later chapters, foreign ownership of enterprises in Japan was limited to 49 percent. In practice, investments in manufactures were limited to those transferring technology that was important to Japan and not available in any other way.

In 1967, the authorities embarked on a program of gradual liberalization, culminating nearly ten years later in 1976. Initially, the liberalization consisted of designating an increasingly large number of very narrowly defined industries (most of them of no interest to foreign investors) in which new rules permitted 100 percent ownership and a smaller number in which 50 percent ownership was permitted. It was not until 1971 that even a minority investment auto assembly was approved. And it was not until 1975 and 1976 that the authorities consented to 100 percent ownership in important industries of interest to U.S. companies, such as chemicals and pharmaceuticals.[2]

In the 1980s, when incentives to financial direct investment

Table 2.1

U.S.–Japan Bilateral Direct Investment Flows, 1950–93 (annual averages, millions of dollars[a])

	United States to Japan			Japan to United States			Net Bilateral Flows	MEMO: Net Flows in Japan's Balance of Payments[c, d]
	Total	Equity and Intercompany Loans	Reinvested Earnings	Total	Equity and Intercompany Loans	Reinvested Earning		
1950–59	18	−11	−7	[b]				
1960–64	−71	−48	−23	−2	−3	1	−73	
1965–69	−125	−53	−73	21	7	14	−104	−24
1970–74	−362	−187	−175	53	−4	57	−309	−196
1975–79	−475	−161	−314	630	474	156	155	−615
1980–84	−313	−27	−286	2,374	1,739	635	2,061	−1,649
1985–89	−634	−36	−598	11,013	11,109	−96	10,379	−12,234
1990–93	−895	−248	−546	8,479	12,443	−3,964	7,584	−13,613

Sources: U.S. Department of Commerce (1981a, 1986). *Survey of Current Business* (February 1973; October 1975; October 1977; August 1983; August 1985; July 1993; August 1994). Unpublished revised data for 1982–89 from U.S. Department of Commerce, Bureau of Economic Analysis. Bank of Japan, *Balance of Payments Monthly* (June issues, 1965–69, and April issues, 1990–94).

a Increase in U.S. assets is minus.

b Not available.

c Japan's balance of payments data exclude reinvested earnings and short-term intercompany loans.

d Increase in Japanese assets is minus.

from Japan to the United States were strong, U.S. policies were enthusiastically positive at the state and local level and, through most of the decade, largely neutral at the federal level. In 1988, a growing ambivalence and uneasiness about foreign investment in the United States resulted in the Exon-Florio Amendment to the Omnibus Trade and Competitiveness Act of 1988. This gave to the president the power to block mergers or acquisitions deemed a threat to national security.[3] These powers have been used sparingly. But they did prevent a few proposed Japanese acquisitions of companies having technology thought to be critically important, as will be described in later chapters. Further, the enactment of the amendment seems to have introduced an element of caution into Japanese companies' investment policies in a few strategic industries. But as indicated in Table 2.1, Japanese investments as a whole remained strong.

The strength of the financial incentives operating in the 1980s was evident not only in the flood of Japanese direct investment into the United States but also in the behavior of U.S. companies' Japanese affiliates. Those already well established in Japan found that they could finance their operations more cheaply in Japan than by drawing on U.S. sources through their parent firm. In fact, some affiliates issued equity shares in Japan at price/earnings ratios two to four times the ratios prevailing in the United States for the U.S. parent company.[4] This financing in Japan reduced the flow of intercompany loans from U.S. parents to their affiliates in Japan throughout the 1980s and, from 1984 through 1986, reversed its direction.

Further, some major U.S. companies, hard-pressed at home, liquidated all or part of their Japanese investments at advantageous prices, repatriating the proceeds to finance operations in the United States. Outstanding examples were (1) International Harvester, which pulled out of a joint venture with Komatsu in 1982;[5] (2) Honeywell, which sold part of its share in a joint venture with Yamatake in 1989;[6] and (3) Chrysler, which gradually reduced its share in Mitsubishi Motors from a peak of 24 percent in 1985 to 4 percent by early 1993.[7]

In view of the diverse reactions of U.S. companies and their Japanese affiliates to changes in the cost of capital in the United States relative to Japan, U.S. financial direct investment flows to, and the U.S. direct investment position in, Japan are not always reliable indicators of the growth and importance of U.S. companies in Japan. The same is true for direct investments by Japanese companies in the United States. For this purpose, affiliate employment, with due allowance for the prevalence of part-ownership, is a better indicator and will be used in our analysis.

Nevertheless, financial direct investment flows, as such, were important. With the rising volume of direct investment flowing from Japan to the United States, the two countries' bilateral direct investments became increasingly important in their global direct investment relations (see Table 2.2). For the United States, investment in Japan remained an insignificant element in total investments. But the share of foreigners' direct investments coming from Japan rose from less than 3 percent in the late 1960s and early 1970s to over 20 percent in the late 1980s. The latter contribution was roughly comensurate with Japan's importance among industrial countries outside the United States. In the early 1990s, Japan's contribution was even greater. In consequence, Japan was the source of over one-third of the net foreign direct investment in the United States in the 1980s, and it continued to be an important net investor even as the United States became a net outward investor once more.

For Japan, that country's balance of payments statistics show that, in the late 1960s and throughout the 1970s, the United States accounted for two-thirds of foreign investment flowing into Japan but closer to one-third of Japan's outward investment. This relationship was roughly reversed in the 1980s and early 1990s when the U.S. contribution to inward flows averaged well below one-third (given the reported disinvestment in the late 1980s) while the importance of the United States in Japan's outward investments rose to over 50 percent. As a result, the share of Japan's net outward investment that was going to the United

Table 2.2

U.S.–Japan Direct Investment Flows in U.S. and Japanese Global Perspectives, 1960–93 (ratios)[a, b]

	In a U.S. Perspective			In a Japanese Perspective		
	To Japan/ to World	From Japan/from World	Net, Japan/ Net, World	To U.S./ to World	From U.S./from World	Net, U.S./ Net, World
1960–64	2.3	–0.5	2.6			
1965–69	2.4	2.9	2.3	40.4	66.0	25.6
1970–74	1.5	2.6	4.7	25.5	61.5	20.7
1975–79	3.0	10.3	–1.6	32.3	61.4	30.6
1980–84	3.2	12.8	39.2	40.8	37.1	41.0
1985–89	2.8	22.6	34.9	50.8	–160.5	51.7
1990–93	2.2	30.9	–56.6	51.5	33.9	52.5

Sources: Same as Table 2.1.

[a] The United States defines direct investment to include equity, intercompany loans, and reinvested earnings, whereas Japan includes only equity and long-term intercompany loans.
[b] Historical cost basis.

States rose from one-fourth in the late 1960s to over half in the late 1980s and early 1990s.

The increasingly important net direct investment of Japan in the United States made a useful contribution to financing the current account surpluses and deficits of the two countries. But it also sensitized U.S. public opinion, already made wary by Japan's trade successes. Some analysts, notably Reich and Mankin (1986), warned that Japanese investment in joint ventures with high-tech U.S. firms gave the Japanese partners access to U.S. technology to use in competition against us. While this was true of many Japanese investments, it was not the predominant motive. In fact the rising Japanese investments in U.S. manufacturing were associated with the first meaningful transfers of Japanese technology to the United States.

Technology Flows

To understand technology flows, we follow the general lines of analysis developed in chapter 1, but probe more deeply. We look first at the technology intensiveness of bilateral investments and their importance to the two economies. Then we examine the evidence regarding the likely direction of direct investment–related technology flows in considerable detail.

Contrasting Technology Intensiveness

The broad industry distribution of U.S.-Japan bilateral direct investment is shown in Table 2.3. It is evident that throughout the postwar period, U.S. investments in Japan have been significantly more technology-intensive and less finance-intensive than Japanese investments in the United States. This was true even though U.S. finance-intensive investments rose in response to Japan's liberalization of official and institutional barriers in foreign exchange and domestic capital markets in the 1970s and 1980s. For the U.S. investments in Japan, the importance of manufacturing (accounting for most technology-intensive invest-

Table 2.3

Industry Distribution of U.S.-Japan Bilateral Direct Investment Positions, Selected Years 1966–93 (%)

	United States in Japan				Japan in United States		
	1966	1977	1982	1993	1966	1980	1993
Technology-intensive industries[a]	80.3	67.6	68.1	55.1	58.3	20.8	19.8
Manufacturing[b]	78.2	66.6	68.0	55.1	58.3	20.8	19.8
Transportation and communications	2.1	1.0	0.1	c	c	c	c
Finance-intensive industries[a]	0.7	5.4	7.2	16.2	21.4[d]	19.0	32.3
Banking	*	3.1	2.5	1.0		13.7	10.2
Finance, insurance, and RI estate	0.7	2.3	4.7	15.2			22.1
Other finance (incl. holding co.)	1.2		2.2			c	11.6
Insurance	−0.6		2.4			c	0.7
Real estate	0.1		0.1			5.3	9.8
Mixed	19.0	27.0	24.7	28.7	20.3	60.2	47.9
Services	c	1.8	0.6	2.4		4.7	12.6
Wholesale trade[e]	17.8	22.6	22.2	18.7[g]		67.3[g]	35.2[g]
Retail trade[f]	*	1.8	1.1	c		1.7	c
Other	1.2	0.8	0.8	0.0		−13.5	0.1
Memorandum:							
Direct investment position ($ mil.)	731	4,593	6,636	31,393	103	4,723	96,213
Of which: in manufacturing[b]	572	3,060	4,511	17,300	60	1,033	17,746

Source: U.S. Department of Commerce (1975, 1981, 1985a). *Survey of Current Business* (February 1973, October 1984, August 1994).

* Negligible.

[a] Includes only those industries for which data are given in table (unless otherwise indicated).

[b] Includes coal and petroleum products.

[c] Not reported separately. Included in "Other."

[d] Includes banking, other finance, and insurance, but not real estate.

[e] Includes petroleum-related.

[f] Excludes gasoline service stations.

[g] Petroleum wholesaling is not reported separately but is included in "Other" in this table. (The Japanese position in the United States was apparently strongly negative in 1980.)

ments) fell from about 80 percent in the 1960s to 55 percent by
1992. But for Japanese investments in the United States, the importance of manufacturing fell from close to 60 percent in the
1960s, when Japanese investments were very small, to 20 percent
in 1992.

Despite the much smaller share of Japanese investment going
to technology-intensive industries, the scale of their total direct
investments was so large that by 1993, U.S. data show Japan's
direct investment position in U.S. manufacturing to have been
roughly equal to that of the United States in Japan. One indicator
of the importance of bilateral investment in manufacturing is
employment in the affiliates of one country's investors as a percentage of total employment in the host countries' industries, as
shown in Table 2.4. The table shows that, in manufacturing as
a whole, these percentages were quite small. However, investors from both countries concentrated their efforts in a few
industries, where their presence became significant and important. The table also shows that, by the late 1970s, U.S.
companies' position in Japanese manufacturing as a whole was
roughly similar to that of Japan in the United States in 1990.
By the latter date, the U.S. position in Japan had expanded
further, notably in pharmaceuticals and instruments. (The industries reported in the table are limited to those where the
presence of at least one country in the other was sigificantly
above average.)

To judge the relative technology-intensiveness of those industries, we draw on recent work by OECD analysts.[8] They divided
all manufacturing into twenty-one industries, classifying them as
being of high, medium, or low technology on the basis of R&D
expenditures relative to gross output in eleven OECD countries in 1980. While definitions of R&D expenditures differ
greatly from country to country, this method of judging R&D
intensiveness may possibly give more weight to product technology than to process technology. The high-R&D industries
proved to be those with strong growth based on new product
technology. The medium- and low-R&D industries, such as

Table 2.4

The U.S. Presence in Japan and Japan's Presence in the United States in High-, Medium-, and Low-R&D-Intensive Manufacturing Industries, Selected Years 1977–90[a] (Employment in investing firm's affiliates as percent of host country employment)

	U.S. Firms in Japan			Japanese Firms in U.S.	
	1977	1982	1990	1980	1990[b]
All manufacturing	1.9	2.2	2.3	0.2	1.6
High R&D (6 industries so classified)[c]					
Computer and office equipment	10.6[d, e]	8.5	10.6[d, e]	1.0[d, e]	5.2
Communications equipment and electronic components	2.2[d, e]	2.0	1.9	1.2	4.6
Pharmaceuticals	6.1	8.2	12.2[d, e]	[d]	2.3
Instruments	4.0	6.3	13.2	0.3	1.0
Other electric machinery	0.2	0.3	1.1	0.3	2.8
Medium R&D (6 industries so classified)[c]					
Motor vehicles	6.6	10.9	11.2	[d]	4.9
Chemicals (excl. pharmaceuticals)	7.0	8.0	7.1[d, e]	[d]	1.8
Rubber and plastic products	[d]	0.7	0.7	0.1	2.5
Nonferrous metals	[d]	0.3	0.4	[d]	1.7
Low R&D (9 industries so classified)[c]					
Stone, clay, glass	[d]	0.4	[d]	0.4	1.8
Petroleum and coal products	36.4	28.2	23.0	0.0	[f]
Ferrous metals	[d]	0.3	0.2	0.3	10.2
Memorandum:					
Affiliate employees, all manufacturing (thousands)	201.9	228.0	261.6	46.0	291.4

Sources: U.S. Department of Commerce (1981, 1983, 1985a, 1993b, 1993c); OECD (1986) and *U.S. Census of Manufactures* (1982); *Japan Statistical Yearbook* (1980); OECD *Industrial Structure Statistics* (1992); *Japan Statistical Abstract* (1980); *U.S. Census of Manufactures* (1982).

[a] Industries classified as in OECD (1986).

[b] Excludes affiliates in which Japanese company's equity is smaller than another foreign company's.

[c] Industry detail limited to industries in which at least one set of affiliates had an above-average presence in the host-country industry.

[d] Not reported by U.S. Department of Commerce to avoid revealing information about a single company in this or another industry.

[e] Estimated. Order of magnitude is correct.

[f] Less than 0.05 percent.

autos and steel, were more mature, and had much lower growth rates.

The stronger U.S. presence in Japan was especially marked in the high-R&D industries. The U.S. position was far stronger in three industries (computers, pharmaceuticals, and instruments), while the Japanese position was stronger in only one (communications equipment and electronic components). In the medium-R&D industries, the relative strength of U.S. auto companies in Japan may be somewhat exaggerated since it consisted of minority positions in three of the smaller Japanese auto companies. In the low-R&D industries, the very large, though falling U.S. presence in Japanese petroleum refining substantially exceeded the Japanese presence in the U.S. steel industry. We will find in later chapters that, at lower levels of industry aggregation, other areas of strength emerge, for example, the U.S. presence in the medium-R&D construction machinery industry in Japan in 1977, and the Japanese presence in the high-R&D U.S. photographic equipment industry.

The Direction and Nature of Technology Transfers

Evidence regarding the direction and nature of technology flows associated with U.S.–Japanese bilateral investments comes from three sources: (1) international payments of fees and royalties indicate the net direction of payments for patented, largely product, technology; (2) patenting data suggest which industries are most likely to have been involved in those payments; and (3) trade data offer clues regarding the likely flow of unpatented technology, such as methods of manufacturing, which we have called process technology.

United States data on net fees and royalty transactions between the United States and Japan from 1970 through 1993 are shown in Table 2.5. Comparing U.S. bilateral transactions with Japan with U.S. transactions with the world as a whole, given in Table 1.9, one finds that net receipts from Japan rose from about 14 percent of net receipts from the world as a whole in the 1970s to close to 20 percent in the late 1980s and early 1990s.

Table 2.5

Net U.S. Receipts from Fees and Royalties in the U.S.–Japan Balance of Payments, 1970–93[a] ($ millions; period averages)

	From Affiliated Companies	Other	Total[b]
1970–74	137	229	365
1975–79	365	268	634
1980–84	435	406	841
1985–89	861	742	1,603
1990–93	c	c	2,715

Source: Survey of Current Business (March 1972–78, June 1979–87, 1993, 1994, September 1992, 1993).

[a] From 1970 through 1981, included payments for intangible property rights and some other services. During that time, payments between affiliated companies were reported on a net basis.

[b] Detail does not always add to total due to rounding.

[c] Payments to Japan not reported in 1991 to avoid revealing information about a single company.

The share of net receipts coming from affiliated companies—those clearly linked to direct investment—was substantially lower in U.S. transactions with Japan than in U.S. global transactions: 38 versus 80 percent in the early 1970s and 54 versus 80 percent in the late 1980s. In good part, this reflects early decisions by big U.S. electrical companies (notably GE and Westinghouse) and later by RCA to license technology to Japanese companies rather than to manufacture in Japan. These events and their consequences are described in chapters 3 and 4. However, reported net transactions of U.S. companies with unaffiliated Japanese companies may also include at least some of the payments to IBM and Texas Instruments for technology which they agreed to sell to Japanese companies as a condition for being permitted to establish wholly owned manufacturing companies in Japan, also described in chapter 3. While those payments came from unaffiliated companies, they were closely linked to U.S. direct investment in Japan.

U.S. data on the share of U.S. patents granted to both Japanese and U.S. inventors for key products in industries where bilateral investments were concentrated, as reported in Table 2.6, sheds

Table 2.6

U.S. and Japanese Shares of U.S. Patents Granted for Selected Technologies, 1975 and 1986 (%)

SIC Code		United States		Japan		Japan/ United States	
		1975	1986	1975	1986	1975	1986
High-R&D industries[a] (unweighted average)		69	57	12	27	0.17	0.50
0.357	General-purpose programmable digital computer systems	77	69	5	19	0.06	0.28
0.366	Telecommunications	66	52	14	26	0.21	0.50
0.367	Semiconductor devices and manufacture	68	57	13	29	0.19	0.51
0.384	Lasers	63	50	14	35	0.22	0.70
Medium-R&D industries[a] (unweighted average)		61	43	15	30	0.25	0.83
0.371	Internal combustion engines	54	28	17	44	0.31	1.57
0.355, 0.356	Robots	63	50	20	29	0.32	0.58
0.354	Machine tools—metalworking	65	51	8	17	0.12	0.33
Low-R&D industries							
0.331	Steel and iron	48	37	18	29	0.38	0.78
All technologies		65	54	9	19	0.14	0.35

Sources: National Science Foundation (1988); OECD (1986).
[a] Industries as in OECD (1986).

some further light on the nature of product technology transfers related to direct investment. The table reveals a strong growth in the Japanese share in high-, low-, and medium-R&D industries. The most interesting feature of the table is that the Japanese share gain, relative to that of the United States, was greater in the medium- and low-R&D industries than in high-R&D industries. Indeed, Japanese inventors received 50 percent more patents for internal combustion engines than did U.S. inventors in 1986. All of this suggests that Japan's very substantial investments in medium- and low-tech industries were accompanied by significant injections of new product technology in some of them.

Still, U.S. patenting data, even for most industries where Japanese companies were investing heavily, show less patenting by Japanese companies than by U.S. companies. However, the trade evidence for the same industries suggests that in some, Japanese technology, broadly defined to include process technology, became superior to that in the United States in the 1980s or even before.

Country performance in international trade in any given industry is often expressed in terms of comparative advantage, as in Table 2.7. A stronger comparative advantage in either country suggests superior technology. However, other factors, such as access to cheaper raw materials, may also affect a country's comparative advantage in some manufacturing industries. It is also important to distinguish between *country* comparative advantage in international trade and the competitive strength of a country's multinationals manufacturing at home and abroad. Kravis and Lipsey (1989) have shown that even though the comparative trade advantage of the United States as a country declined in a number of industries in the 1970s and 1980s, the trade strength of U.S. multinationals remained remarkably stable.

Nevertheless, it seems reasonable to interpret investment abroad in a given industry by a country's multinationals, *following the development of its comparative advantage in trade in that industry*, as having been made to exploit strength in product or process technology. Such investments are likely to involve the transfer of some of this superior technology to the host country.

Table 2.7 shows the development, from 1965 through 1987, in the United States' and Japan's comparative advantages in trade in most industries where bilateral investments have been important. (Refined petroleum is omitted because the industry was dominated by integrated U.S. and European multinationals throughout the period.) For the more heterogeneous industries, trade data are given for those sectors where direct investment has been most important. (For instruments, these sectors include scientific measuring equipment and photographic equipment, including copiers. For industrial machinery, they include construction machinery and metalworking machinery.) The country rows in the table

Table 2.7

Comparative Trade Advantage of the United States and Japan in High-, Medium-, and Low-R&D Industries, 1965–87[a]
(averages of yearly ratios)

R&D Intensity[b]	SITC Code		1965	1970–73	1974–77	1978–82	1983–87
High	75	Computers	6.24	2.05	1.86	1.80	1.28
		United States	1.99	2.29	2.37	2.70	2.30
		Japan	0.32	1.13	1.28	1.50	1.79
	77	Electronic components and other	1.52	1.49	1.28	1.21	1.01
		United States	1.30	1.23	1.15	1.24	1.21
		Japan	0.85	0.83	0.90	1.02	1.19
	76	Telecommunication and sound recording and reproduction	0.21	0.14	0.15	0.16	0.14
		United States	0.82	0.66	0.64	0.62	0.51
		Japan	4.01	4.66	4.20	3.97	3.65
	54	Pharmaceuticals	4.11	4.90	4.55	4.17	5.08
		United States	1.05	1.06	1.08	1.13	1.23
		Japan	0.26	0.22	0.24	0.27	0.25
	87	Professional, scientific, control instruments	1.95	2.43	2.62	3.08	3.07
		United States	2.17	2.19	2.20	2.38	2.41
		Japan	1.11	0.91	0.84	0.78	0.79
	88	Photography, optical, photocopiers	0.69	0.60	0.54	0.44	0.49
		United States	1.14	1.21	1.24	1.16	1.07
		Japan	1.64	2.01	2.33	2.62	2.18
Medium	78	Motor vehicles	1.58	0.86	0.70	0.41	0.49
		United States	1.16	1.20	1.28	0.98	1.04
		Japan	0.73	1.43	1.83	2.41	2.14
	5–54.5	Other chemicals except soaps, etc.	4.34	4.50	5.26	5.93	4.37
		United States	1.72	1.97	1.06	1.11	1.10
		Japan	0.40	0.44	0.20	0.19	0.26
	72	Specialized machinery	4.87	2.84	2.68	2.45	1.45
		United States	1.61	1.28	1.49	1.52	1.18
		Japan	0.33	0.45	0.56	0.62	0.83
	73	Metalworking machinery	6.16	3.68	2.03	0.75	0.50
		United States	1.61	1.13	1.07	0.99	0.84
		Japan	0.26	0.31	0.53	1.36	1.69
	62	Rubber products	1.59	0.92	0.93	0.57	0.61
		United States	1.03	0.76	0.75	0.57	0.61
		Japan	0.65	0.83	0.81	1.00	0.99

(continued)

Table 2.7 *(continued)*

R&D Intensity[b]	SITC Code		1965	1970–73	1974–77	1978–82	1983–87
Low	67	Primary metals, ferrous	0.16	0.18	0.12	0.16	0.25
		United States	0.35	0.33	0.24	0.22	0.19
		Japan	2.18	1.84	2.03	1.38	0.80

Source: OECD (1986); OECD, *Foreign Trade by Commodities,* Series C (1983, 1989).

[a] Ratios in country rows are exporting country's share of OECD imports divided by its share in OECD imports of all manufactures. Ratios in industry rows are U.S. ratio/Japan ratio.

[b] Industry R&D classifications are as in OECD (1986).

show comparative advantage in that product (i.e., country share of industrial country imports of said product relative to its share of industrial country imports of all manufactures). The product rows compare the two countries' comparative advantages.

In many cases the decline in the U.S. comparative advantage from 1965 onward was, at least initially, the result of its direct investment abroad and the technology transfers to other industrial countries related to those investments. This was true of computers, semiconductors (a major element in electronic components), automobiles, and construction machinery. In fact, U.S. investments abroad in those industries were well under way in 1965. The continued rise in the U.S. comparative advantage in scientific measuring equipment in the 1970s probably reflected the development of new technology, followed by direct investment in the 1980s and a tapering off of its advantage in that decade.

Japanese multinationals followed a similar route, but later. Their strength in television and audio equipment, and in optical equipment and photocopiers, began to develop in the 1960s and continued into the 1970s. This was followed by direct investments of Japanese firms in the United States in the late 1970s and into the 1980s. Development of trade strength in automobiles, metalworking machinery, and steel in the 1970s was followed by Japanese direct investment in those industries in the 1980s. Japanese companies were latecomers to these industries, bringing new thinking, new zest, and new capital investment, first to their own country and then to the United States. Although they made some contributions to product technology in these industries, they also brought new methods of manufacturing and new and higher levels of quality that proved a major challenge to their U.S. competitors.

In sum, available evidence regarding international fees and royalty payments, U.S. patents granted, and comparative trade advantage suggests that direct investment–related technology flowed exclusively from the United States to Japan in the early postwar years. It also suggests that the tide began to turn in the 1970s and that flows became strongly two-way in the 1980s. Product technology flows in the high-tech industries continued to be stronger from, than to, the United States. But Japanese technology contributions, mainly process technology, clearly predominated in some very important medium- and low-R&D industries.

Technology Dissemination and Assimilation

Thus far, our discussion of technology transfers associated with direct investment has been related to the initial transfer. However, the benefits to the country receiving the technology transfer depend on whether and how fast that technology is disseminated and assimilated. This may occur in one or more of three ways: (1) sale of product technology by the investing foreign company to host country competitors; (2) joint ventures with, or equity participation in, host-country firms; and (3) competition between the foreign investor and host-country firms. All three methods have been put into play in disseminating technology transfers associated with U.S.-Japan bilateral direct investments.

Technology Sales to Host Country Competitors

In the 1960s, the Japanese government insisted on sales of computer and semiconductor technology to Japanese companies as conditions for permitting IBM and Texas Instruments to establish wholly owned manufacturing affiliates in Japan, a condition to which those companies acceded only reluctantly. But by the 1980s a further innovation, computer networking, led some firms in those very industries to use technology sales to stimulate acceptance of their product as an industry standard. These developments are described at greater length in later chapters.

Joint Ventures and Equity Participations

Joint ventures with, and equity participation in, host-country firms have been extensively used by U.S. firms investing in Japan and, to an important degree, by Japanese firms investing in the United States. Table 2.8 shows their importance as reflected in their share of affiliate employment in industries where bilateral direct investments were important. The table refers to non-majority holdings (i.e., 50 percent or less), because this is the only information available for U.S. firms' affiliates in Japan. However among U.S. affiliates in Japan, there were more majority-held affiliates in which host-country companies retained significant equity than there were among Japanese affilliates in the United States.

The generally high level of shared ownership among U.S. affiliates in Japan in 1982 reflects Japanese barriers to wholly owned foreign investments. With two important exceptions, IBM and Texas Instruments, 100 percent foreign ownership was permitted in those industries where investment was concentrated until 1976. And even after 100 percent ownership was permitted, would-be investors encountered barriers imposed by business firms acting together through a Japanese form of industrial organization known as *keiretsu*. Linear descendants of the prewar zaibatsu, keiretsu are vertical or conglomerate (horizontal and vertical) groupings of firms tied together by cross holdings of equity, strong but not necessarily exclusive supply arrangements, and sometimes, exchanges of key executives and other personnel. Each group is headed by a major bank (in the case of conglomer-

Table 2.8

Employment in Non–Majority-Owned Manufacturing Affiliates in U.S.-Japan Bilateral Direct Investments, Selected Industries and Years, 1982–90 (% of affiliate employment)

	U.S. Firms' Japanese Affiliates		Japanese Firms' U.S. Affiliates
	1982	1990	1990
High R&D[a]			
Computer and office equipment	4.1	3.2[b]	58.8
Communications equipment			14.0
Electronic components	62.6	34.4	25.7
Pharmaceuticals	24.4	11.7	7.1
Instruments	92.5	84.6	18.0
Medium R&D[a]			
Motor vehicles	100.0	100.0	30.8
Chemicals (excluding pharmaceuticals)	59.3	49.3	7.8
Industrial machinery	79.9	80.0	18.8
Rubber tires			0.0
Nonferrous metals[c]			32.8
Low R&D[a]			
Stone, clay, glass			21.1
Petroleum refining	100.0	100.0	
Ferrous metals			60.6

Sources: U.S. Department of Commerce (1985a, 1993a); OECD (1986); MacKnight (1992a); Dalton (1992).

[a] Industries classified as in OECD (1986).
[b] Estimated.
[c] Primary.

ate groups) or manufacturing company (in the case of vertical groups). The keiretsu have been extensively analyzed by Hadley (1970) and by Caves and Uekusa (1976), and Nanto (1990) has provided a useful update.

When official regulations were liberalized to permit wholly owned foreign manufacturing ventures in Japan in the mid-1970s, the keiretsu reacted by expanding cross holdings of equity as a defense against unfriendly foreign takeovers, thereby discouraging any U.S. firms with such ideas. Mark Mason (1992) has described these and other defensive maneuvers of Japanese companies at that time. But in addition, U.S. firms investing in Japan in the 1970s and 1980s often found that joint ventures with keiretsu members facilitated the marketing of their product, gave them access to cheaper financing, and helped them thread their way through the intricacies of government regulations that were initially strange to them. Thus they were willing to trade their technology for those advantages.

Turning to Japan's investments in the United States, we will find that the importance of joint ventures and the motives for forming them varied greatly from industry to industry. Investment in computers was dominated by an investment by Fujitsu in Amdahl, designed to acquire new computer technology. Investment in nonferrous metals was dominated by the Mitsui trading company's investment in Alumax, probably undertaken to provide assured access to an energy-intensive product from a country where energy prices rose much less in response to the oil shock than they did in Japan. Japanese firms' joint ventures in autos and steel may have been motivated in part by the desire to deflect criticism of the sort generated by their trade successes in those industries. But the ventures proved extremely useful to their U.S. partners for the access to Japanese technology that they provided.

Demonstration Effects and Competition

Competition has also been a powerful mechanism for transmitting technology. Innovating firms operating abroad typically provide close-at-hand role models and targets for competing firms in the industry of the host country. Two examples of the many that spring to mind are the competitive impact of IBM in Japan and of Honda in the United States. Further, firms investing abroad to exploit their technology may encounter strong competition from firms with a different mix of skills and technologies; in competing, the investing firm may acquire technologies that it originally lacked. The record provides some interesting cases—for exam-

ple, Xerox and Hewlett-Packard—of U.S. firms learning manufacturing skills and quality controls from their affiliates' battles
to establish and hold their markets in Japan. There is also evidence that some Japanese transplants, initially established in the
United States to exploit superior Japanese technology, also
learned from their competition and collaboration with U.S. competitors. All of these cases will be described at greater length in
later chapters.

Conclusions

In this chapter, we have briefly surveyed the bilateral aspects of
the dramatic changes in the global roles of the United States and
Japan in international direct investment and the growing importance of their bilateral relationship. We have devoted most of our
attention to the transformation of technology flows—nearly all of
them associated with bilateral investments in manufacturing. While
the United States' investments in Japan were more technology-
intensive than those of Japan in the United States throughout the
postwar period, the sheer volume of Japanese direct investment
in the United States from the late 1970s onward carried the Japanese direct investment position in manufacturing in the United
States to rough equality with the U.S. direct investment position
in manufacturing in Japan by 1990. However, the importance of
U.S. companies' affiliates in Japanese manufacturing (as measured by employment) remained somewhat greater and more
concentrated in high R&D industries than that of Japanese companies in the United States.

There is evidence to suggest that the flow of product technology associated with these bilateral investments was very strongly
from the United States to Japan. U.S. investments were more
concentrated in high-technology manufacturing industries, and the
flow of fees and royalty payments between parents and affiliates
in both countries was heavily from the United States to Japan.
But there is also evidence of a strong flow of process technology
from Japan to the United States. Japan's growing trade strength in

the 1970s and early 1980s, especially in medium- and low-tech industries, reflects the development of superior process technology. And Japanese companies' subsequent investments in the United States to further exploit that superiority involved transferring this technology to the United States.

We also took brief notice of the ways in which initial technology transfers from one country to the other were more broadly disseminated in the country receiving technology. These modes included sale of technology (sometimes in exchange for permission to invest and sometimes for strategic reasons); joint ventures; demonstration effects; and competition. The rest of this book describes how direct investment–related technology flows changed and the ways in which they were assimilated, from the early postwar years to the early 1990s. The focus is on manufacturing and related service industries—computer software and communications. We leave for another time the story of technology transfers in banking and finance.

Notes

1. IMF (1993), pp. 369 and 373 for Japan, and pp. 747 and 753 for the United States.

2. Krause and Sekiguchi (1976) describe Japan's early policies, and Christelow (1980) compares Japanese policies with those of other industrial countries.

3. Graham and Krugman (1989), chap. 6, analyze federal, state, and local policies in the 1980s.

4. Fikré (1990–91).

5. *Moody's Industrial Manual* (1991).

6. "Honeywell Sells 16% of Yamatake," *New York Times*, October 25, 1989.

7. "Chrysler Sells Part of Stake in Mitsubishi for After-Tax Gain of About $310 Million," *Wall Street Journal*," September 25, 1989; and "Chrysler Exec. Quits Mitsubishi Board," *Nikkei Weekly*, May 9, 1992.

8. OECD (1986), pp. 58–60.

Part II

Some History

3

Early U.S. Investments and Technology Transfers, 1948–69

In this chapter we take a closer look at the modest one-way flow of direct investments from the United States to Japan and the very important flow of technology that accompanied it in the first two decades after World War II. We preface our account with a description of the state of Japanese industrialization, relative to that of other industrial countries, at the end of the Allied occupation in 1952 and the U.S. contribution to Japan's progress up to that point. This is followed by a description of the major U.S. direct investments in manufacturing and related technology flows in those early years—first in medium- and low-R&D industries and then in high-R&D industries—and the various means whereby this technology was broadly disseminated throughout the Japanese economy.

During those years, the Japanese authorities and industry feared U.S. competition, and U.S. investments were restricted to those assuring crucial petroleum supplies and those bringing technology not available in any other way. Further, the authorities took care, in one way or another, that this technology would be quickly and broadly disseminated to a large part of the Japanese industry. In most cases, this was assured by the participation of the major Japanese players in joint ventures with the investing U.S. firms. In computers and semiconductors—where, in each case, the U.S. industry leader with crucial technology held out for wholly owned investment—this was permitted only on condition that the technology be made available to the entire Japanese industry.

Japan's Industrialization and the United States' Contribution up to 1952

By the end of the Allied occupation in 1952, Japan had already resumed its remarkably successful efforts to catch up with the world's major industrial countries. In the seventy years between 1868, when the Tokugawa shogunate was replaced by the Meiji empire, and the eve of World War II, Japan had transformed itself from a backward, mainly agricultural country to a growing industrial economy.

G. C. Allen (1958), in his early study of Japan's postwar recovery, has described the Japanese position at the end of the 1930s. By then it had developed a strong comparative advantage in textiles and some simple metal manufactures. These industries were developed initially with imported machinery, mainly from England. But by the 1930s Japan had learned to make excellent textile machinery and was in fact exporting some to England. It had also developed considerable competence in making scientific instruments, some other industrial machinery, trucks, ships, aircraft, and basic chemicals required in agriculture and textiles. These industries met a substantial share of domestic needs, and some of them were exported to Japan's colonies, Manchukuo and Formosa. But many were not yet truly competitive in world markets, mainly by reason of lagging technology.

In this early catch-up period as well as later, Japan greatly benefited from the large store of technology already developed in other countries, its accessibility, and Japanese ability to absorb and apply that technology more effectively and rapidly than any other initially less developed country. Two major studies of Japan's early growth—William Lockwood (1955) in his history covering 1868 to 1938, and Kazushi Ohkawa and Henry Rosovsky (1973) in their analysis focusing on 1900–1970—attribute Japan's exceptional success in absorbing foreign technology to the leadership and organization skills of government officials and the zaibatsu groupings of firms in finance, commerce, and a broad range of manufacturing. But they also recognized the importance of required primary education, initiated early in the Meiji period, and the later development of technical schools, colleges, and universities.

Japan acquired most of its early foreign technology by direct purchase unrelated to any foreigner's direct investment. In the case of machinery and ships, the procedure appears to have been to purchase the product from a leader in the industry in Europe or the United States, perhaps through a long-term purchase contract —along with the basic technology and manufacturing know-how required to produce it in Japan. This way of acquiring new shipbuilding technology is described by Tuvia Blumenthal (1976) in her study of the Japanese shipbuilding industry.

But in a few important industries, technology was transferred from the United States to Japan through U.S. firms' direct investment, often in the form of joint ventures with zaibatsu member companies. Mira Wilkins (1974), in her history of U.S. business abroad, offers some tantalizingly brief sketches of these investments, beginning at the turn of the century. In 1899, Western Electric helped establish Nippon Electric Corporation (NEC), taking a part interest in the Japanese Firm. (This and subsequent investments were later absorbed by ITT.) GE followed a few years later in a joint venture with what is now Toshiba, bringing with it the incandescent light bulb. Goodrich entered Japan in 1917, and Libbey-Owens Glass in 1918. The Associated Oil Company (later Tidewater) entered a joint venture in oil refining with Mitsubishi in 1931—the only foreign company to do so. Stanvac, a joint venture between the U.S. companies now known as Exxon and Mobil, had an important presence in Japan in the 1930s, but only as importer and distributor of oil refined in the United States or in the Dutch East Indies.

In automobiles, investments by GM and Ford in wholly owned automobile assembly ventures in Japan in the early 1920s came to be regarded as inhibiting, rather than promoting the development of that industry in Japan. C. S. Chang (1981), in his history of the Japanese auto industry, describes the original view of the authorities that such advanced industries were better left to foreigners, and explains how this view was reversed when militarists gained the upper hand in government and concentrated on military build-up. Both Chang and Michael Cusumano (1985) describe the Japanese government's strategy for subsidizing and encouraging wholly owned Japanese companies and ousting the two foreign companies. The ousting strategies included raising tariffs on knockdown auto sets, enforcing strict output limits that applied only to firms with foreign majority ownership, and instituting foreign exchange controls that frustrated GM's two attempts to form joint ventures with Japanese firms. Both Ford and GM withdrew in 1939. Nevertheless, this prewar demonstration of U.S. mass production methods made a strong impression on young Japanese industrialists destined to lead the Japanese auto industry in the early postwar years, as both Chang and Cusumano stress.

In the late 1930s, IBM also entered Japan. Mark Mason (1992) has described IBM's decision to establish a subsidiary in Japan in 1937, following the success of its model 405 alphabetical tabulating machine in the Japanese market. The new affiliate started to produce punch cards for its machines in 1939. During the war the company was turned over to Tokyo Electric (later Toshiba), which used this opportunity to manufacture copies of the 405 and thus enter the fledgling computer industry.

Since most Japanese industry was still highly dependent on Western technology on the eve of World War II, severance of access to that rapidly growing technology for a decade or more widened the technology gap for most industries. However, military imperatives encouraged independent progress in some industries. Ohkawa and Rosovsky (1973) have noted that Japanese companies that were drafted into the production of military aircraft learned a great deal about manufacturing methods. After the war, they applied what they had learned to industries ranging from sewing machines to motor scooters to automobiles. Further, new technology developed in the process of making gunsights and bombsights found application in postwar development of photographic and optical products.

The Allied occupation of Japan from 1945 to 1952, in which the United States played the main role, proved helpful on balance to Japan's recovery. Patrick and Rosovsky (1976) have described the reversal of U.S. policy from de-industrialization and "social engineering" in 1946 and 1947 to strongly supportive policy as the impracticality of de-industrialization became evident and the cold war was developing. In describing U.S. efforts at "social engineering," they note that land reform, the transfer of ownership to tenant farmers, proved welcome and durable. But they suggest that efforts to alter Japan's industrial organization by abolishing family-owned zaibatsu and establishing a Fair Trade Commission did not go very far. And in late 1949, the introduction of fiscal and monetary reforms, the "Dodge Line" based on the recommendations of a mission headed by Joseph Dodge, helped Japan establish fiscal discipline and eliminate rampant inflation.

Equally if not more important, the U.S. military brought quality control ideas to Japan. Cusumano (1985) provides an interesting account of how Japanese industry absorbed these ideas and ultimately made them their own.[1] After the outbreak of the Korean War, the U.S. military placed large orders with Japanese producers of electrical equipment (in connection with setting up a new communications network in Japan). In order to assure the quality of the Japanese products, the military introduced its Japanese suppliers to newly developed U.S. methods of quality controls which applied statistical sampling techniques to the inspection of products coming off the assembly line. They recruited William E. Deming, a physicist, to teach quality control concepts and methods.

Quality control concepts were enthusiastically accepted in Japan, and the Japanese Union of Scientists and Engineers (JUSE), organized in 1946, became the moving force in promoting quality controls. In 1951, JUSE initiated the Deming prize, an annual award to the company achieving the most progress as a result of quality control policies and programs.

The Japanese also became more receptive than U.S. industrialists generally to further advances in quality control concepts developed by U.S. experts. Both Deming in his later work and J. M. Juran advocated shifting the responsibility for inspecting for defects to workers on the shop floor. And A. V. Feigenbaum, who headed the QC department at General Electric, introduced the idea of "total quality control" (TQC), extending the uses of statistical analysis to include (1) identification of the sources of quality problems (so that they could be remedied), (2) market research (to learn consumer reactions and preferences), and (3) product development, design, and procurement.

In advocating the shift of inspection for defects to the shop floor and Feigenbaum's total quality control ideas, JUSE enthusiasts found that they needed to translate the sophisticated statistical approach found in U.S. analysis into something more easily understood by both workers and management at all levels throughout Japanese industry. Their efforts to accomplish this included a popular NHK radio program and courses for high school teachers (presumably to familiarize future workers with quality control ideas). They also encouraged companies to develop extensive employee education and to establish quality circles where methods of improving quality and inspection techniques could be discussed, as well as seminars for engineers.

Japanese companies pursued the quality control approach in all major industries, as they applied these general ideas to their specific production and manufacturing problems. Progress was sometimes slow. But by the 1970s, Japan's newly acquired process technology skills combined with new foreign technology were responsible for strong Japanese gains in world markets for a number of products.

Postwar Direct Investment and Related
Technology Flows to Japan

Apart from the contributions by the U.S. military, most of the transfers of U.S. technology that fueled Japan's early postwar catch-up were related, directly or indirectly, to U.S. direct investments. A U.S. Department of Commerce (1960) survey of U.S. direct investment abroad in 1957 reported $185 million invested in Japan. The few details available on its distribution suggest that roughly 75 percent was in manufacturing, of which well over half was in oil refining and over 10 percent in transportation equipment, probably mainly a short-lived investment in shipbuilding. A more detailed benchmark survey for 1966 reported U.S. direct investment in Japan to have risen to $731 million. Table 3.1, drawn from that report, indicates that roughly 80 percent was in manufacturing. In the table, those investments are classified according to the OECD measure of R&D intensiveness in 1970, described in chapter 2. Over half of investments in manufactures were in medium-R&D industries, mainly petroleum refining and petrochemicals. Most of the rest was in high-R&D industries, of which the largest part was in computers.

Medium and Low R&D Industries

In some industries classified as low- and medium-R&D industries in 1970, U.S. companies had made technological innovations during or just before World War II. The heavy concentration of U.S. direct investment in those industries during the first two postwar decades helped Japan to catch up, after nearly a decade of isolation.

Shipbuilding

In shipbuilding, an early and short-lived U.S. investment helped Japan to regain and then improve upon its prewar position in world markets. Blumenthal (1976) has described the shipbuilding industry's prewar achievements and the sequence of events that propelled it to a 50 percent share of world markets by the end of the 1960s. Japan had already become an important shipbuilder in the 1930s, when a strong program of military shipbuilding carried its output to 13 to 15 percent of the world total gross tons launched, a distant second to the United Kingdom, whose share ranged from 25 to 50 percent. In terms of technology, however, Japan remained dependent on technology purchased mainly from

Table 3.1

Industry Distribution of the U.S. Direct Investment Position in Japan, 1966

	$ Million	%
Total	731	100.0
Manufacturing	572	78.2
High R&D[a]	214	29.3
Computers and office machinery	115[b]	15.7
Electronic components	11	1.5
Pharmaceuticals	16	2.2
Instruments	7	1.0
Other electrical machinery	65	8.9
Medium R&D[a]	318	43.5
Chemicals (except pharmaceuticals)	71	9.7
Motor vehicles and parts	4	0.5
Petroleum refining	206	28.2
Industrial, construction, mining, machinery	24	3.3
Other nonelectric machinery	6[b]	0.8
Rubber and plastics	7	1.0
Low R&D[a]	37	5.1
Stone, clay, and glass products	11	1.5
Primary and fabricated metals	5	0.7
Lumber and wood products	1	0.1
Food and allied products	14	1.9
Textiles and apparel	1	0.1
Paper and allied products	2	0.3
Printing and publishing	3	0.4
Trade	130	17.8
Petroleum	80	10.9
Other	50	6.8
Transportation, communications, public utilities	15	2.1
Banking, finance, insurance	4	0.5
Other	10	1.4

Sources: U.S. Department of Commerce (1975); OECD (1986).

[a] Classified on the basis of the intensity of R&D expenditures in eleven main OECD countries in 1970. OECD (1986), p. 59.

[b] Of $121 million reported to have been invested in computers and "other" miscellaneous nonelectric machinery, $115 million is estimated to have been in computers, etc., and $6 million in "other."

European companies. Cut off from foreign technology by the war, Japanese shipbuilders devised methods of mass producing standardized ships. But their efforts fell short of U.S. wartime achievements in developing new block-building techniques and the substitution of welding for riveting.

In the occupation period, cold war exigencies led the occupation authorities to reject the Pauley Report proposal to remove shipbuilding equipment as reparations, and Japanese shipbuilders set about acquiring Western technology. This involved importing new welding machinery from the United States and learning the block-building method whereby ships are built in separate blocks simultaneously and then assembled. This was done partly through technological cooperation contracts with foreign firms which, Blumenthal reports, were far more numerous than ever before.

However, some of the crucial technology transfers of the early 1950s were associated with U.S. direct investment in Japan. A pioneer in the new welding techniques, National Bulk Carriers (NBC), a major U.S. builder and operator of ore carriers and tankers, managed to lease a Japanese shipyard from the Japanese government in 1951 to establish a shipyard operation in Japan.[2] The fifteen-year lease on the shipyard in Kure set very low annual payments but also required that NBC sublease a part of the very large shipyard to an affiliate of Ishikawajima-Harima Heavy Industries (IHI), one of Japan's largest shipbuilders, which was already building ships at the yard. NBC introduced U.S. methods of welding, block-building, and assembly to Japanese workers and to IHI as well. While producing in Japan, NBC pioneered in the building of supertankers (producing a series of the world's largest) and ore carriers, while IHI enthusiastically followed the NBC lead. In 1966, when its lease expired, NBC transferred its facilities to IHI and became its biggest customer.

Oil Refining

The largest U.S. investors in the early postwar years were the oil companies, whose joint ventures with, and part ownership of,

Japanese companies gave them a dominant position in oil refining. The story of this early period is told in a company history put out by Toa Nenryo Kogyo (1964), a Japanese oil-refining company, known as Tonen, in which the Standard Vacuum Oil Company (Stanvac) had acquired a 51 percent share in 1949. In the early occupation years, the authorities shut down Japan's Pacific refineries, even considered proposals to scrap them, and placed imports and distribution in the hands of a government corporation. But this policy was reversed in the summer of 1948 with permission for increased petroleum imports and the transfer of petroleum distribution to a designated group of U.S. and Japanese companies and, in 1949, the reopening and rebuilding of Japanese refineries. Stanvac, Caltex, Union Oil, and the British and Dutch–owned Shell established joint ventures with, or acquired strong equity positions in, Japanese firms, and Tidewater returned to its old joint venture with Mitsubishi. Since Stanvac was itself a joint venture undertaken by firms now known as Exxon and Mobil, and Caltex was a joint venture between Standard Oil of California and Texaco, six U.S. oil companies were active in oil refining in Japan. At that early stage, U.S. companies' Japanese affiliates probably accounted for well over half of all Japanese refining, thus assuring a broad dissemination of U.S. refining technology in Japan.

The Tonen history suggests that the greater postwar interest of U.S. oil companies in refining in Japan was related to a change in the world pattern of crude oil supplies—the rise in crude oil supplies in the Middle East and the transformation of the U.S. role from net exporter to net importer—and a worldwide tendency to site refineries in consumer countries in response to the dollar shortage. In discussing Japanese motives, the book notes the importance of assured access to crude petroleum supplies and financial support. But in addition, Tonen's account of its unsuccessful prewar attempts to obtain U.S. technology and its earnest efforts to develop its own refining technology during the war (including experimental conversion of more accessible natural rubber into petroleum) serves to underline Japan's interest in acquiring access to U.S. refining technology, such as the fluid catalytic cracker.

However, foreign part-ownership of well over half of the Japanese oil-refining industry was deeply disturbing to many Japanese, and the government embarked on a long and arduous effort to reduce the foreign position. The initial strategy was to support and encourage Japanese refiners and to limit the growth of foreign-affiliated refiners through allocation of foreign exchange for purchase of crude oil.[3] With liberalization of trade-related foreign exchange controls in 1962, the government enacted a Petroleum Industry Law of 1962 that transferred controls to the Ministry of International Trade and Industry (MITI), authorizing it to establish a petroleum supply plan and to implement it by regulating crude oil imports, new refining capacity, production, sales, prices, and mergers.[4]

Chemicals

Early U.S. investments in petroleum refining were soon followed by U.S. investments in chemicals, largely petrochemicals. U.S. companies established a strong technology lead in this industry in the early postwar period, reflected in Table 2.7, which they exploited by heavy investments in Europe and, to a lesser degree, Japan.

In Japan, government insistence on joint ventures assured the rapid transfer of U.S. technology to Japanese companies. In 1952, Dow Chemical formed a joint venture with Asahi to manufacture a range of basic chemicals.[5] Many others followed later in the 1950s and even more in the 1960s. Several petrochemical complexes of manufacturing plants were developed, centered on a supplier of petroleum-based feedstocks and including numerous joint-venture manufacturers of petrochemical products, especially polyethylene and polyvinyl chloride.[6] Table 3.2 lists U.S. and Japanese partners in major U.S.–Japan joint ventures in petrochemicals operating in the late 1960s. These included numerous U.S. chemical companies and oil companies or their petrochemical affiliates, two U.S. rubber companies, and many Japanese companies. A few U.S. and Japanese companies, notably DuPont and Showa Denko, had several joint ventures with different partners as well as multiple joint ventures with the same partner. Given the number of Japanese participants, drawn from the major keiretsu, it is clear that petrochemical technology introduced to Japan through joint ventures with U.S. companies was disseminated fairly broadly at an early stage.

Industrial Machinery

In the broad field of industrial machinery, the largest U.S. direct investments were those in construction machinery in the early 1960s. At that time, U.S. products and production methods were superior to those in Japan, and U.S. joint-venture investments were therefore welcomed.[7] In both countries, this industry was dominated by a few large firms. Caterpillar, the U.S. industry leader, formed a joint venture with Mitsubishi Heavy Industries, the runner-up in Japan.[8] Komatsu, the Japanese leader, hedged its bets by forming two joint ventures, one with International Harvester to make wheeled vehicles and one with Bucyrus Erie to produce excavators. Since Komatsu held an estimated 60 percent of the market and Mitsubishi 30 percent at the time of the U.S. investments,[9] the three joint ventures brought U.S. technology and production methods to most of the Japanese construction machinery industry.

Motor Vehicle Parts

During the 1960s, the Japanese government blocked U.S. auto companies' efforts to establish joint auto assembly ventures in Japan,[10] no doubt fearful that Japanese companies were not yet strong enough to meet the competition. But they did permit a few joint ventures in auto parts with U.S. and European companies that possessed useful new technology. Important U.S. investments included equity investments by Bendix in two Japanese brake manufacturers—Akebono Brake and Jidosha Kiki[11]—and

Table 3.2

Major U.S.-Japanese Joint Ventures in Chemicals Manufacturing in Japan in the 1960s

U.S. Parent Company	Joint Venture	Japanese Parent Company
Ashland Oil and Refining	Nisshoku Aro Chemicals	Japan Catalytic Chemicals Toyo Menka
Atlantic Refining	Nihon Atlantic	Kao Soap
Chevron Chemical	Nippon Petroleum	Nippon Petrochemicals
Chevron Chemical	Karonite Chemical	Kao Soap and Nomura Trading
Continental Oil	Nissan Conoco	Nissan Chemical
Continental Oil	Toyo Carbon	Toyo Koatsu
Esso Research	Japan Synthetic Rubber	Japan Butyl
Exxon[a] Mobil[a]	Tonen Petrochemicals	Toa Nenryo Kogyo[a]
Phillips Petroleum	Showa Neoprene	Showa Denko
Phillips Petroleum	A. A. Chemical	Showa Denko
Phillips Petroleum	Japan Olefin Chemicals	Showa Denko
Phillips Petroleum	Tsurusaki Yuka	Showa Denko Yawata Chemical
Standard Oil (Indiana)	Furukawa Chemical	Nippon Petrochemicals
Texaco	Mitsui Texaco Chemicals	Mitsui Petrochemical
Diamond Shamrock	Showa Diamond Chemical	Showa Denko
Dow Chemical	Asahi-Dow	Asahi Chemical
Dow Corning	Toray Silicone	Toyo Rayon
DuPont	Toyo Products	Toyo Rayon
DuPont	Mitsui Fluorochemicals	Mitsui Petrochemical
DuPont	Mitsui Polychemicals	Mitsui Petrochemical
DuPont	Showa Neoprene	Showa Denko
Hercules	Teijin Hercules	Teijin
Monsanto	Mitsubishi Monsanto Chemical	Mitsubishi Chemical
Union Carbide	Nippon Unicar	Mitsubishi Rayon
B.F. Goodrich	Japanese Geon	Nippon Light Metal
U.S. Rubber	Sumitomo Naugatuck	Sumitomo Chemical

Sources: Japan Economic Journal (August 20, 1968, and November 26, 1968); *Business Japan* (October 1972 and January 1973); Toa Nenryo Kogyo (1964).

[a] Through part ownership in Toa Nenryo Kogyo, parent of Tonen Petrochemical.

a joint venture between Borg Warner and Aisin Seiki (a Toyota affiliate) to produce automatic transmissions.[12]

Rubber Tires and Related Industries

In another auto-related industry, some rubber tire companies active in prewar Japan returned to Japan in the early postwar years. But their technology contribution to that industry was minor. B.F. Goodrich partially rebuilt its interest in Yokohama Rubber (from 9 percent in 1941 to 23 percent) and also produced synthetic rubber with another Japanese partner.[13] Goodyear Tire and Rubber consigned the manufacture of its tires to Bridgestone Tire, a major Japanese company,[14] but in 1969 it formed a joint venture with Toyobo to produce polyester tire yarn.[15]

However, U.S. tire companies were technology laggards in the 1950s and 1960s and thus were not in a position to bring new tire technology to Japan. The major innovation of those years was the radial tire, invented by a British company, Dunlop, and commercialized by a French company, Michelin, in 1948. U.S. companies did not produce radials until a decade later, and then only in Europe. The tires became popular in the United States only after Michelin invaded the U.S. market in the 1960s.[16]

High-R&D Industries

By the 1960s, companies in the high-tech, high-R&D industries were also beginning to establish a significant presence in Japan. In Table 3.1, the data for 1966 reflect early investments in computers and in industrial control instruments and pharmaceuticals. But they do not catch the entry of Texas Instruments into semiconductors or of Xerox into photocopiers in the final years of the decade.

Computers

IBM's swift moves to reclaim its prewar assets and to reenter Japan in 1949 have been described by Mason (1992). Since

IBM's reentry antedated by one year the enactment of Japan's Law Concerning Foreign Investment, which empowered the authorities to regulate foreign investment in Japan, IBM was able to reestablish itself as a wholly owned company, capitalizing it with the yen proceeds of royalties paid to the Toyota affiliate that operated the company's manufacturing plant during the war. However, its reestablishment as a yen-financed company did not assure its being permitted to remit earnings to the United States and limited its manufacturing in Japan to tabulating equipment.

In the early postwar years, the U.S. computer industry, led by IBM, made enormous technological strides. In the late 1950s, IBM's 1401 computer, produced in the United States, became very popular in Japan. Wishing to bring in substantially more capital in order to manufacture the 1401 in Japan, IBM applied to the foreign exchange authorities, which immediately brought the Ministry of Trade and Industry into the act as well. MITI urged IBM to form a joint venture with a Japanese company. But IBM refused and made sale of its technology to Japanese companies conditional on its sole ownership of its manufacturing affiliate in Japan. Marie Anchordoguy (1988) has described the bargaining that took place between IBM and MITI and the conditions attached to the permission finally granted. Fifteen Japanese firms signed five-year contracts, effective on January 1, 1961, giving them access to IBM technology. And to provide the Japanese companies some much-needed lead time to absorb the technology, MITI required that IBM not start producing the 1401 in Japan until 1963. The Japanese government also provided low-cost finance to a computer-leasing firm jointly owned by the major Japanese producers (Hitachi, Fujitsu, NEC, Mitsubishi, Toshiba, and Oki) to give them an edge in competing with IBM in computer rentals.

Two other U.S. computer firms also made early entries into Japan on a joint venture basis. Univac (a subsidiary of Sperry Rand) formed a joint venture with Oki Electric in the early 1960s.[17] NCR also returned to Japan but concentrated on cash registers and accounting machines, thus playing only a minor role in the industry.[18]

IBM's grand bargain was responsible for the birth of the Japanese computer industry. And at the same time, IBM Japan became the fastest growing affiliate in IBM.

Semiconductors

Computer technology and semiconductor technology go hand in hand, and U.S. firms were the major technology innovators in both industries. Computers of the early 1960s made extensive use of two versions of the integrated circuit (IC) or semiconductor, invented in the late 1950s almost simultaneously at Fairchild Semiconductor and Texas Instruments (TI). The two companies' products, sufficiently distinctive to allow both to be patented, revolutionized the computer industry.

John E. Tilton (1971), in his study of international diffusion of semiconductor technology, includes an interesting chapter on Japan, and Mason (1992) has also chronicled the TI entry into Japan. Japanese firms managed to acquire Fairchild Semiconductor technology in the mid-1960s. But Texas Instruments decided to use its technology to bargain its way into wholly owned investment in Japan. The company applied for a Japanese patent in 1960, but this became mired in administrative procedures. It followed up in 1964 with a request for permission to establish a wholly owned manufacturing company in Japan, refusing to license its technology unless it was permitted to do so. The authorities initially resisted. While Japanese companies were already producing the TI chip, they could not be prosecuted in Japan, since a Japanese patent had not been granted. But when the electronics companies began to export electronic calculators containing the chips in 1967, TI threats of lawsuits forced their withdrawal. In 1968, MITI, the Japanese electronics companies, and Texas Instruments arrived at a compromise solution. TI and Sony were permitted to form a joint venture in semiconductor manufacturing. Sony disclosed its intention to transfer its share of the venture to TI at the end of three years, and TI agreed to make its technology available to the Japanese electronics companies and "to refrain from upsetting domestic production of ICs."[19]

An interesting postscript to this story is that the formal granting of a Japanese patent to Texas Instruments did not occur until 1989, to be effective until 2001.[20] At the end of 1990 the first Japanese company, Toshiba, signed a contract agreeing to pay royalties on its semiconductor sales for ten years.[21]

Radio, TV, and Other Electrical Equipment

In the early postwar years, U.S. direct investment and related technology flows also made a low-key but important contribution to Japan's increasingly successful radio and TV equipment industries. At least four U.S. companies established new joint ventures in Japan. Hughes Aircraft formed a joint venture with Nippon Electric to manufacture telecom equipment for military aircraft and storage direct viewing tubes and circuit boards for the civilian market, and Union Car (later TRW) formed a joint venture with Mitsumi Electric to produce connectors and to import circuit boards.[22] Raytheon formed a joint venture with Japan Radio, and International Rectifier (U.S.) established a Japanese affiliate with Japan to manufacture Japanese equity participation.[23]

Although the large U.S. electrical companies had been the earliest and among the most important U.S. investors in prewar Japan, they had reduced or eliminated their equity positions in the years immediately preceding Pearl Harbor.[24] After the war, GE, ITT, and Westinghouse resumed their remaining modest positions but did not attempt to rebuild them. In the late 1960s, GE held a 10 percent equity share in Toshiba, ITT held a 12 percent share in NEC, and Westinghouse held a 4 percent share in Mitsubishi Electric.[25] (Department of Commerce data classify any equity holding of 10 percent or more as a direct investment.) The U.S. companies apparently had no role in the management of the affiliated Japanese companies. However, they sold technology relevant to radio and television—including transistors and, later, semiconductors—to their Japanese partners and to others as well.[26] In contrast to prewar practice, they imposed no restrictions on the markets in which the Japanese firms might exploit that technology. This change in policy appears to have been the result of a long-drawn-out antitrust suit against GE in the United States, finally decided in 1953. GE was found guilty of participating in international cartels in lamps and electrical equipment and enjoined from making technology agreements with non–majority-held affiliates in foreign countries that would limit the ability of that affiliate to make and sell products incorporating the technology throughout the world. Wilkins (1974), in her analysis of the episode, concluded that the antitrust action and its general disenchantment with foreign operations led to GE's decision not to rebuild its investment in Japanese manufacturing in the 1950s.[27]

However, some of the most important TV technology acquired by Japanese companies in the 1950s and 1960s came from RCA. That company had completely eliminated its 68 percent position in the Japanese Victor Talking Machine company in the years immediately preceding Pearl Harbor[28] and did not return to Japan as a direct investor after the war. In the late 1940s and early 1950s, the Radio Corporation of America (RCA) freely licensed technology for its black-and-white television in order to build a broad market for the color television that it was then developing. RCA's color television was established as the U.S. standard in 1953, and the company was required by U.S. antitrust regulations to make this technology freely available at modest royalty cost. RCA's technology was adopted as the Japanese standard in 1960. Japanese firms obtained RCA's black-and-white technology in 1952 and its color technology in 1960. This technology laid the foundation for Japan's strong performance in that industry in the 1970s.[29]

It should be added that toward the end of the 1960s, GE seems to have reversed its early postwar aversion to expanding its investments in Japan. By 1970 it was searching for investment opportunities and had already formed several joint ventures, with Toshiba and with others, to manufacture a variety of electrical machinery components such as valves, circuit breakers, and motor controls.[30]

Instruments

There were also a number of important early investments in a variety of instruments industries, mainly measurement and control devices and photocopiers. Honeywell formed a joint venture with Yamatake in 1952 to produce control devices for office air-conditioning systems and ship's operating systems,[31] and in 1963, Hewlett-Packard formed a joint venture with Yokogawa Electric to manufacture electronic measurement instruments.[32] In both cases the U.S. companies brought new product technology to their Japanese partners.

A little later in the decade, Xerox brought photocopiers to Japan. In 1959 Xerox, then a small company in Rochester, New York, introduced the first photocopier machine. It was wildly successful, and during the 1960s Xerox concentrated on increasing the speed of its original machine and exploiting its new product by building additional manufacturing facilities not only in the United States but also in Europe and Japan. Its move into Japan took the form of a joint venture between its majority-owned British affiliate, Rank-Xerox, and Fuji Photo.[33]

Pharmaceuticals

In the pharmaceutical industry, U.S. and European companies were far ahead of Japanese companies with respect to R&D and new product development. To exploit its advantage, Merck, one of the largest U.S. companies, formed a joint venture with Banyu in 1953 to manufacture and distribute Merck products.[34] Pfizer also invested early, in a joint venture with Taito. However, most pharmaceutical companies appear to have been deterred by Japan's patent law, in effect until 1976, making manufacturing processes but not products patentable. This encouraged Japanese companies to make "copycat" drugs for their domestic market without incurring large R&D costs or payments of royalties. The disincentive to U.S. firms' investments remained even after Japan's adoption of a national health insurance system which made Japan the world's fastest-growing market for prescription drugs. Under the plan, doctors were permitted not only to dispense the drugs that they prescribed but also to profit from the margin between prescription prices set by government and the lower wholesale prices negotiated with the pharmaceutical companies.[35]

Conclusions

On the eve of World War II, Japan had already passed rapidly through the early stages of industrialization, drawing on foreign technology and its own considerable powers of assimilation and organization. A small part of those prewar acquisitions of technology had come through U.S. direct investments. Its wartime isolation from the West had caused Japan to lose ground in the catch-up race. But assistance of the U.S. occupation authorities in stabilizing the economy, and the introduction of quality control concepts during the occupation period, laid the groundwork for the infusion of direct investment–related technology that followed.

Much of the U.S. investment in Japan in the 1950s and 1960s brought with it technology that had been developed in Japan's period of isolation. This was true of the early and temporary investments in shipbuilding and the larger and longer lasting investments in petroleum refining, and to some extent, chemicals, industrial machinery, and auto parts. But in the 1960s, direct investment–related transfers of new postwar technology in high-R&D industries —computers, semiconductors, electronic measuring equipment, and photocopiers—began to assume greater importance.

Japanese policy during this period generally limited foreign direct investments to those assuring crucial petroleum supplies or providing important technology not obtainable in any other way. Regulations were keyed to assuring that technology transferred with direct investment would be immediately disseminated to major participants in the Japanese industries concerned, either through joint ventures or technology sales to Japanese competitors.

Notes

1. The remainder of this section draws heavily on Cusumano (1985), chap. 6.

2. A recent biography of Daniel Ludwig, the colorful one-man conglomerate, billionaire, and owner of NBC, by Jerry Shields (1986) includes an account of this venture.

3. Masamoto Yashiro (1984). Yashiro, executive vice president of Esso Eastern, described this policy briefly in an address to the Japan Society in New York. His primary emphasis, however, was on Esso Eastern's success in adjusting to doing business in Japan.

4. *Petroleum Industry Law*, Japan (1962).

5. *Moody's Industrial Manual* (1989).

6. *Japan Economic Journal*, Supplement, November 26, 1968.

7. For a brief discussion, see U.S. Department of Commerce (1985b), pp. 22–23.

8. For an account of Caterpillar's initial investment and early setbacks, see "Profiles of Joint Ventures" in *Business Japan*, April 1973.

9. *The Economist*, August 14, 1982, pp. 54–55.

10. "Chrysler May Forge Ties with Daihatsu for Local Assembly," *Japan Economic Journal*, March 31, 1964; and "Nittsu Company May Assemble GM Automobiles in Japan," *Japan Economic Journal*, June 9, 1964.

11. Chang (1981), p. 81.

12. Cusumano (1985), p. 257.

13. *Moody's Industrial Manual* (1968).

14. *Business Japan*, May 1974, pp. 32–33.

15. *Moody's Industrial Manual* (1990).

16. Scherer (1992) describes the origin and dissemination of radial tire technology in the 1950s and 1960s.

17. "Oki Electric Stops Production of Computers; Univac Assisting," *Japan Economic Journal*, June 8, 1965.

18. Corporate Reports, *Japan Economic Journal*, July 23, 1968.

19. "Government Approves Sony Bid," *Japan Economic Journal*, April 30, 1968.

20. "U.S. Chip Gets Patent in Japan," *New York Times*, November 24, 1989.

21. "U.S., Japan Electronics Titans Signal Truce," *Japan Economic Journal*, January 12, 1991.

22. "Profiles of Joint Ventures," *Business Japan*, October 1972 and September 1972.

23. Tilton (1971), p. 138.

24. Wilkins (1974), p. 251.

25. Tilton (1971) p. 147.

26. "Manufacturers Obtain 30% of Foreign Industrial Technical Aid," *Japan Economic Journal*, Supplement on the Electric and Electronics Industries, August 25, 1964.

27. Wilkins (1974), pp. 294–95.

28. Ibid., p. 251.

29. Scherer (1992), pp. 52–54, tells the story of RCA's development of color television.

30. "GE Efforts to Broaden Japan Activities Continue," *Japan Economic Journal*, March 5, 1968.

31. "The Man Behind the Enterprise Cites Good Ties with Parent Firm," *Japan Economic Journal*, April 17, 1973.

32. "The Evolution of Japanese Management," *Japan Economic Journal*, July 29, 1989, p. 22.

33. Clausing, Allen, Berg, Dertouzos, Ferguson, Haavind, Moses, and Penfield (1989), pp. 36–37.

34. "Merck Won Banyo Trust through 1954 Venture," *Japan Economic Journal*, May 20, 1989.

35. MacKnight (1992b) describes the patent law and the national health insurance system.

4

Transition to Two-Way Investment and Technology Flows: The 1970s

The 1970s were a time of transition for U.S.–Japan direct investment relations. As the strength and competitiveness of Japanese industries rose, regulatory barriers to foreign investment in Japan were reduced, thereby encouraging increased U.S. investment. At the same time, their rising technological and financial strength led Japanese companies to make their first significant investments in U.S. manufacturing. Technology transfers related to both flows became distinctly two-directional and developed what has become a characteristic pattern of product technology flows from the United States to Japan and process technology flows from Japan to the United States.

Early in the decade, the Japanese authorities permitted the first U.S. postwar investment in auto assembly. This in turn encouraged U.S. investment and technology transfers in auto parts. But most U.S. investment was devoted to expanding the activities of U.S. companies already operating in Japan. Their presence in Japan generated a two-way flow of technology. Aside from technology transferred to Japanese partners, the competitive challenge posed by the wholly owned ventures of IBM and Texas Instruments spurred the Japanese government to embark on special programs to encourage the development of Japanese technology in computers and semiconductors. In computers, where the focus was on developing advanced product technology, the effort failed because U.S. technology moved faster. But in semiconductors, the drive to improve process technology was an outstanding success. At the same time, Japanese affiliates of some U.S. companies absorbed and benefited from Japanese quality control ideas and associated improvements in manufacturing technology.

Japan's smaller but rapidly growing investments in the United States were also associated with a two-way technology flow. They included significant investments to gain access to IBM-compatible computer technology. They also included investments transplanting superior Japanese manufacturing technology to the United States, largely in consumer audio and video equipment, but also in electronic components, photocopiers, and printers.

Two-Way Financial Flows and Industry Investment Patterns

In the late 1970s, U.S.–Japan bilateral direct investment flows as a whole not only converged but crossed, thereby reversing the direction of net investment. This reversal was described in chapter 2 where Table 2.1 reported the reversal as recorded in U.S. balance of payments data. As noted in the earlier chapter, the reversal of direct investment *flows* was far stronger than suggested by the data. This was because until 1982, the U.S. Department of Commerce reported as flows the revaluation of outstanding direct investments as a result of yen appreciation relative to the dollar.

Nevertheless, actual bilateral direct investment flows in the manufacturing industries—the most technology-intensive sector —probably did not reverse, due to the contrasting importance of manufactures in the two countries' investments. This sector accounted for about 80 percent of U.S. investments in Japan but only 20 percent of Japan's investments in the United States. Reported U.S. investment in Japanese manufacturing (we have estimated the proportion of investment in petroleum refining and distribution that went to refining) was about $3 billion during the decade. This is three times the size of the Japanese direct investment position in manufacturing, nearly all of it made in the 1970s. At a maximum, it is possible that as much as half of new U.S. investments in Japanese manufacturing in the 1970s was attributable to yen appreciation ($800 million on the roughly $1 billion U.S. position in 1970 plus appreciation of investments made during the period). Even so, the flow of U.S. direct investment in manufacturing during the decade, at an estimated $1.5 billion, would have exceeded Japanese direct investment in U.S. manufacturing by roughly 50 percent.

Table 4.1 describes the industry distribution of the two countries' bilateral direct investment positions in manufacturing industries at the end of the decade. (For U.S. investment in Japan, the position in 1982 is given because substantially more detailed information is available for that benchmark survey year.) Industries are grouped according to R&D intensiveness in OECD countries in 1980. The relative importance of the three groups in each country's investments was remarkably similar. In the following sections we review the two countries' investments in those industries where important technology transfers were made during the decade. We give special attention to the modes of technology transmission and dissemination.

U.S. Investment in Japan

Apart from the shifting financial incentives described in the first two chapters, U.S. investment in Japan was buffeted by a changing mix of regulatory, legal, and institutional constraints. As Japan's domestic industries gained strength and became strong exporters, the earlier case for keeping out foreigners' direct investments became untenable, and foreign pressure for liberalization mounted. The gradual liberalization of regulations governing foreigners' direct investments between 1967 and 1976 was briefly described in chapter 2.

As liberalization proceeded in the early 1970s, some in Japan feared that foreign competition would overwhelm domestic firms. With some justification, they worried that freer entry and wholly

Table 4.1

Industry Distribution of U.S.-Japan Direct Investment Positions in Manufactures, 1980 and 1982 (%)

	U.S. in Japan, 1982	Japan in U.S., 1980[a]
High R&D	32.6	31.2
Computer and office equipment	20.0[b]	5.2
Electronic components and communications equipment	4.9	12.1
Electronic components and accessories	4.8	3.0
Communications equipment	0.1	9.1
Pharmaceuticals	5.4	4.0
Instruments	2.0	9.4
Other electrical machinery	0.3	0.5
Medium R&D	29.0	28.9
Motor vehicles and parts	11.9	2.0
Chemicals (except pharmaceuticals)	12.1	11.3
Nonelectric machinery (except computers)	4.7[b]	10.3
Nonferrous metals	0.3	5.3
Low R&D	33.4	34.8
Food and related	3.5	10.2
Petroleum refining	28.4	
Ferrous metals	0.2[b]	0.7
Fabricated metals	1.0	5.1
Lumber and pulp		13.8
Textiles	0.2	7.5
Other[c]	5.1	5.1
Memorandum: direct investment position ($ million)		
All industries	6,636	4,264
Manufacturing	4,511	1,010

Sources: U.S. Department of Commerce (1985a); Hyun and Whitmore (1989); MacKnight (1981).

[a] Industry distributions based on Ministry of Finance data on investment approvals for eight major industry groups as given by Hyun and Whitmore (1989) supplemented by data on employment in Japanese companies affiliated within those groups given in MacKnight (1981).

[b] Distribution of investments between computers and other "nonelectric" machinery and between ferrous and nonferrous basic metals is estimated.

[c] Industries not specified.

owned ventures would make U.S. firms less willing to share their technology with Japanese industry. There was also fear that Japanese joint venture partners, forced into a minority position, would become puppets of their U.S. partners.[1] In some respects, U.S. bashing in the early 1970s in Japan, based on feelings of insecurity, resembled more recent Japan bashing in the United States.

In the event, however, the keiretsu form of industrial organization, briefly described in chapter 2, provided ample defense. Cross equity holdings among keiretsu members rose strongly in the late 1960s and early 1970s, forming an effective barrier to foreign takeovers.[2] And tightly knit supply relationships, often present in vertically organized keiretsu, created marketing problems for some foreigners contemplating wholly owned manufacturing and sales ventures in Japan. As we will see, the keiretsu also acted in other ways to frustrate thrusts by independent challengers.

New Investments in Autos and Technology Transfers

The postwar efforts of the U.S. auto companies to return to Japan finally succeeded in 1971 when Chrysler and General Motors (GM) were permitted to acquire equity positions in Japanese companies. The motor vehicle industry has long occupied an especially sensitive spot in U.S.-Japan direct investments—from its domination of the Japanese industry in the 1920s and 1930s to its ouster in the late 1930s.[3] In the very early postwar period some powerful government officials had originally opposed any support for a domestic auto industry on the grounds that the twenty- to thirty-year technology gap was too great to overcome, while others viewed it as essential to industrial development. The dispute was resolved by the boost given to the industry by U.S. military demand during the Korean War and by the technology provided by the U.S. military in those early years.

Having decided to support the growth of a Japanese auto industry, the government barred the big U.S. auto companies from returning to Japan during the industry's infant years. But bowing to the need for foreign technology, it did permit agreements with

foreign auto companies whereby Japanese companies would assemble foreign cars for sale in Japan in exchange for technology.
(Of the four approved, only one involved a U.S. company, Willys
Knight with Mitsubishi Heavy Industries, in effect from 1953 to
1959.) It also permitted joint ventures in auto parts, noted in
chapter 3. With the very important addition of Japanese companies' own innovative flexible production and assembly methods, described in chapter 5, Japanese small cars began to penetrate
world export markets in the 1960s. By 1970 Japan's share in
OECD auto markets had reached 7 percent (in value terms).[4]

However, some weaknesses remained. The Japanese industry
was still plagued by too many companies to support profitable
operation by all of them. Although the number had been whittled
down from thirteen in the early 1960s to seven by 1970, the
government was still encouraging further consolidation. In fact,
in the late 1960s, Isuzu and Mitsubishi engaged in merger talks
which, however, came to nothing.[5] Further, the U.S. industry was
leading innovation in a number of important components, such as
catalytic converters, power brakes, and automatic transmissions.

By 1970 the government apparently concluded that the industry was strong enough to tolerate carefully regulated U.S. investment yet still weak enough to make U.S. assistance welcome.
Thus, it reacted favorably to Chrysler's efforts to form a joint
venture with Mitsubishi Heavy Industries and to GM's desire to
acquire a part interest in Isuzu. While the U.S. firms appear to
have hoped, initially, for a means of assembling and selling U.S.
cars in Japan and of using Japan as a base for operations in the
Pacific, what they obtained was closer to the Japanese government's apparent objectives: financial support for weak companies and more parts technology.

The first joint-venture agreement, signed in May 1971, was
between Chrysler and Mitsubishi Heavy Industries. It established
a new company, Mitsubishi Motors, in which Chrysler acquired
only 15 percent of the equity with provision for expanding it to
35 percent by 1973. The balance was owned by Mitsubishi Heavy
Industries. Although Chrysler had originally obtained Mitsubishi's

agreement to start their venture by assembling Chrysler cars in Japan,[6] this was disallowed by the government. The final agreement called for export of Mitsubishi cars to the United States and for study of ways to standardize Chrysler and Mitsubishi parts. By 1973 Chrysler had embarked on a program for purchasing parts from Mitsubishi suppliers in Japan for use in Chrysler cars in the United States.[7]

The GM-Isuzu agreement, which followed in July 1971, provided for joint development of a new small passenger car, introduction of GM's advanced management systems, and export of small Isuzu trucks to the United States. The agreement also provided for a GM-Isuzu joint venture with Itochu Motors and Kawasaki Heavy Industries to produce automatic transmissions and gas turbine engines.

Ford's attempt to acquire a share in Toyo Kogyo in 1970 was unsuccessful, although it did form a joint venture with Toyo Kogyo and Nissan to manufacture automatic transmissions.[8] It was not until 1979, after a devastating drop in sales of Toyo Kogyo cars, with their low-polluting but gas-guzzling Wankel engines, that Ford was welcomed as purchaser of a 20 percent stake in the reorganized company, renamed Mazda.[9]

There is no evidence that the investments by GM and Chrysler early in the 1970s influenced the ongoing development of Japan's innovative methods of product planning and auto assembly. But the big three U.S. companies and several major U.S. makers of auto parts clearly did contribute product technology in auto parts to their joint-venture partners, and to the Japanese industry as a whole, early in the decade. But by the end of the decade, the big three found themselves to be the beneficiaries of Japanese manufacturing technology, as imports of small cars from their Japanese affiliates allowed them to meet some of the rising U.S. demand for small cars.

Established Affiliates and Two-Way Technology Flows

Aside from the entry into auto assembly, U.S. investments were directed to industries where a significant U.S. presence had already been established. The largest percentage increases seem to have been in electronic components, pharmaceuticals, and chemicals. The rise in investments in electronic components reflects the expansion of Texas Instruments, whose entry was finally approved and initiated at the very end of the 1960s.

The strong rise in investments in pharmaceuticals came at the very end of the decade in response to the 1976 change in Japanese patent law, described in chapter 3. The new law made combinations of substances in pharmaceuticals patentable for the first time and thus made it possible for foreign companies to obtain meaningful patents on their products in Japan. This improved market prospects for companies already in Japan—notably, Merck and Taito—and encouraged investment by others. In 1979, Rorer purchased a majority share in Kyoritsu.[10]

In chemicals, Dow Chemical was the only firm to respond to Japan's new willingness to permit wholly owned foreign investments. Its experience did not encourage others to try. A long-standing partner of Asahi, Dow elected to form a new wholly owned company in 1974. However, when the new affiliate announced its intentions to manufacture soda in Japan, using its own advanced technology and refusing to sell the technology to its Japanese competitors, it evoked a storm of alarmed protest from the latter. This led to a two-year delay in obtaining government permission to build the new plant, followed by further obstacles to finding a suitable manufacturing site. Dow finally abandoned its caustic soda project, limiting its activities to less contentious projects.[11] However, a few U.S. chemical companies formed new joint ventures with Japanese companies, bringing new technology with them. One example is the Olin joint venture with Asahi Glass, established in 1974, to build and operate a urethane polyol plant in Japan.[12]

In industrial machinery, major U.S. construction machinery companies—Caterpillar, International Harvester, and Bucyrus-Erie —appear to have added to their investments, at least in the form of reinvested earnings. But there is little evidence of additional technology transfers from these U.S. companies to their Japanese partners. However, a number of new joint ventures were established in various other types of industrial machinery, and this may have generated a modest flow of technology from the United States to Japan. For example, MGD Graphic Systems Company, a subsidiary of North American Rockwell, entered a joint manufacturing venture with Ikegai Iron Works to manufacture rotary presses for color offset printing of newspapers.[13] Accuride, a subsidiary of Standard Precision, formed a joint venture to manufacture ball bearing sliding parts for computers.[14] And Dresser Industries converted a long-standing license agreement with Mitsubishi Heavy Industries, relating to centrifugal compressors used in oil refineries and petrochemical complexes, into a joint venture. The new investment took the form of an additional technology transfer.[15] (It seems possible that income from technology transfers of this type is recorded in Department of Commerce statistics as dividend income rather than fees and royalty payments. If so, data on the latter understate the importance of technology transfers from the United States to Japan.)

In computers, there were no new U.S. entrants in the 1970s. The importance of Oki-Univac's output in Japan probably diminished as a result of Oki's decision in 1969 to return to making large computers on its own. One of its major clients, government-owned Nippon Telephone and Telegraph (NTT), announced that it would not purchase computers from partly foreign-owned firms.[16]

Technology Transmission by Competitive Challenge

As U.S. companies became well established in Japan, competition between them and their host-country competitors provided another avenue for two-way transmission of technology. The challenge posed by the superior product technology being exploited by U.S. investors spurred Japanese companies to intensify their R&D efforts, including reverse engineering. At the same time the superior process technology on display at Japanese competitor companies spurred Japanese affiliates of U.S. companies to competitive imitation. We look first at the Japanese response to competition from U.S. companies, then at the response of U.S. companies to experience in Japan.

Because both IBM and Texas Instruments were conducting successful wholly owned manufacturing ventures in their respective industries in Japan, the competitive challenge that they posed was especially strong. In 1971 the Japanese government, concerned by IBM's dominant position and technology leadership in the Japanese computer market and fearful that Texas Instruments might become similarly powerful in semiconductors, embarked on a number of new programs designed to foster the growth of strong independent domestic computer and semiconductor industries. The government programs included financing R&D in advanced technologies and attempts to organize efforts in the two closely related industries.[17] In Japan, the big electronics companies were the largest makers of semiconductors and computers, so coordination of all concerned was relatively easy.

In the computer industry, efforts were initiated in 1971 to develop a new, more powerful mainframe computer incorporating more advanced, LSI (large-scale integrated) semiconductors than the semiconductors used in the IBM 360 then dominating the market. By 1975, however, it was clear that this effort had failed, since the U.S. semiconductor industry had moved on to VLSI (very large-scale integrated) semiconductors, and IBM and others in the United States were incorporating them in even more powerful computers.

Perhaps learning from the failed computer effort, the government moved on in 1976 to a strong push to improve process technology in semiconductors. This involved a government-funded research project undertaken by the Ministry of International Trade and Industry (MITI), NTT, and five major electronics companies (NEC, Hitachi, Toshiba, Fujitsu, and Mitsubishi) to develop Japanese manufacturing capability in VLSI semiconductors. Roughly one-third of the government funds were apparently used to buy semiconductor manufacturing equipment (SME) made by U.S. companies, the undisputed world leaders at the time, and to spur the development of Japanese SME producers. (We return to this industry in chapter 8.) The electronic companies devoted their efforts to improving manufacturing processes, concentrating on DRAM (dynamic random access memory) semiconductors for which they had already acquired the basic patents, since DRAMs best lent themselves to mass production methods. By the end of the decade, Japanese companies were generating an estimated 16 percent of world semiconductor output and were well on their way to their triumphs of the 1980s.

In other industries as well, Japanese companies often responded vigorously to new foreign competition, even when the competition took the form of joint ventures with other Japanese companies. The Japanese response to the photocopiers introduced by Fuji-Xerox is a case in point. The Japanese camera companies—Canon, Minolta, and Ricoh—had little difficulty grasping the basic technology involved and were soon providing strong competition, especially at the low end, to Fuji-Xerox products in Japan.[18]

Turning to U.S. companies investing in Japan to exploit their superior product technology, their affiliates there often encountered competition from Japanese adept in process technology. In meeting this competition, the Japanese affiliate, and ultimately the U.S. parent, acquired that process technology. Largely led and staffed by Japanese personnel, the affiliates absorbed quality control thinking and adopted the same sort of process technology employed by their Japanese competitors and by leaders in other industries. This seems to have been true of IBM, Texas Instruments, Fuji-Xerox, Yokogawa–Hewlett-Packard, and, very likely, others as well.

Continuing the Fuji-Xerox story, the affiliate was battered by Japanese competition in the early 1970s. By 1975, Fuji-Xerox (whose president was Japanese) recognized that its competitors offered a higher-quality product produced by more efficient and cheaper methods. Having some independence in its policy making, it decided to develop its own product line, better adapted to Japanese needs, and to establish new companywide quality control procedures. The efforts were so successful that the company won the prestigious Deming prize in Japan in 1980.[19]

The Yokogawa–Hewlett-Packard joint venture, producer of electronic measurement equipment, faced somewhat similar problems at about the same time. In response, it embarked on a five-year program to improve quality controls and to integrate product planning and manufacturing. By the end of the period, it had cut manufacturing costs by 42 percent, inventory by 64 percent, product failure by 60 percent, and product development time by one-third.[20]

In the two cases just cited, the presence of a strong Japanese partner no doubt facilitated the absorption of Japanese process technology. But even in the case of the two major wholly U.S.-owned affiliates, IBM and TI, many senior officers were Japanese. And their staying power in the Japanese market, in the face of government preferences and support for their Japanese competitors, strongly suggests that they too had absorbed the best of Japanese process technology.

While the Japanese affiliates themselves benefited greatly from their exposure to Japanese process technology in the 1970s, it appears that in some cases, the U.S. parent companies did not apply what their affiliates had learned to operations at home until the 1980s, as we will see in later chapters.

Japanese Investment in the United States[21]

As Japan developed the financial strength to invest in the United States, its direct investments in manufacturing pursued three major objectives: (1) to gain access to cheap raw materials and energy-intensive products; (2) to acquire new technology; and (3) to exploit Japan's new technology strengths.

Access to Cheap Raw Materials and Energy

In view of Japan's dependence on imports for most raw materials, the Japanese trading companies often spearheaded aggressive investment abroad in raw materials extraction throughout the postwar period. This sometimes led to primary processing of those materials. In this case, they invested in lumber and fish processing. Investments in lumber were among Japan's earliest and accounted for a significant part of Japan's very modest manufacturing investments in the first half of the decade. In fisheries, several Japanese companies fishing the Pacific waters off the Alaskan coast and the Marubeni trading company acquired part or whole ownership in a number of Alaskan fish-freezing and fish-canning plants. These probably accounted for well over half of Japanese investments in the food industries by 1980.

After the first oil price shock of 1974, the interest of Japanese trading companies was focused on energy-intensive primary metals production. Energy costs rose more in Japan than in the United States because the Japanese authorities allowed the effect of rising world oil prices to be more fully reflected in domestic prices. This greatly increased the cost of producing energy-intensive products such as aluminum. In response, Mitsui and Company (a major Japanese trading firm), with minor participation by Nippon Steel, formed a joint venture with AMAX, a major U.S. aluminum producer, to manufacture primary aluminum and aluminum products. The joint venture, known as Alumax, started operations in 1974 and accounted for much of Japan's investments in primary and fabricated metals in 1980.

Similar incentives were probably partly responsible for Japanese trading company financial support for investments by small Japanese steel companies in the minimill sector of the U.S. steel industry in the second half of the 1970s. Minimills were then a new and lustily growing sector of the steel industry in both countries. Typically small and relying on electric furnaces and scrap metal, they were the low-cost producers of billets suitable for rolling into bars and small structural shapes.[22] In the United States, the price of scrap metal was low relative to that of iron ore, whereas in Japan the reverse was true.[23] This and lower energy costs in the United States after the oil shock may have appealed to Japanese minimill companies. The Sumitomo trading company joined Kyoei in establishing Auburn Steel in Maine in 1975, and Mitsui joined Tokyo Steel in acquiring a part interest in Tamco in California in 1976.

Acquiring New Product Technology

In the computer and semiconductor industries, Japanese companies supplemented their efforts to develop their own technology by investments in the United States to acquire U.S. technology. In computers, Fujitsu invested in a financially weak but technologically promising U.S. firm, Amdahl, not only to acquire technology but also to develop a base for marketing computers in the United States. Founded in 1970 by Gene Amdahl, a leading computer designer at IBM who had left to form his own company, Amdahl moved rapidly to take advantage of new developments in VLSI semiconductors to simplify the design and improve the speed and efficiency of mainframe computers. Early on, Amdahl ran into financial difficulties and, in 1973, welcomed equity participation from Fujitsu. Amdahl brought its first computer to market in 1975, a little ahead of IBM's similar mainframe.[24] By 1980, Fujitsu's share in Amdahl was 28 percent. In making this investment, Fujitsu gained access to IBM-compatible computer technology, which, as we have seen, had leapfrogged Japan's early efforts to beat IBM.

In semiconductors, Japan's technology-seeking investments started even earlier. The tendency of bright, ambitious U.S. researchers and engineers to leave established U.S. semiconductor companies to strike out on their own, only to run into financial constraints, invited technology-seeking investment by foreign firms, both Japanese and European.[25] In 1971, one of Japan's smaller semiconductor companies, Rohm, acquired a 25 percent interest in Exar, a new California company in need of financial assistance. In 1973, Seiko Epson acquired a 51 percent interest in Micro Power Systems. In 1979, NEC acquired Electronic Arrays, and in 1980, Toshiba acquired Maruman.

Exploiting a Lead in Process Technology

Roughly one-fourth of the investments made by Japanese firms in U.S. manufacturing in the 1970s were related to these firms exploiting their own technological advances, primarily in product

development and manufacturing methods. The biggest investments were in telecommunications equipment and some of their
components. But there were also modest investments in instruments (mainly photocopiers), motor vehicles, and machine tools.

Audio and TV receivers account for most of Japan's investment in communications equipment, shown in Table 4.1 (although
producers of private branch exchange systems also established a
foothold). In audio and TV receivers, Japanese firms combined
patents purchased from RCA and other U.S. companies in the
1950s and 1960s, some product innovations of their own in transistors and capacitors,[26] manufacturing skills, quality controls,
and astute product development to achieve their first lead in a
high-technology industry. Japan began to make some headway in
exporting to the United States in the 1960s and early 1970s. The
first success was Sony's small black-and-white TVs. This was
soon followed by Sanyo sales to Sears Roebuck for its private
label products, and then by growing sales by a number of other
Japanese companies to meet other retailers' private label de-
mands. Market gains were driven by Japan's growing reputation
for high quality, low defect rates, and low costs.[27]

Following up on early trade successes, Japanese companies
gradually established assembly plants in the United States. The
pioneers were Sony in TV receivers and Foster Electric in audio
speakers in 1972. They were followed by Matsushita in 1974 and
Sanyo in 1975. A second wave of investment by these same
players and others took off in 1977, in response to the three-year
orderly marketing agreement of 1977 limiting Japan's exports to
the United States. By the end of the decade, all of the major
Japanese firms in this field were assembling in the United States.
A number of associated firms also established plants whose products included semiconductors and other important electronic
components, tapes, ceramic wafers, and plastic, rubber, and fabricated metal parts.

The new technology transferred to the United States by Japanese investors in the assembly of TV and audio receivers was
mainly superior manufacturing methods, with their quality con-

trols and dramatically lower defect ratios.[28] However, there is little evidence of any prompt secondary diffusion of this technology to U.S. companies. Rather than rise to the challenge posed by the Japanese display of manufacturing skills, most of the major U.S. producers seemed to have lost interest in what they considered to be a mature industry, distracted by a variety of other seemingly more promising opportunities for expansion in other fields. RCA devoted much of its attention and R&D to computers (where it was ultimately unsuccessful), and Motorola concentrated its efforts on other sectors of telecommunications and on semiconductors. Indeed, Motorola gladly sold its TV division, with its two plants in Illinois, to Matsushita in 1974. Two other U.S. firms, Sylvania and Magnavox, sold out to Philips. By the end of the decade, only Zenith and RCA remained important U.S. suppliers in U.S. markets.[29] As we will see in chapter 7, Zenith ultimately mounted a strong competitive response, taking a leading role in the development of digital high-definition TV.

In other industries where strides in process technology were strengthening their competitiveness, a few Japanese firms established beachheads in U.S. manufacturing in the 1970s. In the photocopier industry, Ricoh and Canon followed up on successful competition with Fuji-Xerox in Japan by establishing plants in California to manufacture copiers and toner for copiers—Ricoh in 1973 and 1979, and Canon in 1974. These investments and an earlier investment in computer printers probably encouraged Dainippon Ink to acquire two U.S. companies producing printer's ink: Kohl and Madden in 1976 and Polychrome in 1979.

In motor vehicles, early entrants on the U.S. scene included two motorcycle producers—Kawasaki Motors and Honda—as well as Toyota, which started producing cargo beds for pickup trucks (an early Toyota specialty) in 1974. In 1979, Yamazaki Mazak opened the first Japanese plant producing numerically controlled machine tools in Florence, Kentucky, very close to Cincinnati, Ohio, long a machine tool center and an easy delivery run to Marysville, Ohio, where Honda was starting to manufacture motorcycles.

Conclusions

In the 1970s, U.S.-Japan bilateral direct investments were clearly approaching the turn of the tide. At the same time, associated technology flows became two-directional, with product technology continuing to flow from the United States to Japan and process technology beginning to flow from Japan to the United States. In addition, the threat posed by strong wholly owned U.S. companies operating aggressively in the Japanese computer and semiconductor industries galvanized Japanese government efforts to push Japanese technology into the lead. A program to develop advanced product technology in computers was leapfrogged by advances in U.S. semiconductor technology. But a program to strengthen process technology in some mass-produced semiconductors was dramatically successful. Competitive responses in other industries also improved Japanese technology. The same competitive forces led numerous Japanese affiliates of U.S. companies to absorb Japanese process technology innovations.

Japan's growing investments in the United States gradually shifted their focus from assuring access to raw materials and energy-intensive primary products to obtaining important computer and semiconductor technology and, even more, to exploiting Japan's growing success in manufacturing technology. In consumer audio and TV equipment, where Japanese successes were greatest, the initial response of U.S. companies was often to withdraw from the industry and to turn their attention to industries considered to have a higher growth potential. But Zenith showed some resilience, remaining to fight another day. Smaller Japanese investments in photocopiers, motor vehicles, and machine tools were harbingers of Japanese advances in the 1980s.

Notes

1. See, for example, "U.S. Computer Makers Unveil True Intentions," *Business Japan*, April 1976.

2. Mason (1992), pp. 206–7.

3. Unless otherwise indicated, factual material in this and the following five paragraphs is drawn from Chang (1981), chapters 3 and 4.

4. OECD, *Foreign Trade by Commodities*, Series C, Part 1 (1983).

5. "Isuzu-Mitsubishi Tie-up Looms as Future Reorganization Trend," *Japan Economic Journal*, June 4, 1968.

6. "Delay Seen in Chrysler Tie-Up Deal," *Japan Economic Journal*, February 10, 1970.

7. "Chrysler Plans to Buy Japanese Auto Parts," *Japan Economic Journal*, February 12, 1973.

8. "Joint Venture Starts for Car Transmissions," *Japan Economic Journal*, February 3, 1970.

9. "Ford's Reward for Waiting," *The Economist*, May 25, 1979.

10. *Moody's Industrial Manual* (1987).

11. Mason (1992), pp. 212–18, describes Dow's experiences.

12. *Moody's Industrial Manual* (1987).

13. "Ikegai Goss," *Business Japan*, April 1973.

14. "Accuride Is Planning to Set Up Joint Venture in Japan," *Japan Economic Journal*, August 13, 1974.

15. Letter to author, May 30, 1993, from John Lawrence, Chairman of the Board at Dresser Industries in the 1960s and early 1970s.

16. "Oki Electric Returns to Computers," *Japan Economic Journal*, May 28, 1968.

17. The description of Japanese government programs for computers and semiconductors given here draws heavily on Borrus, Millstein, and Zysman (1983), especially pp. 205–11 and 221–23.

18. Clausing, Allen, Berg, Dertouzos, Ferguson, Haavind, Moses, and Penfield (1989), pp. 37–38.

19. Ibid.

20. Young (1988).

21. Unless otherwise indicated, references to Japanese investors, their affiliates' products, and employment are from MacKnight (1981, 1992a).

22. Barnett and Crandall (1986), pp. 4–10.

23. Ibid., p. 24.

24. "Will IBM Trounce Its 'Imitators' with Its Next Computer?" *The Economist*, February 3, 1979.

25. Borrus, Millstein, and Zysman (1983), pp. 164–65 and 172.

26. Staelin, Bozdogan, Cusumano, Ferguson, Filippone, Reintjes, Rosenbloom, Solow, and Ward (1989), p. 12.

27. Scherer (1992), pp. 52–56, provides an interesting short history of technology developments in color TV receivers.

28. Staelin et al. (1989), p. 16.

29. Ibid., p. 45.

Part III

The New Relationship

5

Japanese Technology Contributions to the U.S. Auto Industry

In the 1980s, Japan's superior process technology became increasingly evident in medium- and low-technology industries. In a number of them, rising imports from Japan triggered U.S. trade restraints. Japanese firms responded by investing in the United States, thereby introducing their process technology to the United States. Experience in the U.S. auto industry is notable for the scope of the technology introduced, the vigor of the U.S. companies' response, and the associated speedy dissemination of the technology throughout the U.S. industry.

Much of the Japanese auto companies' process technology derived from quality control ideas developed in the United States and first introduced to Japan during the Occupation period by William E. Deming, as described in chapter 3. Adapting those ideas to the needs of their industry as it developed and flourished, the Japanese auto companies created a manufacturing system which produced autos of superior quality and at lower cost than those produced elsewhere. Following up on success in exports, the big three Japanese auto companies—Toyota, Nissan, and Honda—established manufacturing operations in the United States in the early 1980s. They were followed late in the decade by the three smaller Japanese companies—Mazda, Mitsubishi, and Isuzu—in which the U.S. big three had already acquired an equity position, as described in chapter 4. Each of the big three U.S. auto companies devoted much effort to absorbing Japanese process technology in its own distinctive way. Their strategies included joint ventures and other collaboration with the Japanese big three and drawing on the skills of the smaller Japanese companies in which they had invested. By the early 1990s, they had succeeded in greatly reducing the technology gap between themselves and their Japanese competitors—with signs of more to come.

Japanese Market Gains and Factors Attracting U.S. Consumers

Japan's gains, relative to those of the United States, in international trade (noted in chapter 2) were reflected in the U.S. domestic market, where the number of cars and light trucks imported from Japan rose from negligible proportions in the early 1960s to 4.2 percent in 1970 and 21.4 percent in 1980. While the "voluntary restraints" on Japanese auto exports to the United States agreed to by Japan in 1980 limited any further expansion in the share of imports from Japan, they also encouraged Japanese direct investment in U.S. manufacturing and modest investments in Canada as well. By 1991, the Japanese share of U.S. retail sales of cars and light trucks had risen to 28.3 percent. Roughly half of that was produced by the Japanese companies' U.S. and Canadian affiliates. By 1993, this share had receded slightly to 26.3 percent (see Table 5.1).

In the late 1970s, U.S. consumers had become increasingly attracted to Japanese cars by the fuel economy associated with their small size, performance as good as or better than other small cars, and superior repair records. Tests by *Consumer Reports* (*CR*) (1981) of small cars sold in the United States put Japanese cars on a par with European cars and far superior to U.S. cars in that size group (see Table 5.2). At that time, however, Japanese production and export efforts were concentrated on small cars, while U.S. firms' efforts were focused on larger cars.

Table 5.1

Japanese Companies' Share of the U.S. Market for Cars and Light Trucks, 1963–93

	1963	1973	1980	1983	1991	1992	1993
	Sales (thousands of vehicles)						
Cars and light trucks[a]							
Total U.S. market	8,801	14,380	11,238	11,901	12,335	12885	13917
Produced by Japanese companies	8	823	2,408	2,285	3,490	3,584	3,664
Cars							
Total U.S. market				9,153	8,176	8,211	8,518
Produced by Japanese companies				1,953	2,761	2,889	2,895
Of which: by U.S. and Canadian affiliates				50	1,442	1,443	1,563
Light trucks[a]							
Total U.S. market				2,748	4,159	4,674	5,398
Produced by Japanese companies				332	728	695	769
	Japanese Companies' Share in U. S. Markets[b]						
Cars and light trucks[a]	0.1	5.7	21.4	19.2	28.3	27.8	26.3
Cars				21.3	33.8	35.2	34.0
Light trucks				12.1	17.5	14.9	14.2

Sources: Cusumano (1989) Appendix C; *Automotive News* (January 11, 1993, and January 10, 1994); MacKnight (1992c, 1994).

[a] Light trucks include minivans and sports-utility vehicles.

[b] Includes vehicles sold by the big three U.S. companies but made in plants managed by Japanese companies; excludes vehicles sold by Japanese companies but made in big three plants.

During the 1980s and early 1990s, probably initially in response to quantitative "voluntary" export restraints forced on them by the United States, Japanese companies moved up-market to larger cars with higher profit margins. These included compact, midsize, luxury, and sporty cars, plus minivans and sport-utility vehicles. As they entered these new markets, the Japanese companies moved quickly to top *CR* overall test ratings in most and top reliability ratings in all of these categories.

Table 5.2

Consumer Reports Tests of Small Cars in the U.S. Market, 1980–81
(by location of manufacture)

	United States	Japan	Europe
Models in market	10	18	11
Models tested[a]	4	10	6
Models preferred	1	7	4
as percentage of tested	25	70	67

Source: Consumer Reports (April 1981).

[a] Of the twenty cars tested, two were tested in 1979, sixteen in 1980, and two in 1981.

Further, there is general agreement among those who have studied the U.S. and Japanese auto industries that by the early 1980s, Japanese firms had probably achieved a higher level of man-hour productivity than U.S. firms. But measuring the size of the gap has proved extraordinarily difficult in view of differences between the two countries' manufacturing and assembly systems. Some useful measurements will be reported later in this chapter.

Evolution of Japan's Technology

The success of Japanese companies in world auto markets from the late 1970s onward had its roots in their enormous innovative efforts during the first quarter century after World War II to adapt U.S. manufacturing methods and quality control concepts to their own rapidly changing market opportunities. This produced a distinctive flexible manufacturing system, methods of product planning and development, and supplier relationships. Beginning in the 1970s, Japanese companies also offered interesting product innovations, which further enhanced the popularity of Japanese cars.

Flexible Manufacturing Systems

The innovative flexible manufacturing methods developed by Japanese auto companies in the early postwar years evolved as a response to the small size of their domestic market and the large number of assemblers. In 1955 Japanese auto output was less than 70,000 and, after a decade of headlong growth, had reached 1.9 million in 1965.[1] At that time, after some thinning of the ranks, there were still eleven Japanese assembly companies.[2] This ruled out trying to duplicate the long production runs of identical products and job specialization on the assembly floor that had been adopted in the United States in the 1920s (and later supported by labor unions as a means of protecting jobs). It also put a premium on assembly methods that permitted rapid shifts from producing one product to another.

The Japanese assembly firms responded to their special problems by developing manufacturing systems more flexible than their U.S. prototypes.[3] Assembly floor workers were organized in teams whose members were expected to perform numerous tasks (including quality inspections) interchangeably. All of the auto companies used time-motion studies to reduce the time required to adjust equipment to perform new tasks such as changing dies in a stamping press. (In the 1970s in Japan, where there was a frequent need for such changes, the time required to do so had been reduced to five minutes, while in the United States, where such changes were infrequent, the change required eight to twenty-four hours.[4]) The companies also greatly reduced inventory costs by requiring frequent small deliveries of parts to meet day-to-day assembly line needs—the "just-in-time" system.

However, in the 1950s and 1960s, the auto assemblers did differ in their approach to automation and inventory management.[5] Toyota, placing greater reliance on general-purpose machine tools, required its workers to make the frequent adjustments that permitted them to perform a wide variety of tasks, and arranged assembly lines in configurations that permitted one worker to tend a number of machines. It also pioneered in the development of just-in-time inventory controls. By contrast, Nissan moved more quickly to single-function high-speed machine tools, introducing transfer machines for flexibility, and rapidly increased its reliance on computers to schedule the organization of assembly lines and parts purchase, and on robots to maintain machinery. Other auto companies' assembly systems appear to have fallen between these two extremes.

By 1970, when Japanese car output had topped 5 million, the original rationale for flexible assembly methods had receded. But the general approach had yielded many other advantages, such as reliance on workers to conduct continuous quality inspection, the just-in-time inventory system, the variety of models that could be offered, and the ease of adjusting models for export (for example, producing right-hand and left-hand drive cars on the same production line). Thus, the basic flexible approach was preserved. However, during the 1970s and 1980s, Toyota, Nissan, and the other assemblers, recognizing the advantages of one another's somewhat different assembly systems, brought their systems closer together. Toyota increased reliance on automation, and Nissan tightened its inventory controls.

New Model Planning and Development

By the late 1970s or before, the Japanese system of new model planning and development had also acquired distinctive and much-admired features. One was the closer integration of its various stages—initial concept study, product planning, advance engineering, product engineering, process engineering, and pilot run—resulting in more overlap and shorter time elapsed between the initial concept and the pilot run. A broad sample survey of U.S., European, and Japanese companies in the mid-1980s found the average time elapsed to have been sixty-two months for the U.S. and European companies, as compared to only forty months for the Japanese companies.[6]

A second very important feature of product planning was the permeation of quality control concepts to all stages of the process. Drawing on past experience and consumer responses, planners sought to avoid defects by choice of materials and product design. A third and related feature was inclusion of major suppliers of critical parts in the product planning and development process.

Supplier Relationships

Japan's distinctive organization of parts suppliers seems to have helped Japanese assemblers to achieve a more reliable final product, possibly at lower cost, than that of their U.S. counterparts. The development of auto parts supply groups has been traced in detail by Cusumano (1985) and by Smitka (1991). The system, developed early in the postwar period, maintained the same broad structure thereafter. In the 1980s, each assembly company was dealing with a group of a few hundred suppliers with whom they maintained long-run supply relationships. (For Toyota and Nissan, this included a dozen or so companies in which they had a strong but usually minority interest.) Some suppliers dealt largely with a single assembler, but some (especially tires, glass, and electronics) dealt with two or even more assemblers. The supply groups sometimes included more than one supplier of a given product for different car models thereby maintaining a degree of competition tension. Some first-tier supply group members were themselves assemblers of major car components and maintained their own groups of suppliers, and some in second-tier supply groups even organized their own supply groups.[7] These long-term supply relationships lent themselves to the "just-in-time" system of delivery and inventory management.

Relationships of Japanese assembly companies with their suppliers evolved over time, shifting from heavy pressure to reduce costs in the 1950s and 1960s to more help with quality controls in the 1970s and 1980s. This crucial shift was speeded by another jolting new idea from the United States.[8] In 1966, the U.S. Congress enacted legislation requiring government inspection for safety defects of cars sold in the United States, and that the makers of defective vehicles recall them and make repairs at their own expense. The Japanese Ministry of Transport, its sights already set on the U.S. market, reacted by setting up a similar system for Japan. In 1969, the first inspection year, there were recalls for safety defects on 2.5 million Japanese cars, trucks, and motorcycles (roughly equal to the average annual output in the preceding five years). The auto companies found that most of the defects could be traced to parts acquired from suppliers, who may have chosen inferior materials in response to price pressures from the assemblers, or to defective design. As this came to be recognized, the auto companies increased their emphasis on product design and specifications with a view to reducing defects, and broadened their special relationship with suppliers. This included insisting on better quality controls, helping them achieve those controls, and pulling major suppliers into the product planning process.

In the early 1980s, the relationship of Japanese assembly companies with their suppliers was very different from the system prevailing in the United States. U.S. companies produced more of their own parts than did Japanese companies. (Estimates differ as to how much more.) But for the rest, they determined their requirements and put them out to competitive bidding. At any given time, they might be purchasing largely standardized parts from suppliers numbering in the thousands who worked to fill short-term contracts. This system permitted little cooperation or exchange of helpful information between assemblers and suppliers, as well as lower-quality parts and higher defect ratios.[9]

Product Technology

For much of the postwar period, the Japanese auto industry drew on European and U.S. sources for product technology. In the 1950s, all Japanese auto companies assiduously studied small European cars, considered to be better adapted than U.S. cars to Japan's narrow roads and city streets.[10] Encouraged by the Japanese government, three companies contracted to assemble European cars in Japan—Nissan for Austin, Isuzu for Rootes, and Hino for Renault—while Shin Mitsubishi did the same for Willys Overland.[11] By contrast, Toyota decided very early to rely more heavily on reverse engineering, whereby they purchased foreign vehicles and parts and copied their essentials without violating patent law.[12] Many parts companies also relied on technology agreements with European (mainly German) and U.S. companies.[13] This was followed in the 1960s and 1970s by the U.S.–Japan joint ventures in manufacturing parts in Japan, as described in chapters 3 and 4.

But by the late 1970s, Japanese companies were developing product technology of their own—for example, Honda's CVCC engine and Mazda's adaptation of the Wankel engine. In the 1980s, Japanese companies pioneered multivalve cylinders in auto engines and four-wheel drive. In 1987, as noted in chapter 2 (Table 2.6), Japanese companies were awarded more U.S. patents for internal combustion engines than U.S. companies were. Womack (1989) suggests that these Japanese product successes reflected their superiority in exploiting technologies "on the shelf" in their research departments.[14]

Japanese Investment and U.S. Absorption of Japanese Technology

The fairly rapid dissemination of Japanese innovations in process and product technology throughout the U.S. auto assembly and parts industries in the 1980s and early 1990s owes much to Japan's direct investment in those industries in the United States, beginning in 1982. The transplants demonstrated that Japanese process technology was indeed transferable to the U.S. environment, and they immediately raised technology levels in the United States by an amount proportionate to their importance in the industry. At the same time, U.S. companies energetically absorbed the technology by various means, forming joint ventures or other collaborative arrangements with the big three Japanese companies and drawing on the smaller Japanese companies in which they held minority equity positions. Some small U.S. auto parts producers who became suppliers to the Japanese transplants gained from a forced-march learning experience.

Japanese Direct Investment in the United States[15]

While the Japanese auto makers had made a cautious start in U.S.

manufacturing in the late 1970s—Toyota in cargo beds for trucks in California and Honda in motorcycles in Ohio—the voluntary export restraints accepted by Japan in 1980 no doubt accelerated the migration. Honda was the first to manufacture cars in the United States, establishing an assembly plant in Ohio in 1982 and, in partnership with associated companies, a plant to manufacture automotive seat assemblies and steel wheels. Nissan followed in 1983 with a plant to assemble trucks in Tennessee. And Toyota joined with GM to establish the New United Motor Manufacturing, Inc. (NUMMI), joint venture, which started assembling cars in California in 1984.

In the latter half of the 1980s, Toyota established its own assembly plant in Kentucky; the three smaller Japanese companies in which the U.S. big three already held large minority interests also established manufacturing plants in the United States, and investments by Japanese auto parts makers gathered momentum. These new ventures pushed employment in assembly, stampings, and parts produced in the same plants to over 24,000 in 1990. At the same time, the establishment of many additional plants producing basic auto parts (principally, engines and parts, transmissions, catalytic converters, brakes, steering systems, clutches, wheels, and suspension systems) pushed employment in Japanese companies' affiliates in the SIC motor vehicles and parts industry as a whole to over 34,000 (see Table 5.3).

During the decade, there was also substantial investment in the United States by Japanese firms manufacturing other car components not counted in the motor vehicle industry in national and international statistics. These included engine parts, a wide variety of electrical equipment, tires and other rubber auto parts, car seats, safety equipment, and audio equipment. Drawing on employment data collected by the Japan Economic Institute and further information drawn from other sources, Dalton and Yoshida (1992) concluded that total employment in Japanese companies' U.S. affiliates in autos, parts, and other closely related industries was about 90,000 in 1990.

Table 5.3

Employment in U.S. Affiliates of Japanese Companies in Auto and Parts Manufacturing, 1990

SIC Code		Japanese Companies' U.S. Affiliates (in thousands)	All U.S. Businesses (in thousands)	Japanese Affiliated, All U.S. Businesses (%)
371	Motor vehicles and equipment	34.5	704.4	4.9
3711	Motor vehicles and car bodies	24.2	239.5	10.1
3713,5	Trucks, bus bodies, and truck trailers	0.4[a]	62.0	0.6
3714	Motor vehicle parts and accessories[b]	9.9[a]	388.7	2.5

Sources: U.S. Department of Commerce (1993c); Office of Management and Budget (1988).

[a] Estimated from ranges given in source.

[b] Establishments primarily engaged in producing parts and accessories rather than complete motor vehicles. Excludes establishments primarily producing auto stampings, vehicular lighting equipment, ignition systems, storage batteries, carburetors, pistons and rings, and engine intake and exhaust values.

As noted earlier, the mere presence of Japanese companies assembling cars and producing auto parts had an immediate effect on U.S. productivity. A rough notion of the size of this initial impact is provided by the ratio of employment in Japanese-affiliated companies to that in the entire U.S. auto and parts industries, given in Table 5.3. It appears that by 1990 those companies accounted for about 10 percent of U.S. employment in auto assembly. In car parts produced in separate plants and classified as auto parts (SIC 3714)—engines, transmissions, brakes, wire harness sets, and a wide variety of other items—Japanese companies clearly did not move to the United States on the same scale as the assemblers did, since their share of U.S. employment was only 2.5 percent. This was partly due to continuing reliance on suppliers in Japan, as reflected in the rise in U.S. imports from Japan. But it was also due to the transplants' rising use of U.S. suppliers in a concerted effort to meet the complaints of U.S. parts makers, who were suffering from the declining share of their main customers, the U.S. auto companies, in the U.S. market for motor vehicles.

U.S. Companies' Strategies for Learning

The success of the Japanese small car in U.S. markets in the late 1970s generated rising respect in the U.S. industry. In the 1970s, GM and Chrysler drew on their recently acquired Japanese affiliates for small cars and trucks to sell under their own marques in the United States. In the 1980s, as Japanese companies demonstrated the applicability of Japanese process technology to the manufacture of larger cars, the U.S. auto companies developed strategies for absorbing and adapting that technology to their own operations. In each case, the U.S. company formed a joint venture or other collaboration with one of the Japanese big three auto companies and also drew on the small Japanese companies in which they had invested—Isuzu, Mitsubishi Motors, or Mazda— encouraging these companies to manufacture in the United States (see Table 5.4). Despite these broad similarities, the ways in which each of the three U.S. companies, Japanese technology was distinctive.

GM continued to draw on Isuzu for its imports of small cars and trucks and, late in the 1980s, supported that company in its joint venture with Subaru to manufacture in the United States. (It also formed a new manufacturing joint venture in Canada with another small Japanese company, Suzuki.) But GM's learning efforts were concentrated on NUMMI, its joint manufacturing venture in the United States with Toyota. Toyota was the only one of the Japanese big three to devote part of its investment in the United States to a full-fledged, separately incorporated joint venture. One reason for doing so appears to have been a desire to placate Congress's increasingly negative views of the Japanese industry. But in addition, Toyota's attitude toward foreign investing was more conservative than that of Honda or Nissan. It valued the opportunity to learn more about U.S. parts suppliers and U.S. labor unions in a joint venture experiment before striking out on its own.[16]

NUMMI started operations in 1984 in an idled GM plant in California, redesigned, reequipped, and managed by Toyota. Initially, NUMMI assembled a car already designed by Toyota, to be sold as a Corolla and as a Chevrolet Nova. It planned to obtain about half of its parts (including engines and transmissions) from suppliers in Japan, and the other half from suppliers in the United States.[17] GM dispatched a rotating succession of managers and engineers to work and learn under the Japanese. The many lessons to be learned from NUMMI included (1) Toyota's assembly methods, including quality controls on the assembly line; (2) Toyota's relations with suppliers and the importance of low defect ratios in auto parts supplied; and (3) Toyota's method of dealing with labor union realities in the United States. Although Honda and Nissan, already producing in the United States, had succeeded in discouraging UAW organization of their workers, Toyota agreed to recognize the UAW as bargaining agent for workers at the plant and to use laid-off GM workers as the primary source for new hires. In exchange, the UAW agreed to be flexible about work rules. This permitted Toyota to introduce its own system of work teams and job classifications.[18] In addition, GM observers visited and studied Toyota's operations in Japan, including methods of product planning and development and its relationship with their suppliers in Japan.

Reports of life at NUMMI in the early 1990s suggest that there may have been a bit of a relapse as the joint venture aged and that productivity was not as high at NUMMI as at Toyota's wholly owned plant in Kentucky, which started operations in 1988. It was also reported that Toyota officials attributed the differences to staffing, suggesting that the thirty managerial and technical employees assigned to NUMMI by Toyota were simply not enough to assure the thorough penetration of the Toyota management style.[19]

Table 5.4

U.S.-Japan Joint Ventures and Collaborations in Auto Assembly in the United States

Starting Date	U.S. Partner	Japanese Partner	Products[a]	Assembly By[a]	Design By[a]	Major Parts From[a]
Joint ventures						
1984	GM	Toyota	Small cars Toyota Corolla GM Nova	Toyota	Toyota	Toyota
1989	GM[b]	Subaru-Isuzu	Small cars Pickup trucks Sport-utility vehicles	Subaru-Isuzu		

1987	Ford[c]	Mazda	Sporty cars
			Mazda MX6
			Ford Probe
			
			Compact cars
			Mazda 626
				Mazda	Mazda
					Ford
					  Styling and
					  dashboard
					  for Probe
						Mazda
						Engine transmission
						Ford
						Other
						
						Ford
						Other

1988	Chrysler	Mitsubishi	Small cars Mitsubishi Mirage Eagle Summit Sporty cars Mitsubishi Eclipse Eagle Talon Eagle Summit	Mitsubishi	Joint	Chrysler Engine transmission Mitsubishi Other

Collaborations						
1990	Ford	Mazda	Small car Ford Escort	Ford	Mazda chassis transmission Ford other	Mazda engine
1991	Ford	Mazda	Sport-utility vehicles Mazda Navajo Ford Explorer	Ford		
1993	Ford	Mazda	Pickup trucks	Ford		
1993	Ford	Nissan	Small vans Mercury Villager Nissan Quest	Ford	Nissan	Nissan body panels engine

Sources: MacKnight (1992a); press reports.

[a] Refers to initial products in the case of joint ventures. Joint venture plants also produced body stampings and molded plastic parts.

[b] Through part ownership of Isuzu.

[c] Initially through part ownership of Mazda. Ford acquired 50 percent ownership of the Michigan plant in 1992.

Nevertheless, early GM observers at NUMMI and at Toyota in Japan were very favorably impressed with the Toyota style and did their best to apply what they had learned throughout GM. The most successful of these endeavors was the establishment of an entirely new company, Saturn, in a new locality, Tennessee. Saturn adopted Toyota's integrated approach to product planning and development and a modified version of the supply group system.[20] Major suppliers were selected early so that they could be brought into the planning process. They included eleven GM affiliates—one a joint venture with a Japanese company (Akebono Brake)—at least six Japanese parts companies, a few U.S.-Japan joint ventures, and numerous U.S. companies. All had contracts for the duration of the model. Key components were all single-sourced, and most suppliers were linked electronically to Saturn in order to facilitate just-in-time deliveries and payments.[21] A newly assembled labor force working under an unusually flexible UAW contract similar to the one at NUMMI seems to have enthusiastically embraced the new cooperative work environment.

GM's efforts to apply some of the lessons learned from NUMMI and Saturn to the rest of its operations in the 1980s were piecemeal and less successful. Its 1987 contract with UAW included provision for acceptance of the Japanese team concept in exchange for greater job security at a few plants. However, implementation is reported to have been stalled by resistance from some managers and workers.[22] The replacement of key players in GM's top management in 1992 and 1993 brought many changes, such as a start on new relationships with suppliers,[23] and a reduction in the number of vehicle frames to seven from twenty,[24] with signs of many more changes to come.

Ford, by contrast, seems to have decided to learn by actively participating—in a joint venture, a series of collaborations with Mazda (in which it had a 25 percent equity position), and one collaboration with Nissan. As described in chapter 4, Ford acquired its interest in Mazda in 1979. Soon thereafter, it embarked on a series of collaborations with that company. The first collaborative manufacturing effort aimed at the U.S. market was in Mexico. In 1983 Ford received permission from the Mexican government to establish an auto assembly plant for the assembly of Mazdas, using Mazda engines and transmissions imported from Japan, to be sold mainly in the United States.[25] This was followed by Mazda's purchase of a Ford plant in Michigan, where it started assembling its MX6 and the Ford Probe in 1987. Engines and transmissions for both cars were designed and manufactured in Japan, while Ford was responsible for the body styling and dashboard of the Probe and for the supply of some parts for both cars.[26] Management was entirely in the hands of Mazda, which negotiated a contract with the UAW allowing it to use Japanese style job classifications and work procedures.[27] Mazda also advised Ford on quality controls in the manufacture and procurement of parts and worked to expand its own purchases of parts produced in the United States.[28] By 1992, this heavy reliance on locally produced parts allowed Mazda to become the first Japanese transplant to claim 75 percent U.S. domestic content, the minimum required to be classified as domestic for purposes of EPA fuel economy regulations. But even then, Mazda continued to obtain engines and transmissions from Japan.[29]

Ford and Mazda also engaged in a number of other collaborations, dividing between themselves in various ways the tasks of design, manufacture and procurement of parts, and final assembly. Mazda assisted in the design and engineering of the Ford Escort, and Ford designed and assembled a sport-utility vehicle sold as the Mazda Navajo and the Ford Explorer.[30] To allow Mazda to avoid a 25 percent tariff, Ford developed and produced a pickup truck for Mazda.[31]

In 1992 Ford purchased a half interest in Mazda USA and appointed several senior officers at the firm. While press accounts interpreted this as an effort to gain closer control over the operation and to protect its interests,[32] the move would also give Ford closer experience with Japanese manufacturing methods.

As its ventures with Mazda were moving forward, Ford also began to cultivate relations with Nissan. In 1988, after two years of negotiations, the two companies announced their intention to jointly develop and produce a front-wheel-drive minivan, to be brought to market under both companies' nameplates in 1992. It was agreed that Nissan would design and engineer the vehicle (mostly at its new R&D facilities in the United States), providing the engine, power train, and main body panels from its plants in Tennessee, and that Ford would contribute one of its existing plants, at Avon Lake, Ohio, and the labor force already employed there. It was also agreed that Nissan would be responsible for organizing the assembly operations and parts supplier relationships and that thirty Nissan "advisers" would remain at the plant for several months after production started before turning over plant operations to Ford.[33]

Interestingly, part of the plant at Avon Lake continued to produce the Ford Econoline van. This part of the plant employed 1,700 persons working under a standard UAW contract. The Nissan-Ford part of the plant, also employing 1,700, operated under a radically revised UAW contract permitting the Japanese team system of manufacturing and assembly. One may speculate that the close-at-hand comparison of the two systems involving Ford workers in both parts of the factory may yield some conclusions of value to both labor and management.

Its experiences with Mazda and Nissan seem to have contributed to Ford's sustained restructuring efforts throughout the 1980s and early 1990s. The building of improved labor relations in the mid-1980s (following massive layoffs and outsourcing early in the 1980s) drew on observation of Mazda operations in Japan.[34] Advice from Mazda regarding parts procurement led to a number of modifications in Ford's mode of operations. In 1990 Ford began to experiment with the team approach to new model planning and development.[35] And, possibly reacting to its dependence for engines on its Japanese partners in joint ventures and collaborations, it stepped up its R&D on engines and, in 1992, introduced a new V-6 engine incorporating the multivalve cylinders commonly found in Japanese engines.[36]

Chrysler, like Ford, gave its attention first to the Japanese firm in which it already held a strong minority interest, Mitsubishi Motors. However, it was the last of the U.S. big three to move aggressively into learning relationships. It formed a joint manufacturing venture with Mitsubishi Motors, called Diamond Star, which started producing small and sporty Mitsubishis and Chryslers in Illinois in 1988. Chrysler provided half of Diamond Star's capital which, taken with its interest in Mitsubishi Motors, made Chrysler the ultimate majority owner. The chairman of Diamond Star was a Chrysler official, but day-to-day management was in the hands of Mitsubishi appointees. Chrysler supplied engines and transmissions developed jointly with Mitsubishi.[37] Diamond Star's contract with the UAW was thought to give the workers even more job security than there was at NUMMI, Mazda, or Saturn—in exchange for reducing job classifications from dozens to three and accepting the team concept.[38]

In 1991, Chrysler responded to serious operating losses throughout its entire company, as well as at Diamond Star, by selling its half interest in Diamond Star to Mitsubishi Motors. But it retained its rights to half of Diamond Star's output and its role as supplier of engines and transmissions.[39] In 1993, Chrysler eliminated its interest in Mitsubishi Motors itself, profiting from the high value of the yen relative to the dollar at the time.[40]

Chrysler also developed a special relationship with Honda. This link seems to have been looser and less comprehensive than any of the joint ventures and collaborations described thus far, but it helped to correct weaknesses at both companies. The rising popularity of sport-utility vehicles in the United States and Japan in the 1990s seems to have caught Honda by surprise. The company responded by starting to develop its own vehicle. But given the time required to develop an entirely new product and to establish suitable production facilities, Honda filled the gap in its product offerings in Japan by selling the Cherokee Jeep for Chrysler. Chrysler had long admired Honda, had studied it intensively since the late 1980s, and seems to have welcomed the opportunity to work with that firm. Consultations between technical personnel in the two companies contributed to Chrysler's decision to offer a right-hand-drive vehicle in 1992, its first in Japan, and to establish a special R&D section to work on quality improvements at its Ohio plant which manufactured the Cherokee.[41]

In reaction to its associations with Mitsubishi and Honda, Chrysler experimented with a new system of product development, adopting a team concept patterned closely on the Honda system but that also drew heavily on its experience at Diamond Star.[42] The first Chrysler platform team, organized in 1989, brought its first products (the LH cars) to market in the fall of 1992. Whereas platforms at Chrysler had previously been planned piecemeal in separate "chimneys" with imperfect coordination of the pieces, the LH platform team brought together representatives from management, labor, design, engineering, purchasing, manufacturing sales and marketing, finance, service, and major suppliers. The high-powered team leader was the ex-chairman of the Diamond Star joint venture, who brought further ideas from his experience there. As the LH team completed its work in 1992, the core team, some 300 strong, turned its attention to the development of a new compact car, targeted for market in 1995.

In summarizing the approaches of the big three U.S. companies to learning from their Japanese partners, GM appears to have left the initial organization and operation of its joint venture in Toyota's hands, concentrating on observing and applying or adapting what it had learned to GM operations as a whole and to a greenfields venture of its own. By contrast, Ford's approach to its joint venture with Mazda and to its collaborations with Mazda and Nissan was energetically participatory, involving numerous divisions of the Ford company in making a wide range of vehicles. Chrysler's efforts appear to have fallen somewhere between those two extremes.

Progress Report

In their efforts to absorb Japanese process technology, the big

Table 5.5

**Reliability of U.S. and Japanese Cars Sold in the United States
as Reflected in Repair Records, 1980-90[a]** (problems per 100 cars)

	1980	1985	1990
Cars new when surveyed			
GM	112	55	40
Ford	100	47	33
Chrysler	90	57	32
Average, U.S. big three	101	53	35
Nissan	47	28	16
Honda	35	20	15
Toyota	24	18	17
Average, Japan's big three	35	22	16
U.S. big three/Japan's big three	2.85	2.41	2.19
U.S. big three/Toyota	4.19	2.94	2.06
Cars five years old when surveyed			
GM	265	250	190
Ford	280	235	170
Chrysler	300	280	200
Average, U.S. big three	282	255	187
Nissan	265	170	140
Honda	265	155	85
Toyota	165	110	100
Average, Japan's big three	232	145	108
U.S. big three/Japan's big three	1.22	1.76	1.72
U.S. big three/Toyota	1.71	2.32	1.87

Source: Consumer Reports (April 1991).

[a] Read from *CR* chart. Based on *CR* reader replies (averaging "several hundred thousand") to annual questionnaires. Records for GM, Ford, and Chrysler exclude models that are foreign in design, manufacture, or both.

three U.S. auto companies were pursuing a moving target, but they nevertheless managed to gain ground. The extent of their gains with respect to quality of the product is suggested by *Consumer Reports'* annual tests of a broad sample of cars sold in the United States and their analysis of reliability based on frequency-of-repair records derived from answers to its questionnaire sent annually to all *CR* subscribers.

In 1991, *CR* published a special comparison of repair records of cars designed and manufactured entirely by the Japanese big three and by the U.S. big three in each year from 1980 through 1990. Their findings, summarized in Table 5.5, reveal that there were two catch-ups in process during the decade. Nissan and Honda were catching up with Toyota, and by 1990 Honda had at least temporarily wrested the lead from Toyota. At the same time, the U.S. big three were narrowing but not eliminating the gap between themselves and their Japanese counterparts.

Consumer Reports' annual report on their tests for performance and evaluations of comfort and convenience, as well as their latest reliability reports, is summarized in Table 5.6. In overall testing scores, all of the sedans in all price groups are rated by a single standard, while sporty cars, minivans, and sport-utility vehicles are rated according to standards specific to those types. In summarizing the report, we have grouped companies according to the nationality of the company actually operating the assembly plant. In most cases, the assembling company also designed the product. A single important exception is the top-rated minivan, assembled by Ford but designed by Nissan and in a plant designed by Nissan, as described earlier.

In the overall ratings (excluding reliability) for small cars, the few U.S. cars tested did very nearly as well as those of the Japanese companies. In compact cars, midsize cars, and luxury cars—all fields new to the Japanese in the 1980s—the ratings of Japanese cars averaged higher than those of U.S. cars. In large cars, where there were no Japanese entries, U.S. cars did very well. In sporty cars, U.S. and Japanese companies seemed evenly matched. In minivans, we have already noted that Nissan contributed to Ford's top rating. But in sport-utility vehicles, U.S. companies, Ford and Chrysler, were clear winners. In terms of reliability ratings, however, the rating for Japanese companies averaged higher than U.S. company ratings in every group in which the Japanese were active.

With respect to manufacturing productivity, available evidence suggests that a significant gap between Japanese and U.S. producers remained in the early 1990s, but might be closing. The

International Motor Vehicle Program at MIT spent several years in the late 1980s and early 1990s comparing performance at selected assembly plants in Japan, North America, Europe, and four newly industrializing countries. Some of their findings on man-hours per unit of output and the quality of the output (measured in terms of defect ratios) for U.S. and Japanese assembly plants are given in Table 5.7.

The study reports separately on Japanese-owned plants in Japan, Japanese plants in North America (including joint ventures with U.S. companies), and plants in North America that were wholly owned by U.S. companies. Their measures of both man-hour productivity and quality in 1989 averaged 50 percent higher in Japanese-owned plants in Japan than in U.S.-owned plants in the United States. Plants in the United States that were wholly or partly owned by Japanese companies occupied a middle ground; their man-hour productivity was lower than, but product quality was equal to, Japanese plants in Japan.

An interesting feature of IMVP findings was that the difference between the best and the worst man-hour productivity and defect ratios among the Japanese plants in Japan and among the wholly U.S.-owned plants in the United States was greater than the difference between the average performance of those two groups. Moreover, the performance of the best of the wholly U.S. owned plants with respect to both man-hour productivity and defect ratios was roughly equal to that of the best in the Japanese transplant group. Since there is intense competition among the U.S. big three, the achievements of one of them could lead to a further narrowing of the performance gap between U.S. and Japanese assembly plants.

Conclusions

To summarize, Japan's emerging strength in world car markets in the 1970s was based on innovative process technology involving a flexible manufacturing system, integrated product

Table 5.6

Consumer Reports' 1994 Ratings of New Cars Produced by U.S. and Japanese Companies and Sold in the United States
(number of car models)

Type and Producer	Overall Testing Score[a]						Reliability Ratings[b]					
	P	F	G	VG	E	Total	MW	W	A	B	MB	Total[c]
Small cars		2	6	4		12	1		3	1	5	10
Japanese		1	4	3		8			1	1	4	6
U.S.			2	1		3			2		1	3
Other		1				1	1					1
Compact cars (under $20,000)	1	2	6	3		12	2	1	6	1	2	12
Japanese			1	3		4			1	1	2	4
U.S.	1	2	5			8	2	1	5			8
Compact cars (over $20,000)				2	1	3			1		1	2
Japanese				1		1						1
Other				1	1	2			1			1
Midsized cars (under $25,000)		1	1	4	1	7			4		3	7
Japanese				2	1	3					3	3
U.S.		1	1	2		4			4			4
Midsized cars (over $25,000)			2	7	3	12		1	2	2	5	10
Japanese				5	1	6			2		4	6
U.S.			1	2		3		1		1		2
Other			1		2	3				1	1	2
Large cars				6	2	8		2	4	2		8
U.S.				6	2	8		2	4	2		8
Luxury cars			2	2	1	5		1		1	2	4
Japanese				2	1	3				1	2	3
U.S.			1			1		1				1
Other			1			1						
Sporty cars (under $25,000)	1	2	3	6		12	1	1	3		4	9
Japanese		2	3	3		8		1	3		3	7
U.S.	1			3		4	1				1	2

continued

Type and Producer	Overall Testing Score[a]						Reliability Ratings[b]					
	P	F	G	VG	E	Total	MW	W	A	B	MB	Total[c]
Sporty cars (over $25,000)				1	4	5	1	1	1	1		4
Japanese				1	3	4		1	1	1		3
U.S.				1		1	1					1
Minivans	3		2	3	1	9		2	5		1	8
Japanese	1			1		2			1		1	2
U.S.	1		2	2	1	6		2	4			6
Other	1					1						
Sport-utility vehicles		1		3	2	6	1	1	3			5
Japanese				2		2			1			1
U.S.		1		1	2	4	1	1	2			4

Source: Consumer Reports (April 1994).

[a] From *CR*'s extensive testing. Covers performance, comfort, and convenience, but not reliability. P = poor; F = fair; G = good; VG = very good; E = excellent. All sedans are rated by a single standard. Three separate standards apply to sporty cars, minivans, and sport-utility vehicles.

[b] Based on frequency-of-repair data for past models as reported in response to annual questionnaire sent to *CR* readers. MW = much worse than average; W = worse; A = average; B = better; MB = much better than average.

[c] Totals for reliability ratings are smaller than for overall testing scores because there were no reliability records for new or recently redesigned models.

planning and development, and close long-term relationships with suppliers—all permeated by commitment to quality controls. Japanese companies maintained and expanded this mode of operation as they broadened their offerings from the small economy cars, in which they first made their mark, to a wider range of products in the 1980s and early 1990s. Japan's technology was transferred to the United States by direct investment and absorbed quite rapidly by the United States' big three auto companies through joint ventures and other collaborations with their Japanese counterparts and through drawing on the smaller Japanese companies in which they held an equity interest. By the early 1990s, the performance gap between U.S. and Japanese cars was greatly narrowed in those areas where the two competed, and in sport-utility vehicles, U.S. companies were in the lead. The reliability gap—though narrowed—remained substantial.

Table 5.7

Labor Productivity and Defect Ratios at Selected Assembly Plants in North America and Japan, 1989

	Man-hours per Vehicle			Number of Plants
	Best	Average	Worst	
Japanese-owned in Japan	13.2	16.8	25.9	8
Japanese-owned in North America[a]	18.8	20.9	25.5	5
U.S.-owned in North America	18.6	24.9	30.7	14
	Assembly Defects Ratios[b]			Number of Plants
	Best	Average	Worst	
Japanese-owned in Japan	37.6	52.1	88.4	20
Japanese-owned in North America[a]	36.4	54.7	59.8	6
U.S.-owned in North America	35.1	78.4	168.6	42

Source: International Motor Vehicle Program as reported in Womack, Jones, and Roos (1990, figures 4.3 and 4.4).

[a] Includes joint ventures with U.S. companies.

[b] Defects per 100 cars traceable to the assembly plant, as reported by owners in first three months of use. Tabulated by IMVP from data provided by J.D. Powers Associates. Covers only cars sold in the United States.

Notes

1. Cusumano (1985), Appendix D.
2. Smitka (1991), p. 8.
3. Cusumano (1985) provides a detailed description of the development of the Japanese system from the early postwar years to the mid-1980s. Womack (1989) describe the Japanese system in the mid-1980s.
4. Womack (1989), p. 21.
5. Cusumano (1985), chapter 5.
6. Reported in Womack (1989), pp. 29–31.
7. Ibid., pp. 35–36.
8. Cusumano (1985), pp. 334–40, describes the episode, including the assemblers' response.
9. Womack (1989), pp. 34–35.
10. Cusumano (1985), p. 88.
11. Ibid., pp. 89–90.
12. Ibid., pp. 60–67.
13. Ibid., pp. 246–47.

14. Womack (1989), p. 49.

15. Dates of establishment and products of Japanese-affiliated manufacturing plants in the United States are drawn from MacKnight (1992a).

16. Weiss (1987) describes the agreement and the preceding negotiations.

17. "Toyota and GM Agree on Forming Joint Venture," *Japan Economic Journal*, February 22, 1983.

18. Weiss (1987), p. 33.

19. "Two Toyota Factories Seen as Different as U.S. and Japan," *Japan Economic Journal*, April 20, 1991.

20. "Team Saturn: Suppliers Are Integral Players," *Wards Automotive Yearbook*, 1991, pp. 55, 57.

21. "GM Saturn Plant Makes Friends," *New York Times*, January 23, 1990.

22. "GM's New Teams Aren't Hitting Any Homers," *Business Week*, August 8, 1988.

23. "Why GM Buyer Unnerves Suppliers," *New York Times*, September 30, 1992; and "GM Agrees to Allow Parts Suppliers to Use Some of Its Idled Employees," *Wall Street Journal*, November 30, 1992.

24. "GM to Cut Number of Vehicle Frames to 7 from 20," *Wall Street Journal*, May 15, 1992.

25. Ford had urged Mazda to establish an assembly plant in the United States but Mazda had demurred, fearful that the action would invite an Arab boycott, already applied to Ford. See "Ford to Make Toyo Kogyo Subcompacts in Mexico," *Japan Economic Journal*, August 1, 1983. The article also reported that the Mexican plant was in fact a joint production venture of Mazda and Ford.

26. "Mixing Cultures on the Assembly Line," *New York Times*, June 5, 1988.

27. "UAW Faces Test at Mazda Plant," *New York Times*, March 27, 1990.

28. "Mazda Gives Know-How to Ford Motor," *Japan Economic Journal*, January 5, 1988.

29. "Domestic Label for Mazda Would Be First for Japan," *New York Times*, February 7, 1992.

30. "Ford Will Build Compact Pickup for Japan's Mazda," *Wall Street Journal*, August 8, 1991

31. "Ford Agrees to Build Trucks for Mazda," *Nikkei Weekly*, August 17, 1991.

32. "Ford Motor Agrees to Buy 50% in Mazda's Car Factory in Michigan," *Wall Street Journal*, April 16, 1992.

33. "Ford/Nissan Click on New Minivan," *Ward's Auto World*, April 1992.

34. "Team Spirit: A Decisive Response to Crisis Brought Ford Enhanced Productivity," *Wall Street Journal*, December 15, 1992.

35. "Running Strong: Picking a Chairman Is the Next Big Challenge," *Wall Street Journal*, July 16, 1992.

36. "Ford Is Ready to Invest $1.2 Billion to Develop New Group of Engines," *Wall Street Journal*, February 24, 1992.

37. "Mitsubishi, Chrysler Reach Model Accord," *Japan Economic Journal*, November 10, 1990.

38. "UAW Accepts Chrysler Mitsubishi Pact Offering Unprecedented Job Protection," *Wall Street Journal*, August 28, 1989.

39. "Mitsubishi Buys Chrysler's 50% Stake in Their Diamond Star Venture," *Wall Street Journal*, October 30, 1991.

40. "Chrysler to Sell Final Holdings in Mitsubishi Motors," *Nikkei Weekly*, July 5, 1993.

41. This paragraph draws on information provided in: "Chrysler Can't Live with Honda or without It," *Nikkei Weekly*, January 18, 1992; "Honda First in OEM Auto Sales," *Nikkei Weekly*, June 14, 1993.

42. "Chrysler's L-H Team," *Ward's Auto World*, March 1992.

6

Technology Flows in Other Low- and Medium-R&D Industries: Steel, Tires, and Machine Tools

Japanese direct investment also brought useful process technology to three other mature medium- and low-R&D industries—steel, rubber, and machine tools (a small but important sector of the industrial machinery industry). In the 1960s and 1970s, most companies in these industries had been slow to innovate or to adopt new technology developed in other countries. In the 1980s, the U.S. technology lag, its adoption of protective trade policies in response to rising imports, and the broad financial incentives described in chapters 1 and 2 encouraged the flood of direct investment into the United States from industry leaders in the rest of the industrial world. By 1990, foreign-affiliated manufacturing plants accounted for about one-fourth of U.S. employment in blast furnaces and steel mills, over one-half in tire plants, and almost 10 percent in machine tool plants. The Japanese share in this foreign presence ranged from over 80 percent in blast furnaces and steel mills to a little less than half in tires and machine tools.

In steel, Japanese companies' joint ventures with all of the big U.S. steel companies financed plant modernization and introduced Japanese process and product technology to the entire integrated steel industry in the United States. At the same time, modest Japanese investments in the new and vigorous minimill steel sector in this country generated a reverse flow of new technology to Japan. In tires and machine tools, where Japanese investments were buyouts or wholly owned new ventures, the competitive challenge that they posed seemed to have speeded efforts to adopt new technology by their U.S. competitors.

The resulting improvement in U.S. technology in these industries, combined with superior U.S. technology in some high-R&D industries, helped the United States maintain a technology lead in manufacturing as a whole in the early 1990s.

U.S. Weakness, Foreign Strength, and Japanese Investment

In the United States, the steel, tire, and machine tool industries had contributed greatly to the country's industrial strength before and during World War II. But in the first three postwar decades, innovation in these industries lagged—with the important exception of the new steel minimills. Moreover, U.S. companies, reluctant to write off outdated equipment, were often slow to adopt technology developed in other countries or even to apply technology developed in other U.S. industries. By contrast, Japanese companies in all three industries, starting *de novo* after World War II, eagerly purchased foreign technology. Applying their skills in manufacturing and incremental product improvement, they had moved to the forefront in all three industries by 1980.

Emerging Japanese strength and U.S. weakness in steel, tires, and machine tools is suggested by the two countries' changing comparative advantages in trade in those industries, as shown in Table 2.7. As noted in chapter 2, a country's trade performance may be a poor indicator of the competitiveness of that country's multinationals, which may exploit technological superiority by investing abroad rather than exporting. But Japan's growing trade strength in these industries in the 1970s and early 1980s *prior to investing abroad* did reflect the growing technological strength of Japanese companies. Table 2.7 indicates that Japan's strength in steel developed early while its strength in machine tools developed only in the late 1970s, and its position in rubber products where European exports were strong improved gradually but remained modest.

By the 1980s, the three industries faced weak domestic growth prospects in all industrial countries. In the United States, many companies reacted by giving more attention to diversifying out of, rather than improving, their performance in those industries.

In Japan many companies, especially steel companies, diversified as well. But for companies in Japan and in some European countries, superior manufacturing skills and technology permitted continued expansion in their original industries through exports to, and direct investment in, the United States. There were other incentives to investment in the United States as well. One was the protective trade measures adopted by the United States in the 1980s for steel and machine tools. Another, for Japanese companies, was investment in the United States by a major customer, the Japanese auto industry. And finally, there were the generally higher returns on investment that were seemingly more available in the United States than in Japan or many European countries, as described in chapter 1.

The importance of both Japanese and other foreign companies, in terms of employment, in these U.S. industries in 1987 and 1990 is shown in Table 6.1. By 1990, the foreign presence was highest, at over 50 percent, in tire manufacturing plants. In this case, the plants were wholly owned by foreigners, leaving only Goodyear and Cooper to face the foreign competition. In blast furnaces and steel mills, the 24 percent foreign presence included numerous joint ventures with U.S. companies. The foreign position in machine tools was relatively modest at around 9 percent.

The position of Japanese companies relative to that of other foreigners reflects in part the relative strength of Japanese technology. In steel, where Japanese companies had not only incorporated European technology but also had made important contributions—notably, in electro-galvanized steel for automobiles—the Japanese

Table 6.1

The Position of Japanese and Other Foreign-Affiliated Companies in U.S. Primary Ferrous Metals, Rubber Products, and Industrial Machinery Industries, 1987 and 1990

	Employees (in thousands)		Percentage of U.S. Industry	
	1987	1990	1987	1990
Ferrous metals (SIC 331,2)				
All foreign-affiliated companies	45.9	71.6	12.0	18.3
Japanese-affiliated companies	13.9	39.8	3.6	10.2
Wholly U.S.-owned companies	336.7	319.7	88.0	81.7
All companies in U.S. industry	382.6	391.3		
Blast furnaces and steel mills (SIC 3312)				
All foreign-affiliated companies	23.4	45.4	12.5	24.1
Japanese-affiliated companies	12.2[a]	37.3	6.5	19.8
Wholly U.S.-owned companies	164.7	143.1	87.5	75.9
All companies in U.S. industry	188.1	188.5		
Rubber products (SIC 30–308)				
All foreign-affiliated companies	28.3	61.7	12.2	26.0
Japanese-affiliated companies	4.5	16.9	2.0	7.1
Wholly U.S.-owned companies	203.7	169.7	87.8	71.5
All companies in U.S. industry	232.0	237.5		
Tires and inner tubes (SIC 3011)				
All foreign-affiliated companies	13.9	35.5	21.3	52.5
Japanese-affiliated companies	3.8	17.5[a]	5.7	25.8
Wholly U.S.-owned companies	51.5	32.2	78.7	47.5
All companies in U.S. industry	65.4	67.7		
Industrial machinery (SIC 35–357)				
All foreign-affiliated companies	92.9	160.6	6.1	10.1
Japanese-affiliated companies	9.3	25.4	0.6	1.6
Wholly U.S.-owned companies	1,423.8	1,428.4	93.9	89.9
All companies in U.S. industry	1,516.7	1,589.0		
Machine tools (SIC 3541,2)				
All foreign-affiliated companies	2.9	3.9	6.3	8.8
Japanese-affiliated companies	1.0[a]	1.8	2.2	4.0
Wholly U.S.-owned companies	42.6	41.0	93.7	91.2
All companies in U.S. industry	45.5	44.9		

Source: U.S. Department of Commerce (1992b, 1993c).
[a] Approximated from ranges given in source data.

position was over 80 percent of the total foreign presence. In tires, Japan's lesser relative position, at a little less than half of the foreign presence, reflects the strength of Michelin, the leading innovator in tires. That company had been producing tires in the United States since the 1970s.

In industrial machinery as a whole, Japan's relative position was smaller still (about one-sixth of the foreign presence), since the United Kingdom, Germany, Switzerland, and Canada were also active. But in the machine tool sector of industrial machinery, Japanese companies accounted for nearly half of the foreign presence. Japanese and German companies (the second largest investor group) are generally considered the exemplars of machine tool technology.

In the following three sections, we take a closer look at each of these three industries, the Japanese investments in the United States, the related technology flows, and the response of U.S. firms in the 1980s and early 1990s.

Steel

The Dual Industry

The steel industry in the United States, Japan, and other major industrial countries consists of two distinct segments, integrated steel production and minimills.[1] Traditional integrated companies produce steel on a very large scale from iron ore, coal, and limestone in a succession of five to six production stages. Coal is converted to coke in coking ovens, and iron ore is converted to pellets or sinter strands in other plants. Coke and pellets or sinters are then combined in blast furnaces to make pig iron, moved on to basic oxygen furnaces to make molten steel, then passed on to one or two casters, and finally, moved to rolling mills. In both countries, this part of the industry is dominated by a few large firms with production capacities ranging from 1 million to over 25 million tons of raw steel per year. They are the main source of large semifinished shapes, slabs, and sheet steel used in automobiles, aircraft, and many other consumer and capital goods. This group includes a few smaller producers of high-quality specialty steels.

The second group of steel producers, minimills, make steel out of scrap in three short stages: an electric furnace, a single continuous caster, and a rolling mill. Minimills began to produce on any scale only in the 1960s and are estimated to have supplied about 20 percent of the U.S. market by 1990.[2]

In the United States, there are well over forty minimill companies with annual production capacities ranging from less than 100 thousand to 2.5 million tons of raw steel. Most of the firms have only one plant and serve regional markets, but the leading firms have several plants and serve national markets. Being a new industry, minimills started with new technology and amortized it quickly, with a view to continuing to take advantage of new technology as it developed. In Japan, minimill companies are also small. Most, but not all, are loosely linked to one or another of the big integrated steel companies. The latter typically have minority equity positions in a number of minimills.[3]

By the early 1990s, minimills in both countries had taken over much of the market for bars, small structural shapes, and rods—where their capital and labor costs were far lower than those of integrated companies. They were also gaining ground in larger structural shapes and were beginning to develop technology that would permit them to compete successfully in the important sheet market.[4]

Innovation and International Competitiveness

The international competitiveness of U.S. and Japanese companies in the two steel sectors in the 1980s was quite different. The actual competitiveness of either sector at any given time was complicated by changing price relationships with respect to raw materials, energy, and the yen/dollar exchange rate. However, U.S. minimills were estimated to have been slightly more efficient in terms of man-hours per ton of standard product.[5] But in the case of integrated mills, various studies suggest that the United States lagged well behind both Japan and Germany in the 1970s and into the early 1980s.[6]

In the integrated steel industry, the basic problem was that the U.S. industry, reluctant to write off equipment not yet fully amortized, was slow to incorporate new manufacturing technology that was developed largely in Europe. In Japan, by contrast, where few old plants survived wartime destruction, there was every incentive to do so. By 1970, Japan was producing over 80 percent of its crude steel in basic oxygen furnaces, as compared with 50 percent in the United States.[7] And by 1975, continuous casting—a process that allows skipping the ingot stage and results in higher quality steel—accounted for 31 percent of Japan's steel output but only 9 percent of the United States' output.[8]

In the United States the combined pressures of the declining long-term trend in the demand for steel (under way since the early 1970s), the recession of the early 1980s, and competition from minimills and imports forced the U.S. integrated industry to cut output, scrap much of its obsolete plant and equipment, and shed workers in the early 1980s. By 1985, output of raw steel was down 35 percent from 1979; capacity was down 14 percent; and employment at blast furnaces and steel mills was down a devastating 49 percent (see Table 6.2)

This drastic downsizing brought man-hours per ton of standard products roughly into line with that of German companies but was still short of Japanese companies' performance. For example, Barnett and Crandall (1986) estimated that, in 1985, the cost of producing cold rolled coil in an efficient integrated firm operating at 90 percent of capacity was 5.75 hours in the United States, 5.85 hours in West Germany, and 5.35 hours in Japan.[9] Moreover, Japanese companies were leading in the development of new products of special interest to the automobile industry—in particular, electro-galvanized steel sheet.

Despite wrenching adjustments in the U.S. steel industry, the surging U.S. dollar gave a new impetus to steel imports, pushing

Table 6.2

Output, Capacity, and Employment in the U.S. Steel Industry, 1972–92

	Output[a]	Capacity[a, b]	Capacity Utilization[b]	Employment[c]
	(in millions of short tons)		(%)	(in thousands)
1972	133.2			552.9
1973	150.8			591.8
1974	145.7			611.0
1975	116.6	153.0	76.2	531.8
1976	128.0	158.2	80.9	532.1
1977	125.3	159.8	78.4	529.7
1978	137.0	157.8	86.8	534.3
1979	136.3	155.2	87.8	544.4
1980	111.8	153.6	72.8	489.9
1981	120.8	154.3	78.3	477.4
1982	74.6	154.1	48.4	365.7
1983	84.6	150.5	56.2	314.0
1984	92.5	135.2	68.4	312.9
1985	88.3	133.6	66.1	278.0
1986	81.6	127.9	63.8	249.1
1987	89.2	112.2	79.5	253.5
1988	99.9	111.2	89.2	265.8
1989	97.9	115.9	84.5	260.8
1990	98.0	116.7	84.0	258.8
1991	87.9	118.5	74.2	245.9
1992	92.9	113.0	82.2	

Sources: Business Statistics 1963–91; Survey of Current Business (March 1993); *Census of Manufactures* (1982, 1987); U.S. Department of commerce, Bureau of the Census, *Annual Survey of Manufactures* (1988, 1990, 1992).

[a] Raw steel.

[b] Data not available for years before 1975.

[c] Blast furnace and basic steel products (SIC 331).

them from 16 percent of U.S. consumption in 1980 to 26 percent in 1984. Table 6.3 shows the long-term downward trend in U.S. steel consumption and the growing share of imports in the 1970s and 1980s. All of this led Bethlehem Steel and the United Steel Workers to petition the International Trade Commission for relief from "unfair" competition. In response, the U.S. government negotiated voluntary export restraints with major steel exporter countries, including Japan.

Table 6.3

The U.S. Market for Basic Steel Products, 1963–92
(in million net tons)

	Shipments	Exports	Imports	Apparent Con-sumption[a]	Imports as % of Con-sumption	Net Imports as % of Con-sumption
1963	75.6	2.2	5.4	78.8	6.9	4.1
1965	92.7	2.5	10.4	100.6	10.3	7.8
1970	90.8	7.1	13.4	97.1	13.8	6.5
1971	87.0	2.8	18.3	102.5	17.9	15.1
1972	91.8	2.9	17.7	106.6	16.6	13.9
1973	111.4	4.1	15.2	122.5	12.4	9.1
1974	109.5	5.8	16.0	119.6	13.4	8.5
1975	80.0	3.0	12.0	89.0	13.5	10.2
1976	89.4	2.7	14.3	101.1	14.1	11.5
1977	91.1	2.0	19.3	108.5	17.8	16.0
1978	97.9	2.4	21.1	116.6	18.1	16.0
1979	100.3	2.8	17.5	115.0	15.2	12.8
1980	83.9	4.1	15.5	95.2	16.3	12.0
1981	88.5	2.9	19.9	105.4	18.9	16.1
1982	61.6	1.8	16.7	76.4	21.8	19.4
1983	67.6	1.2	17.1	83.5	20.5	19.0
1984	73.7	1.0	26.2	98.9	26.4	25.5
1985	73.0	0.9	24.3	96.4	25.2	24.2
1986	70.3	0.9	20.7	90.0	23.0	22.0
1987	76.7	1.1	20.4	95.9	21.3	20.1
1988	83.8	2.1	20.9	102.7	20.3	18.3
1989	84.1	4.6[b]	17.3[b]	96.8	17.9	13.2
1990	85.0	4.3	17.2	97.8	17.5	13.1
1991	78.9	6.3	15.7	88.3	17.8	10.6
1992	76.6	4.3	17.0	89.3	19.0	14.2
1970–74	98.1	4.5	16.1	109.7	14.7	10.5
1975–79	91.8	2.6	16.9	106.0	15.9	13.5
1980–84	75.0	2.2	19.1	91.9	20.7	18.3
1985–89	77.6	1.9	20.7	96.4	21.5	19.5
1990–92	80.2	5.0	16.6	96.7	17.2	12.0

Source: Business Statistics 1963–91, Survey of Current Business (March 1993).
[a] Shipments − exports + imports.
[b] Break in series. New product classification system.

Japanese Investments and Two-Way Technology Flows

In Japan in the early 1980s, the integrated steel industry was also faced with a leveling off of demand in domestic and world markets and increasingly strong competition from the newly industrializing countries. The big steel companies reacted by cutting back production and diversifying into a wide variety of high- and low-technology industries.[10] (Their joint venture investments in semiconductors will be described in chapter 7.) They also turned their attention to investing in the U.S. steel industry. Overtures in the early 1980s—Kobe to both Wheeling-Pittsburgh and Mc-Louth Steel, and Nippon Kokan to both Kaiser and Ford's Rouge Steel—came to nothing.[11] But Japan's acceptance of voluntary export restraints in 1984, coupled with the Japanese auto companies' investments in the United States, greatly increased the pressure on the Japanese steel companies to invest in U.S. manufacturing. At about the same time, financial constraints made U.S. firms receptive to the idea of joint ventures with Japanese partners. Japanese joint venture investments in integrated steel mills between 1984 and 1991 are listed in Table 6.4.

Japanese investments in 1984 in effect permitted total or partial withdrawal from the steel industry by two of its weaker members. Kaiser, which had shifted its focus to mining coal and iron ore, sold part of its California steel plant to a joint venture (California Steel) between Kawasaki Steel and a mining company owned by the Brazilian government. In a much larger transaction, Nippon Kokan acquired a half interest (raised to 70 percent in 1990) in National Steel. The U.S. holding company making the sale had already diversified into other industries[12] and seems to have treated the sale as a means of gradually withdrawing from the steel industry.

Subsequent Japanese investments, all of which were joint ventures with U.S. companies, tended to strengthen the steel-producing capabilities and product offerings of the U.S. partners rather than to facilitate their departure from the industry. Four were joint ventures with strong integrated U.S. companies: Kobe with U.S.

Table 6.4

U.S. Affiliates of Japanese Companies: Blast Furnaces and Steel Mills,[a] 1991

Year Plant Opened or Acquired	U.S. Affiliate	Japanese Parent Companies[b]	U.S. Parent Companies[b]
Minimills			
1975	Auburn Steel	Kyoei Steel (10) Sumitomo Corp. (90)	None
1976	Tamco	Tokyo Steel (25) Mitsui & Co. (25)	Ameron Inc. (50)
1988	Nucor-Yamato	Yamato Kogyo (49)	Nucor (51)
1989	Arkansas Steel Associates	Yamato Kogyo (50) Sumitomo Corp. (25) Auburn Steel (25)	None
Integrated Steel Mills			
1984	National Steel Corp.	NKK Corp. (70)	National Intergroup (30)
1984	California Steel Industries	Kawasaki Steel (50) [Comp. Vale do Rio Dolce S.A. (50)]	None
1986	L-S Electro-Galvanizing	Sumitomo Metals (40)	LTV (60)
1991	L-S II Electro-Galvanizing	Sumitomo Metals (50)	LTV (50)
1988	Wheeling Nisshin Inc.	Nisshin Steel (80)	Wheeling-Pittsburgh (20)
1989	ARMCO Steel L.P.	Kawasaki Steel (45)	Armco (55)
1989	USS/Kobe Steel	Kobe Steel (50)	U.S. Steel (50)
1989	Inland Steel Industries, Inland Steel	Nippon Steel (14)	Inland Steel (86)
1990	I/N Tek	Nippon Steel (50)	Inland Steel (50)
1991	I/N Kote	Nippon Steel (50)	Inland Steel (50)
Specialized Steel Mills			
1970	Hitachi Metals, Hi-Specialty America Division	Hitachi Metals (100)	
1989	Copperweld Steel	Daido Steel (33) [Imetal S.A. (33)]	

Source: MacKnight (1992a).
[a]SIC 331.
[b]Equity shares and non-Japanese foreign owners are given in parentheses.

Steel; Kawasaki with Armco; Nippon Steel with Inland; and NKK (acting through National Steel) with Bethlehem (expected to start production in 1994). Two of these involved joint ventures with U.S. firms in chapter 11 bankruptcy: Sumitomo with LTV and Nisshin with Wheeling-Pittsburgh. In addition, Daido acquired a part interest (along with a French company, Imetal S.A.) in Copperweld, a specialty steel company.

The Japanese steel companies brought important new capital equipment embodying new technology to the U.S. steel industry. Commerce reports on expenditures for plant and equipment by affiliates of Japanese and other foreign companies, along with Census data for the steel industry as a whole for 1987–91 are given in Table 6.5. They show Japanese-affiliated firms' share of the industries' capital expenditures to have been two to six times as large as their share in industry employment in the first four years, moderating to 1.6 times in 1991. (Capital spending by other foreign-affiliated companies was also strong in 1987 and 1988 but moderated thereafter.)

A large portion of Japanese investment in new plant was devoted to the production of electro-galvanized steel of the sort favored by Japanese automobile companies. Other important investments included continuous casting facilities at National;[13] a vacuum degassing system, which minimized the carbon content of steel, also at National;[14] installation at I/N TEK of continuous cold mill process equipment, designed and manufactured by Nippon Steel, for converting steel coil into high-quality finished steel products;[15] and computerized controls for BOF steelmaking at several plants.

Beyond this, it is evident that the U.S. joint-venture partners were impressed by Japanese methods of planning and installing new plant and equipment, their emphasis on quality, their organization of labor on the plant floor, and their relationships with customers in the auto and other industries. Even though many of the new joint-venture plants did not start operations until 1989 or 1990, their impact on the behavior of U.S. companies was already evident in 1991 and 1992. In 1991 at U.S. Steel's huge

Table 6.5

Employment and Capital Expenditures by Japanese and Other Foreign-Affiliated Companies in U.S. Primary Ferrous Metals Manufacturing, 1987–91[a]

	Employment (in thousands)					Capital Expenditures (in $ millions)				
	1987	1988	1989	1990	1991	1987	1988	1989	1990	1991
All foreign-affiliated companies[b]	39.3	38.0	52.2	73.9	86.8	638	981	1,275	1,337	1,229
Japanese-affiliated	14.9	15.1	28.9	49.3	47.6	220	594	1,022	1,024	768
Other	24.4	22.9	23.3	24.6	39.2	418	387	253	313	461
All U.S. companies in U.S. industry	382.6	403.1	398.1	391.3	371.3	2,103	2,725	3,518	3,532	3,808

Percentage of U.S. Establishments

	1987	1988	1989	1990	1991	1987	1988	1989	1990	1991
All foreign-affiliated companies[b]	10.3	9.4	13.1	18.9	23.4	30.3	36.0	36.2	37.9	32.3
Japanese-affiliated	3.9	3.7	7.3	12.6	12.8	10.5	21.8	29.0	29.0	20.2
Other	6.4	5.7	5.9	6.3	10.6	19.9	14.2	7.2	8.9	12.1

Sources: U.S. Department of Commerce (1990a, 1991a, 1992a, 1993a, 1993d and Annual Survey of Manufactures, 1988–1991).
[a] SIC 331 and 332.
[b] Data refer to all employment and expenditures for plant and equipment by *affiliates* whose largest revenues derived from the manufacture of primary ferrous metals.
[c] Data refer to employment and *all* capital expenditures of *establishments* manufacturing primary ferrous metals rather than to the companies owning the establishments.

Gary Works, installation of a new continuous slab caster (which completed Gary's conversion to this more efficient process) was accomplished in a mere five months from initial planning to full-scale operation, a far shorter period than usual, and with extraordinarily few difficulties, by virtue of adopting teamwork between the equipment supplier and the operating, maintenance, and training personnel at Gary.[16] Seeking higher quality steel, a number of companies installed degassers.[17] At U.S. Steel, where a serious labor dispute had shut down all operations for six months in 1986–87, the installation in 1990 of a new company president (who had had exposure to the joint venture with Kobe steel) was followed by improved labor relations. Changes included reorganization of workers into teams, flexible work assignments, and regular consultation with union officials regarding a wide variety of company policies affecting them.[18]

The U.S. recession of 1990–91 produced poor operating results for a number of the joint ventures, disappointing both partners. But all of the ventures remained intact.

Turning to the very much smaller Japanese investments in U.S. minimill production, it is likely that these were associated with more technology transfers to Japan from the United States than the reverse. As noted in chapter 4, Japanese companies invested in the United States in the mid-1970s, probably attracted by cheaper scrap and energy costs than in Japan. Kyoei, financed largely by Sumitomo trading company, established a minimill, Auburn, in the New York State city of that name. Tokyo Steel contributed equally with another trading company, Mitsui, to a joint venture with a U.S. company. But the investments may have also provided a learning experience for the Japanese steel companies.

Much later, in 1988, another Japanese firm, Yamato, established a joint venture with Nucor, one of the strongest and most innovative U.S. companies, to build a new minimill in Arkansas to manufacture structural steel shapes. Since Nucor was a leader in developing methods to produce larger structural shapes in minimills,[19] one can conclude that Yamato learned these methods in the course of its joint venture. In 1989, Yamato acquired a second, smaller plant in Arkansas, this time with Japanese partners (Auburn and Sumitomo), to produce steel railroad tie plates. In 1992 Kyoei Steel, long familiar with the U.S. industry through its operations at Auburn, bought out Florida Steel, the sixth-largest but financially weak U.S. minimill.[20] It is not clear whether Kyoei hoped to gain technology from Florida or was simply seeking a means of expanding its U.S. presence.

In 1993, Yamato and Nippon Steel (part owner of Yamato) obtained Nucor assistance in their efforts to expand in Southeast Asia. The two companies and the Industrial Bank of Japan brought to Nucor an invitation from the government of Malaysia to establish a steel plant there. The Japanese group offered to help in the financing in exchange for equity in the new enterprise.[21]

The United States' Competitive Response

All in all, Japan's investments appear to have helped the U.S. integrated steel companies to catch up with world leaders. While the U.S. companies themselves did much of the catching up in the early 1980s, Japanese investment provided welcome financing and new technology that helped complete the job. The experience also appears to have made the U.S. industry newly eager to adopt and to further develop new technology.

New U.S. attitudes were evident in the industry's response to the emergence of new technology for energy-efficient direct reduction of iron ore in the late 1980s. The new technology substitutes ordinary coal for coking coal, capturing coal gas byproducts for use in a prereduction process or for power generation. This eliminates the atmosphere-polluting coke oven and provides energy savings as well.[22] The development of the new technology offers a sharp contrast to that of the basic oxygen furnace in the early postwar years. Then, innovation occurred in Europe and was adopted swiftly in Japan but slowly and reluctantly in the United States. The new direct-reduction technology was also conceived in Europe, at Klockner Stahlforschung in

Germany in 1987. But development of the basic idea to arrive at commercially viable direct-reduction methods proceeded simultaneously in the United States, Japan, and Europe.

In these competitive development efforts, an Austrian company, Voest-Alpine, was first off the mark. Its system, Corex, uses the unburned gas by-product to generate electricity. Its first plant, sold to ISCOR in South Africa, went into operation in 1990, and the second, for Pohang in South Korea, was scheduled to open in 1994. The third was likely to be an LTV plant in Cleveland, Ohio, built with the cooperation of an electric utility company there.

However, development efforts in the United States and Japan were mainly focused on a technology that used by-product coal gases in prereducing iron ore. Government-backed groups of integrated steel companies in the United States and Japan, and HIsmelt, a private joint venture (between a U.S. maker of direct-reduction plants, Midrex, and Australia's largest mining and metals company, CRA), were each working independently. HIsmelt in Australia and a Japanese plant, using its DIOS technology, were each scheduled to start small operations in late 1993. The U.S. effort, directed by the American Iron and Steel Institute, with substantial help from its suppliers (including the German Mannesman Demag), hoped to have a larger plant in operation by 1995. Since U.S. coking ovens are considerably older than the Japanese ones, the need to replace them to meet revised clean air standards could hasten development in the United States.

In the minimill sector, Nucor took the lead in exploring the possibilities of substituting directly reduced iron for scrap in its electric furnaces—but using natural gas rather than coal in the direct reduction process. This would enable minimills to make higher-quality steel and thus to broaden the scope of minimill competition with integrated steel companies. In early 1993, Nucor announced plans to build a small direct reduction plant in Trinidad using natural gas (plentiful and cheap in Trinidad). It stated that it would ship the reduced iron to its electric furnaces in the United States.[23]

Tires

Postwar Innovation and the U.S. Technology Lag

In the tire industry, U.S. companies were early prewar investors in Japan. (Their financial and technology contributions were briefly noted in chapter 3.) But from the 1950s to at least the mid-1970s, they were technology laggards and thus were in no position to transfer product technology to Japan. The major tire product innovation of the postwar period, the steel-belted radial tire, greatly increased the safety and durability of tires, and made for better handling and fuel efficiency in cars so equipped.[24] Radials were invented at Dunlop, in Britain, and first commercially exploited by Michelin, in France, in 1948. Goodyear offered radials in Europe some ten years later, in 1958, and in the United States in 1965. But radials were not well received in the United States, at least partly because U.S. auto companies were reluctant to redesign suspensions to accommodate radials' different handling properties. It was not until the 1970s, when European cars became popular in the United States, that the radials on which they rolled were perceived as desirable. Only then did the U.S. auto companies begin to design cars to accommodate radials. The U.S. tire industry responded by investing in equipment to produce them.

Following up on radials' newfound popularity in the United States and responding to U.S. imposition of countervailing duties in 1973, Michelin established a large manufacturing plant in South Carolina in 1975. Thus, it was Michelin, rather than a Japanese company, that first demonstrated the virtues of quality controls in a U.S. tire plant. The Michelin competitive demonstration appears to have spurred the U.S. tire makers to give more attention to quality and to introduce product innovations of their own, such as puncture-sealing linings, all-weather treads, and lightweight spare tires in the 1970s. Still, some quality gaps between U.S. tire makers and Michelin remained, especially in the case of Firestone.

In the 1980s, the prospect of slow growth in global demand for

Table 6.6

Output, Employment, and Labor Productivity in the U.S. Tire Industry, 1972–92

	Tire[a] Output (in millions)	Establish-ments[b]	Production Workers		
			Number (in thousands)	Man-hours (in millions)	Tires/ Man-hour
1972	229.6	126	83.1	168.9	1.4
1973	223.4		88.3	172.8	1.3
1974	211.4		89.8	177.8	1.2
1975	186.7		80.0	152.7	1.2
1976	188.0		78.8	136.0	1.4
1977	231.6[c]	126	88.3	176.4	1.3
1978	223.4		81.0	160.9	1.4
1979	206.7		81.0	154.6	1.3
1980	159.3		66.1	121.7	1.3
1981	181.8		62.3	118.3	1.5
1982	178.5	99	54.6	101.1	1.8
1983	186.9		52.2	103.5	1.8
1984	209.4		56.3	112.3	1.9
1985	196.9		55.9	105.2	1.9
1986	190.3		51.7	98.8	1.9
1987	203.0	97	52.6	103.7	2.0
1988	211.4		54.6	111.1	1.9
1989	212.9		54.6	108.5	2.0
1990	210.7		54.7	106.1	2.0
1991	202.4		52.4	99.5	2.0
1992	230.3				

Sources: Business Statistics, 1963–91; Survey of Current Business (March 1993), *Census of Manufactures* (1982, 1987), *Annual Survey of Manufactures* (1988, 1990, 1992).

[a] Pneumatic casings.

[b] Establishments with twenty employees or more. Smaller establishments numbered eighty in 1972, seventy-four in 1977, sixty-five in 1982, and sixty-six in 1987. Data were collected only in census years.

[c] Break in series. Excludes tires for motercycles and mobile homes.

tires provoked differing national responses. In the United States, weakening domestic demand and rising imports led to a 23 percent drop in tire output, from a high in 1977 to a low in 1982, and a corresponding reduction in the number of operating plants. Employment was cut by 38 percent over those same years and remained at those lower levels even as output made a partial recovery, thus raising productivity in terms of tires per man-hour by nearly 50 percent (see Table 6.6). As compa-

Table 6.7

U.S. Affiliates of Japanese Companies Manufacturing Tires, 1990

Year Acquired	U.S. Affiliate	Japanese Parent
1982	Bridgestone-Firestone, Inc.	Bridgestone Corp.
1988	Bridgestone-Firestone, Inc.	Bridgestone Corp.
1986	Dunlop Tire Co.	Sumitomo Rubber, Inc.
1989	Mohawk Rubber Co.	Yokohama Rubber Co.
1991	GTY Tire Co.	Yokohama Rubber (33.4%)
		Toyo Tire and Rubber (15.6%)

Source: MacKnight (1992a).

nies retrenched in this industry with meager growth prospects, the attractions of other, faster-growing industries led some tire companies to devote more attention to diversification opportunities than to the tire industry. Goodyear, the strongest tire company, moved into oil fields and pipelines.[25] Goodrich continued its long-term move into chemicals and also ventured into new materials with aerospace applications. In 1986 it merged its tire business with that of Uniroyal, later sold to Clayton Dubilier.[26] The weaker rubber companies seem simply to have looked for buyers.

In Europe and Japan, by contrast, strong tire companies producing high-quality tires in efficient plants concluded that there was still room for expansion in a familiar industry by acquiring U.S. companies. For Japanese tire companies, the decision of the Japanese auto industry to assemble cars in the United States created strong incentives to follow. By 1990, the four largest Japanese tire companies were manufacturing tires in the United States (see Table 6.7).

The Infusion of Foreign Technology by Takeover and Japan's Role

As early as 1982, Bridgestone made a first modest investment, purchasing a single run-down Firestone plant in Lavergne, Tennessee. The Bridgestone purchase offer was conditional on worker acceptance of Japanese-style work rules, an offer that was accepted only when Firestone made clear that the alternative was plant closure. After buying the plant, Bridgestone spent $100 million totally reequipping it. U.S. observers reported that tire quality, productivity, and labor relations were much improved.[27] In 1986, Sumitomo Rubber purchased the Dunlop Tire Company (a British company), including Dunlop's two tire plants in the United States.

By 1988, when the tire industry was nearing its cyclical peak, a bidding war broke out among Japanese and European tire companies for the major U.S. tire companies. Bridgestone managed to outbid Pirelli (an Italian company) by paying $2.6 billion for Firestone's U.S. plants, plus others abroad. In succeeding years it is reported to have spent an additional $1 billion upgrading existing plant plus $350 million for a new plant in Tennessee.[28] In 1989, Yokohama Rubber, Japan's second largest tire company bought Mohawk, a smaller U.S. tire company. In 1991 Yokohama and Toyo acquired an interest in a German-owned general tire plant.

At roughly the same time, European companies were buying other large chunks of the U.S. tire industry. Michelin purchased Uniroyal-Goodrich from Clayton Dubilier. Continental AG (a German company) purchased General Tire, and Pirelli purchased Armstrong. Goodyear, the world's largest tire company until 1990, borrowed heavily to escape being acquired by the British raider, Sir James Goldsmith.[29] By 1990 Goodyear and one smaller company, Cooper, remained the only U.S.-owned tire companies operating in the United States.

The United States' Competitive Response

In what remained of U.S.-owned tire industry in the United States in the early 1990s, Goodyear responded to the new and sharper competition from foreigners. While it had long been a leader in premium-price, high-performance tires, it devoted more attention than before to manufacturing tires in the medium priced range and developing new products. With respect to medium-priced tires, a study by *Consumer Reports*[30] rated six brands of medium-priced tires in each of two popular size groups made by Japanese, European, and U.S. companies producing in the United States. *CR* recommended all but one tire (one of three Michelin tires tested) and emphasized that the difference between those recommended was very small. Nevertheless, in the two *CR* listings, in the order of *CR*'s preferences, Goodyear was at the bottom and a Japanese brand was at the top.

In the area of new products, Bridgestone introduced a run-flat tire in 1992, capable of running fifty miles after losing its air, but requiring special wheels, then available only on some customized Chevrolet Corvette models. Goodyear promptly countered with an announcement that it would introduce, in 1994, a run-flat tire capable of running 200 miles and mountable on standard auto wheels.[31] All of this suggests that Japanese investments contributed some high-quality tires and innovative products to the U.S. market and served as a useful competitive goal to Goodyear and, very possibly, to Cooper as well.

Machine Tools

The Japanese Lead

Machine tools are power-driven, increasingly computerized machines that cut, form, and shape metal. Serving nearly all durable goods industries, the machine tool industry is an important but small part of the broad industrial machinery industry. According to U.S. Census data, machine tools accounted for only 2 percent of employment in the broad industrial machinery group in 1990. There were a great many small companies in both the United States and Japan. But a rationalization process had been under way in both countries for at least two decades.

Numerical control (NC) was the major technological innovation in the postwar machine tool industry. "NC" is a generic term that has been used to describe three routines: (1) simple NC, consisting of computerized instructions punched into a tape to control a stand-alone machine tool; (2) CNC, a computerized numerical control that replaces the tape with a microprocessor in the machine itself; and (3) FMS (flexible manufacturing systems), the hardware and software used to bring related CNC machines performing a variety of functions under a centralized computer control.[32]

In a useful analysis of the machine tool industry in the United States, Japan, and Germany, Artemis March (1989) has compared technology developments and industry rationalization in the United States and Japan. With respect to technology, the United States took an early lead in developing numerical controls; but broad application of the new technology was frustrated by its sophistication relative to the available semiconductor components. In 1949, the U.S. Air Force, interested in the potential of numerical controls for the milling of aircraft wing panels, commissioned a group at MIT, Servolab, to develop such a system. The software that Servolab developed, the Automatically Programmed Tool (APT) program, is still in use in updated form.[33] A number of the machine tool companies produced NC machines incorporating APT for the aircraft industry. But in the 1950s and early 1960s, before the appearance of the microprocessor that revolutionized the computer industry, programming manufacturing processes was not easy. Manufacturers apparently experienced great difficulties in applying APT to the simpler machine tools that constituted the bulk of their business. Even after the introduction of microprocessors, Allen Bradley and General Electric, principal makers of NC controls for machine tools, seem not to have been responsive to the needs of machine tool makers and users, as they reportedly reveled in sophistication and complicated design.

By contrast, Japanese machine tool builders did not shift to NC in any volume until the 1970s. Up to that time, they had been building machine tools based on non-NC technology purchased from U.S. and European companies. Thus, when they moved to

NC, they were able to incorporate microprocessors from the start. And with encouragement from MITI, the two main producers of NC controls for machine tools, Fanuc and Mitsubishi Electric, produced standardized and simple products. Other distinguishing characteristics of Japan's technology, as in so many other manufacturing industries, were its greater emphasis on quality controls in manufacturing and closer relationships with both suppliers and customers.

Industry rationalization, under way in both countries as stronger firms bought weaker ones, also went more smoothly in Japan. In the United States, some of the buyers were conglomerates, whose managements used profits generated in their new, highly cyclical machine tool subsidiaries to finance other ventures. This deprived the machine tool companies of the capital needed to develop new products, and led to the ultimate failure of several respected small companies. In Japan, by contrast, MITI appears to have encouraged an orderly rationalization and specialization by the remaining firms.

While the stronger machine tool companies in both countries grew by acquiring smaller firms, Japanese firms grew faster and became bigger. In 1991, seven out of the world's ten largest machine tool companies were Japanese. Amada, the largest, had worldwide sales of $1.3 billion. The largest U.S. company, the still family-controlled Ingersoll Milling, was number eleven, with world machine tool sales of $400 million. The second largest U.S. company, Cincinnati Milacron (also family controlled) was number eighteen, with world machine tool sales of $384 million.[34] The modest standing of Cincinnati Milacron, once the largest U.S. company, resulted from its wandering interest in the 1980s, away from machine tools and into plastics-forming machinery, robots, and other industrial specialties.[35]

Japan's leap to leadership in world trade in the late 1970s, following its adoption of NC and the gradual decline of U.S. world competitiveness in the 1970s, is illustrated in Table 2.7. These same developments were strongly evident in the U.S. market. By 1980, U.S. imports were nearly twice as large as exports

Table 6.8

Shipments, Exports, Imports, and Consumption of Machine Tools in the United States, 1963–92 (millions of dollars)

Year	Shipments	Exports	Imports	Apparent Con-sumption[a]	Net Trace/ Consumption (percent)
1963	895.8	185.4	37.7	748.0	19.8
1964	1,164.4	254.5	36.4	946.2	23.1
1965	1,425.6	222.4	56.3	1,259.5	13.2
1966	1,685.2	208.9	117.7	1,594.0	5.7
1967	1,806.0	224.7	178.2	1,759.5	2.6
1968	1,726.9	216.6	163.6	1,673.9	3.2
1969	1,597.6	242.4	156.1	1,511.2	5.7
1970	1,443.1	292.1	131.8	1,282.8	12.5
1971	997.9	251.5	90.1	836.5	19.3
1972	1,018.7	238.1	114.0	894.6	13.9
1973	1,501.0	325.5	167.1	1,342.6	11.8
1974	2,030.6	410.5	270.7	1,890.8	7.4
1975	2,451.7	536.7	317.6	2,232.6	9.8
1976	2,059.7	514.9	318.3	1,863.0	10.6
1977	2,280.8	426.7	400.9	2,254.9	1.1
1978	3,013.5	533.1	715.3	3,195.6	−5.7
1979	3,876.6	619.1	1,043.8	4,301.2	9.9
1980	4,691.8	734.1	1,298.5	5,205.0	10.7
1981	5,095.6	949.6	1,437.0	5,560.5	5.7
1982	3,604.4	615.0	1,253.3	4,242.7	−15.0
1983	1,845.1	406.0	946.5	2,385.6	−22.7
1984	2,285.9	409.3	1,356.6	3,233.2	−29.3
1985	2,545.2	452.4	1,738.5	3,831.3	−33.6
1986	2,578.5	590.3	2,251.6	4,239.8	−39.2
1987	2,323.7	650.4	1,995.4	3,668.7	−36.7
1988	2,399.1	768.3	2,058.7	3,689.5	−35.0
1989	3,195.6	949.8	2,406.6	4,652.4	−31.3
1990	3,299.9	1,062.5	2,305.1	4,542.5	−27.4
1991	2,673.5	1,076.1	2,135.7	3,733.1	−28.4
1992	2,596.0	1,029.2	1,718.1	3,708.9	−18.6

Sources: Business Statistics, 1963–91; Survey of Current Business, March, 1993; The Economic Handbook of the Machine Tool Industry, 1992–93; AMT Statistical Department.

[a] Shipments − exports + imports.

and accounted for roughly one-fourth of all U.S. purchases. By 1986, imports were four times as large as exports and accounted for over half of U.S. purchases (see Table 6.8) Imports from Japan included some by U.S. machine tool companies; as a defensive measure, they contracted to sell them under their own

Table 6.9

Japan's "Voluntary" Export Restraints on Machine Tools, 1987–93
(percentage share of U.S. market[a])

	Ceilings for 1987–91[b]	Ceilings for 1993
CNC lathes	57.47	60.27
Machining centers	51.54	54.03
CNC punching and shearing machines	19.25	21.56
CNC milling machines	7.17	7.47

Source: JEI Report, No. 18B, May 8, 1992.

[a] Number of machines.

[b] When VERs were extended for two years in April 1992, 1987–91 limits were continued for 1992.

names.[36] By 1986, Japan was supplying over half of all U.S. imports, followed by Germany, which supplied 16 percent, and Taiwan, Switzerland, the United Kingdom, and Italy—each supplying around 5 percent.[37]

Reacting to this surge of imports, the Reagan administration requested Japan and others to apply voluntary export restraints (VERs). Under an ensuing agreement, Japan agreed to limit its exports of four types of numerically controlled types of machine tools to its shares of the U.S. market (in terms of number of machines) in 1981 (see Table 6.9). But for the two markets where Japan had been strongest—computerized numerically controlled lathes and milling machines—its share of the U.S. market was, and remained, over 50 percent.

Japanese Investment in the United States

Japanese machine tool builders invested in U.S. manufacturing both before and after the United States requested voluntary export restraints (see Table 6.10). Yamazaki Mazak, the world's third largest machine tool company, began producing NC lathes and machining centers at a new plant in Kentucky in 1979. In

1981 Makino Milling Machines bought a U.S. company, Le-Blond, where it produced machining centers, and Amada Sonoike (part-owned by Japan's number one, Amada) built a small plant to make NC turret punch presses. The 1986 trade restraints produced another wave of investment in 1986 and 1987, including one large acquisition, two sizable new plants, and several smaller establishments, as shown in Table 6.10. Others followed in 1988 and 1989, but most of them were very small, with fewer than forty employees, and thus may have been limited to final assembly processes, what are sometimes called "screwdriver" plants.

All but one of Japan's U.S. machine tool affiliates (Sumitomo's minority investment in a very small company) were wholly owned and operated by the Japanese investing companies. However, Fanuc abandoned an effort to make a sizable minority investment in the Moore Special Tool Company following strenuous congressional objections. The U.S. company, a maker of machine tools used in making nuclear weapons but experiencing losses in its operations as a whole, had sought Fanuc's participation in order to carry out a long-term plan to modernize its plant and manufacturing processes.[38]

Japanese investments in machine tool building were supported by investments by the two principal Japanese makers of controls for NC tools and other industrial machinery. Mitsubishi Electric Corporation established a wholly owned affiliate to assemble NC equipment from imported knockdown sets in 1983. In 1988 it expanded to full-scale manufacturing and partial reliance on U.S. components (such as microprocessors from Motorola).[39] Fanuc formed a manufacturing joint venture with GE in 1987.[40] If reported complaints regarding GE's early NC controls for machine tools were justified, GE's partnership with Fanuc should prove helpful to U.S. machine tool makers.

The United States' Competitive Response

Since manufacturing affiliates of Japanese machine tool makers in the United States were almost entirely wholly owned and

Table 6.10

U.S. Affiliates of Japanese Companies Manufacturing Machine Tools, 1990

Year Plant Opened or Acquired	U.S. Affiliate	Japanese Parent Company	Products
1970	Ooya USA	Ooya Machinery Works	Machining centers, radial drills
1979	Mazak Corp.	Yamazaki Mazak	NC lathes
1981	LeBlond Makino	Makino Milling Machines	Machining centers Machining centers
1981	U.S. Sonoike	Amada Sonoike	NC turret punch presses
1986	Okamoto Corp.	Okamoto Machine Tool	Surface grinders
1986	Toyoda Machinery USA	Toyoda Machinery Works Ltd.	Machining centers, NC lathes
1987	Toyoda Machinery USA	Toyoda Machinery Works Ltd.	Grinders
1988	Toyoda Machinery USA	Toyoda Machinery Works Ltd.	Machining centers
1986	Hitachi Zosen Clearing	Hitachi Zosen Corp.	Stamping presses
1987	Miyano Machinery USA	Miyano Machinery	NC lathes
1987	Okuma Machine Tools	Okuma Machinery Works	NC lathes, grinders
1988	Wheeler Manufacturing	Rex Industries	Tools for pipeline installation and maintenance
1988	Amada Manufacturing	Amada Sonoike	NC metal forming machines and flexible manufacturing cells
1989	Hitachi Seiki USA	Hitachi Seiki	NC lathes
1989	Sugino USA	Sugino Machines	Automatic drilling/ tapping machines
1989	Swisstronics	Sanko Senzai Kogyo	Screw machine parts
1989	Murata Wiedemann	Murata Machinery	NC punch presses
1990	American Precision	Mitsubishi Heavy Industries	Machining centers, NC lathes
1990	Debur	Sumitomo (minority)	Polishing/finishing equipment

Source: MacKnight (1992a).

probably accounted for only 4 to 5 percent of U.S. machine tool output by 1990, productivity gains in the United States depended largely on the competitive response of U.S. companies to the performance of the Japanese investors. There were some signs of such a response, at least from the larger companies. Cincinnati Milacron, recognizing the failure of most of its diversification efforts of the 1980s, decided in 1990 to return to the basic machine tools that it had abandoned to the Japanese in the 1980s. It developed a five-year plan, "Wolfpack," to design and bring to market a range of new products and to improve the efficiency of its manufacturing processes.[41] Its methods, already applied in its only successful diversification (into plastics machinery),[42] appear to be very similar to the Japanese system described in chapter 5. These efforts helped the company return to profitability in 1992, after two years of operating losses.[43]

In a quite different response, Giddings and Lewis (the largest U.S. machine tool builder in 1992 after its acquisition of Cross and Trecker in 1991) rose to prominence as a developer of large integrated systems. (This was a field in which Japan was not an active exporter.) An example is the integrated flexible system sold to Navistar to inspect and monitor production processes in the manufacture of diesel engines.[44]

The response of the U.S. industry to the Japanese challenge was accompanied by a drop in U.S. imports and a rise in U.S. exports. This reduced the ratio of net imports to domestic consumption to 18 percent in 1992, a big improvement over the 37 percent peak in 1986. This improvement was too large to be entirely accounted for by the presence of new foreign-affiliated producers in the United States. But some of the improvement was no doubt due to the rise in the yen and the deutsche mark to levels so far above their purchasing power parity as to be untenable in the long run. Nevertheless, on balance it would appear that the goad provided by Japanese competition, especially the demonstration effect in the United States, was raising U.S. productivity and international competitiveness in the early 1990s.

Conclusions

In the first three postwar decades, U.S. companies in the integrated steel industry, tires, and machine tools—all of which were mature medium- or low-technology industries—became technology laggards slow to adopt product and process technology developed in foreign countries. In the 1980s, this U.S. backwardness and its resort to protective trade policy, along with higher expected rates of return on business investments in the United States and lower costs of capital elsewhere, attracted direct investment flows to the United States. By 1990, foreign-affiliated companies accounted for half of U.S. employment in the tire industry, about one-fourth in steel, and 9 percent in machine tools. Japan's share of the foreign presence ranged from over 80 percent in blast furnaces and steel mills to around half in tires and machine tools.

Japan's investments brought important product and process technology to its affiliated plants in the United States. But there was also heartening evidence of broader technology ripples throughout those U.S. industries. In the integrated sector of the steel industry, where Japanese investments included joint ventures with all of the major U.S. companies, most of the U.S. industry was strengthened by direct exposure to Japanese manufacturing methods. In all three industries, U.S. companies were strengthened by their efforts to meet the challenge of Japanese competition. At the same time, the strong and growing minimill sector of the U.S. steel industry attracted Japanese investments eager to keep abreast of the new technology. Since bilateral investments in these three industries probably generated more technology gains for the United States than for Japan, they helped the United States maintain its technology lead in manufacturing as a whole relative to Japan and other industrial countries.

Notes

1. The description of the U.S. steel industry given in this section draws heavily on Barnett and Crandall (1986).
2. Estimates by AUS Consultants: the WEFA Group reported in "An In-

dustrial Comeback Story: U.S. Is Competing Again in Steel," *New York Times*, March 31, 1992.

3. "Nippon Steel Moves to Consolidate Minimills," *Japan Economic Journal*, September 15, 1990.

4. "Minimill Inroads in Sheet Market Rouse Big Steel," *Wall Street Journal*, March 9, 1992.

5. Barnett and Crandall (1986), pp. 26–27.

6. Flemings, Clark, Cohen, Eager, Elliot, Gutowski, Thurow, and Tuller (1989), p. 31.

7. Ibid., pp. 47 and 13.

8. Barnett and Crandall (1986), p. 39.

9. Ibid., p. 46.

10. See, for example, "Nippon Kokan to Increase Shift to Non-Steel Sales," *Japan Economic Journal*, December 27, 1986; and "Diversification in Nippon Steel's Future," *Japan Economic Journal*, May 16, 1987.

11. "Nippon Kokan–Rouge Steel," *The Economist*, July 31, 1982.

12. "America's Steel Men Yearn to Make Anything But Steel," *The Economist*, November 2, 1985.

13. "National Steel Holds Course Despite Setbacks," *Japan Economic Journal*, March 11, 1989.

14. "NKK Still Seeking Payoff for U.S. Venture," *Japan Economic Journal*, September 8, 1990.

15. "A Faster Path to Finished Steel," *New York Times*, April 7, 1991.

16. "Unified Approach Casts Team's Success," *Iron Age*, September 1992.

17. "Steelmakers Push for Purity," *Iron Age*, March 1992.

18. "An Industrial Comeback Story," *New York Times*, March 31, 1992.

19. See n. 4.

20. "Steel Industry to Consolidate in Two Deals," *Wall Street Journal*, June 30, 1992.

21. "Nippon Steel, Yamato Kogyo to Help Nucor Build Plant in Malaysia," *Nikkei Weekly*, July 5, 1993.

22. Discussion of new technology for direct reduction of iron ore and related developments in this and the following two paragraphs draws heavily on McManus (1993).

23. "Nucor to Build Plant to Help Steel Minimills," *Wall Street Journal*, January 7, 1993.

24. Scherer (1992), pp. 61–63, provides a brief history of the development and dissemination of radial tire technology.

25. *Moody's Industrial Manual* (1992).

26. Ibid. (1988, 1992).

27. "Bridgestone's New U.S. Challenge," *New York Times*, February 22, 1988.

28. "Spinning Wheels: Bridgestone Discovers Purchase of U.S. Firm Creates Big Problems," *New York Times*, April 1, 1991.

29. "Debt Focuses the Mind," *Forbes*, January 7, 1991.

30. *Consumer Reports*, February 1992, pp. 75–79.

31. "No Pressure? No Problem. New Tires Run Flat," *New York Times*, September 2, 1992.

32. March (1989), pp. 75–76.

33. "Is APT Over the Hill?" *American Machinist*, May 1992.

34. "The Top Machine Tool Companies," *American Machinist*, July 1992.

35. "Can High Tech Put Milacron Back on the Cutting Edge?" *Business Week*, November 17, 1986.

36. March (1989), p. 89.

37. Association for Manufacturing Technology (1992).

38. "Japanese Drop a U.S. Investment," *New York Times*, February 20, 1991.

39. "Mitsubishi's NC Unit in the Spotlight," *Japan Economic Journal*, September 8, 1990.

40. "Fanuc Robots Are on the March Worldwide," *Japan Economic Journal*, July 14, 1990.

41. "Milacron Wolfpack Goes in for the Kill," *Wall Street Journal*, August 14, 1990.

42. "Creating Teamwork in Engineering," *American Machinist*, March 1992.

43. "The Top Machine Tool Companies," *American Machinist*, August 1993.

44. "Transfer Line Inspection with CMMs," *American Machinist*, January 1992.

7

Two-Way Technology Flows in High-R&D Industries: Computers, Semiconductors, and Communications Equipment

In the medium- and low-technology industries described in chapters 5 and 6, Japan's greater financial and technological strength generated strong net flows of direct investment and related technology from Japan to the United States. But in the high-technology industries that we will be observing in this and the next chapter, a strong U.S. lead in innovative product technology produced more balanced two-way direct investment flows, a strong flow of U.S. product technology to Japan, and a useful backflow of Japanese process technology to the United States.

The three industries described in this chapter—computers, semiconductors, and telecommunications equipment—share a common technology heritage. Innovations during the 1980s and early 1990s tightened the technology ties among these three industries and made the U.S. industry structure more integrated and more like the Japanese structures. Further, the complementarity of the two countries' technologies encouraged a two-way flow of investment and technologies. At the same time, a convergence of the two countries' formerly contrasting policies on trade and investment—a very slow move toward liberalization in Japan and a stronger move toward managed trade and investment in the United States— influenced and generally encouraged those two-way flows.

Technology Linkages and Industry Structure

The computer, semiconductor, and communications equipment industries have long been linked by common technology and interdependencies. AT&T's Bell Labs (and its precursor, American Bell Telephone) originated or developed much of their basic technology, on which these three industries are based, from the telephone in the nineteenth century to the transistor (basic to semiconductors) in the 1950s. Semiconductors are in fact the most critical component of both communications equipment and computers. And some communications equipment, especially switching equipment, might be regarded as specialized computers.

Major technology developments of the 1980s and early 1990s tightened these linkages by blurring the functional distinction between computers and communications equipment. The networking of computers (in the 1980s in the United States and the 1990s in Japan) created another communications system. At the same time, the increased digitization of wired telephone networks, previously based on analog signals, made telephone and computer network systems similar and compatible. This was followed in the early 1990s by a start on digitizing recently developed cellular radiotelephone systems. This, and the projected digitization of TV systems, raised visions of tying the four systems together in one great multimedia system.

In the early development stages of these industries after World War II, industrial structure in the United States and Japan differed greatly. In the United States, four separate industries took shape, with little overlapping membership. In Japan there was something closer to one great omnibus electronics industry. But in the 1980s, the two countries' industrial structures became a bit more similar.

The early development of separate industries in the United

States owes much to AT&T's policies, designed to protect its privately owned near-monopoly as a telephone system (a unique position when contrasted with other industrial countries' government-owned systems) and its related monopoly as producer of communications equipment.[1] A separate consumer audio and video industry was created in the 1920s and 1930s by AT&T's cross-licensing agreements with GE, RCA, and Westinghouse. These gave the latter three companies exclusive rights to manufacture household audio and TV equipment, while allocating similar exclusive rights to radio and TV transmission equipment to AT&T's manufacturing affiliate, Western Electric. In 1956, as part of an antitrust settlement that permitted it to maintain its ownership of Western Electric, AT&T agreed to freely license all of its technology and to confine its own commercial manufacturing to communications equipment. The result was a speedy diffusion of AT&T's recently developed transistor technology and the birth of numerous innovative companies in a new semiconductor industry.[2] It also kept big computer companies and AT&T out of one another's businesses.

Technological change and procompetitive decisions by the courts and the Federal Communications Commission (FCC) ultimately eliminated the AT&T monopolies and blurred industry distinctions. The FCC's Carterfone decision of 1968 encouraged new entrants in consumer premises equipment. The development of microwave telephone transmission and FCC decisions allowing new companies to offer microwave telephone services in the 1970s also encouraged new producers of telephone switching and transmission equipment. Its monopolies seriously eroded, AT&T gladly settled a U.S. Department of Justice antimonopoly suit in 1982 by agreeing to divest itself of the regional telephone companies in exchange for permission to enter other industries. By the early 1990s, AT&T had become a leader in the computer industry. IBM, already a leader in computers and semiconductors, had ventured into communications equipment. Motorola was a leader in semiconductors and communications equipment. Still, some fast-growing companies continued to specialize.

In Japan, many of the big electric companies were founded as joint ventures with U.S. or European makers of communications equipment and/or other electrical equipment in the early twentieth century.[3] As described in earlier chapters, they acquired computer, semiconductor, and communications equipment technologies as they became available and often operated in several of the industries as we have defined them here. But partly as a result of government encouragement and partly as a practical matter, most specialized in a limited number of products. Further, telephone service was a government monopoly until 1985 and, after liberalization, the electronics companies did not enter that industry.

By the end of the 1980s, industrial structures in the United States and Japan had some similarities as well as important remaining differences. This is illustrated in Table 7.1, listing world leaders in the four related manufacturing industries and also indicating which of those companies also had a strong presence in communications services. In both countries, a few giant corporations were world leaders in three industries, not always the same ones. However, among the other leaders, U.S.-based companies were almost entirely one-industry leaders, while Japan-based companies were fairly evenly distributed between one-industry and two-industry leadership.

Bilateral Investments and Government Policies

In these high-tech industries as in others, the higher cost of, and returns on, capital in the United States than in Japan or most other industrial countries in the 1980s contributed to stronger flows of direct investment from Japan to the United States than the reverse in that decade. But the United States' technological strength continued to encourage an expansion of U.S. companies' existing operations in Japan and the establishment of some new ones. By 1990, employment in U.S. affiliates of Japanese companies had pulled roughly even with employment in Japanese affiliates of U.S. companies in the three industries combined (see Table 7.2). However, the presence of U.S. companies in Japan, as

Table 7.1

World Leaders in Four Related Manufacturing Industries and Their Rankings, 1988 and 1991

	Computers (1991)	Semi-conductors (1988)	Communications Equipment (1988)	House-hold Video[a] (1988)	Memo: Active in Communications Services[b]
Leaders in three industries					
AT&T	7		1		c
Motorola		5	6		c
IBM	1	2	8[d]		
NEC	3	1	4		
Fujitsu	2	7	10		
Hitachi	6	4		6	
Leaders in two industries					
GTE			9		c
Toshiba		3		9	
Mitsubishi		9		8	
Matsushita		10		3	
Siemens	9		3		
Northern Telecom			5		c
Leaders in one industry					
DEC	4				
Hewlett-Packard	5				
Unisys	8				
Apple	10				
Texas Instruments		6			
Intel		8			
Zenith				1	
Sanyo				4	
Sharp				7	
Sony				6	
Alcatel			2		
Ericsson			7		
Philips				2	
Samsung				10	
Memorandum: Number of leaders					
U.S.-based	6	4	4	1	3
Japan-based	3	6	2	7	
Other	1	0	4	2	1

Sources: Datamation (June 15, 1992), p. 12; Stevens (1992); U.S. Department of Commerce (1993b), pp. 45–46; Staelin, Bozdogan, Cusumano, Ferguson, Filippone, Reintjes, Rosenbloom, Solow, and Ward (1989), p. 45.

[a] U.S. market for color TV sets only.

[b] Includes only leading companies in manufacturing industries listed. No rankings.

[c] Denotes a major presence in communications industry.

[d] IBM-Rolm. IBM transferred controlling interest in Rolm to Siemens in a joint venture agreed to in 1989.

Table 7.2

U.S. Presence in Japan and Japanese Presence in the United States in 1990: Computers, Electronic Components, and Communications Equipment

	Affiliate Employment (in thousands)		Percentage of Host-Country Employment	
	U.S. in Japan[a]	Japan in U.S.[b]	U.S. in Japan	Japan in U.S.
Computers and office equipment	30.6[c]	14.9	10.6c	5.2
Communications equipment and electronic components	19.5	38.1	1.9	4.6
Electronic components	19.5	22.1	d	4.1
Of which semiconductors		12.0	d	6.8
Audio, video, and communications equipment	0.0	16.0	0.0	5.4
Household audio and video		11.5		25.7
Other communications equipment		4.5		1.8
Total	50.1	53.1		

Sources: U.S. Department of Commerce (1993b, 1993c); OECD, *Industrial Structure Statistics* (1992).

[a] Employment in affiliates whose largest revenues are derived from indistry indicated.

[b] Employment in establishments in industry indicated.

[c] Data suppressed in U.S. Department of Commerce (1993a).

[d] Japanese employment data not available at this level of industry disaggregation.

measured by percentage of industry employment, was greater than that of Japanese companies in the United States in computers, and possibly roughly similar in semiconductors. But in the broadly defined communications equipment industry, the Japanese position was nearly 26 percent in household audio and video equipment, but less than 2 percent in other important communications equipment, while the U.S. position in Japan was nil. The table does not include the U.S. position in closely related Japanese service industries—computer software and communications services. Both sorts of investments rose further in the early 1990s and played an important role in technology transmission.

Because U.S. companies led in developing new product technology in these industries, while Japanese companies developed a lead in process technology in some of them, bilateral direct investment was associated with a strong flow of product technology to Japan in the 1980s and into the 1990s, and a healthy flow of Japanese process technology to the United States. However, the character of the technology transfers and the investments themselves were strongly influenced by the policies of the two governments with respect to technology, trade, and investment.

In the 1980s, both governments' policies were gradually changing as Japan's technological strength pulled closer to that of the United States, thus changing each country's perception of national interest. Both governments had long given financial support to R&D in those industries. But the United States' focus was typically on breaking new ground and staying ahead, while Japan's focus was on catching up with and, possibly, leapfrogging superior foreign technology. But we will find that in the 1980s, some U.S. government support went to catch-up efforts in semiconductors, while some Japanese government support went to maintaining a temporary lead in television equipment.

At the same time, the two countries' policies with respect to international trade and investment were converging. Japan continued to move very cautiously away from protectionist management toward deregulation. Its success in world markets for a broad range of products had led to the lifting of restrictions of foreign investments in most manufacturing industries in the late 1970s, as described in chapter 4. A parallel move to freer trade was evident in Japanese tariff reductions, agreed to in the Tokyo Round of multilateral trade agreements, which became effective in 1980. But numerous intangible barriers to trade, such as product standards, elaborate import inspection requirements, and preferential purchasing practices by government and industry and institutional barriers to unfriendly takeovers (described earlier) remained. Some of these remaining barriers began to be reduced in 1985, when the government-owned Nippon Telephone and Telegraph Corporation (NTT), then the sole provider of telecommunications services in Japan, embarked on a gradual privatization process. At the same time, the government opened up the communications industry to private enterprise other than the partly privatized NTT, but subject to detailed regulation. Foreign investors were permitted to establish wholly owned value-added networks (VANs) and to acquire a minority interest in other communications companies. This provided foreigners with new opportunities for investment and for sales of communications equipment in Japan.[4]

Over the same period, the United States was moving rather more rapidly away from laissez-faire policies toward managed trade and investment. As noted in chapters 5 and 6, it reacted to rising imports of products in low- and medium-R&D industries by requesting Japan and a few other countries to exercise "voluntary export restraints." These VERs, increasingly popular in Europe as well as the United States, were in effect a bilateral version of the quota restrictions long practiced by many countries but by then on the wane. But beginning in 1986, the United States carried its managed trade approach one step further. The cumulative pressures created by Japan's developing superiority in semiconductor process technology, U.S. outrage over Japanese companies' predatory export pricing policies, and U.S. frustration concerning Japan's regulatory and institutional barriers to imports led the United States to embark on a new experiment in bilateral managed trade. Following punitive tariffs on some imports from Japan and threats of more, a U.S.-Japan Semiconductor Agreement was signed in 1986. It not only ended Japanese predatory pricing but established somewhat vague and unspecified goals for foreign (in effect, largely U.S.) penetration of Japanese markets over a five-year period. In a subsequent two-year extension of the original agreement, targets were made a bit more specific and applied to Japan's purchases from foreign-based companies, whether manufacturing abroad or in Japan.[5] The semiconductor agreement was followed by other bilateral agreements designed to improve U.S. companies' access to Japanese markets in a number of industries, including communications equipment. Most referred to specific remedial actions to be taken by the Japanese government and/or Japanese companies rather than targets for Japanese purchases, although U.S. negotiators continued to push for the latter.

With respect to direct investment by foreigners, the U.S. Congress took a modest step toward regulation in 1988, partly in response to the enthusiasm of Japanese companies for investing in technology-rich U.S. companies. As noted in chapter 2, the Exon-Florio Amendment to the Omnibus Trade and Competitiveness Act of 1988 gave the U.S. president the power to block foreign acquisitions or mergers judged to be a threat to national security.

The combined effect of Japan's moves to open up new areas for foreign investment and the United States' efforts to force greater access to Japanese markets contributed to increased U.S. investments in Japan's semiconductor and communications industries and to a substantial related two-way technology flow. Nevertheless, the U.S. position in the Japanese semiconductor industry remained substantially smaller than the U.S. presence in the computer industry, achieved without the benefit of those particular U.S. policies. At the same time, the Exon-Florio Amendment and the congressional sentiment that it reflected influenced Japanese investment and investment strategy in the United States. It prevented the Japanese from purchasing several technology-rich companies in the semiconductor and related industries and may have encouraged a bit more reliance on joint ventures and equity participations than on takeovers to acquire desired technology.

The following three sections examine in some detail the relative technology strengths of companies based in the United States and Japan and the bilateral investments and related technology transfers to which they gave rise.

Computers

In the computer industry, the global lead of U.S. companies in product technology in the 1980s was based on a series of important innovations made possible by the rapidly rising capabilities of semiconductors.[6] Powerful minicomputers proved popular alternatives to mainframes with office users. The introduction of personal computers (PCs) led to a new and rapidly growing consumer industry. Even more important, PCs arranged in networks began to supplant mainframes in a wide variety of business uses. The subsequent introduction of high-powered desktop workstations, which could also be networked, broadened the onslaught on mainframes. Supercomputers, first using a single high-powered processor and then, massively parallel, using large numbers of smaller cheaper processors, met sophisticated computing needs.[7]

While some of this innovation germinated in large companies, especially IBM, it was more aggressively developed by newer companies. The development of minicomputers by Digital Equipment Company (DEC) propelled it to a leading market position. Other new leaders included Apple, Compaq, and Dell in personal computers; Sun Microsystems and Hewlett-Packard in workstations; and Cray and Thinking Machines in supercomputers. Independent software companies also flourished: Microsoft in PC operating systems and Novell in networking.

The older mainframe producers—IBM and "the BUNCH" (Burroughs, Univac, NCR, Control Data, and Honeywell)—ultimately responded in a variety of ways. Burroughs and Univac merged to become Unisys, while Honeywell gradually withdrew from the industry. NCR was acquired in 1991 by AT&T (following AT&T's earlier experimental joint-venture forays into the industry). IBM, world industry leader, was the only one to take an innovative lead in PCs. But it moved slowly on workstations, supercomputers, and networking, probably inhibited by its heavy commitment to mainframes.

In the late 1980s, both IBM and AT&T came to recognize that networking placed a new premium on computer compatibility. Toward the end of the decade, each organized a group of companies manufacturing computers, components, and peripherals to support competing versions of a universally applicable Unix computer operating system. Unix originated in AT&T's Bell Labs in the 1970s. But its numerous licensees had developed so many versions that some standardization seemed to be required. After an extended period of competition between the IBM-sponsored Open Software Foundation (OSF) and the AT&T-sponsored Unix International (UI), and the purchase of UI by Novell, the two groups reached an uneasy truce in 1993 in order to fend off a new competitive offering, Windows NT by Microsoft.[8]

Bilateral direct investment played a major role in transferring these U.S. product innovations to Japan. It also facilitated the transfer of some Japanese manufacturing technology for peripherals to the United States.

U.S. Firms in Japan: Bringing New Products and Acquiring Skills

By the 1980s, bilateral direct investment had already been instrumental in transferring much U.S. computer technology to Japan, as described in earlier chapters. In the 1960s, IBM's bargain with the Japanese authorities had made its early technology available to all of the big Japanese electronics companies in exchange for permission to expand its operations in Japan. And in the 1970s, Fujitsu kept abreast of rapidly evolving U.S. technology partly through its investment in Amdahl.

In the 1980s, IBM remained the dominant U.S. computer company manufacturing in Japan. Nihon Unisys concentrated on sales of computers manufactured elsewhere and on services, although it also had a manufacturing joint venture with Oki Electric.[9] DEC established a plant to manufacture its minicomputer in Japan,[10] but remained a smaller player in the Japanese market. NCR continued to specialize in point-of-sale devices and distribution processing terminals until it was acquired by AT&T in 1991.[11] Apple developed an extensive sales operation in Japan in the early 1990s.[12]

IBM's strong presence in Japan had a profound effect on the development of the Japanese computer industry and its technology. As a role model and the company to beat, IBM led Japanese companies to devote most of their energies to mainframes and to underestimate the importance of PCs, workstations, and networking until late in the decade. Japanese companies' success in pursuing the Pied Piper is evident from IBM's declining share of the Japanese mainframe market, which fell from 42 percent in 1978 to 33 percent in 1989.[13]

IBM's strategy in the Japanese PC market during much of the 1980s may also have slowed the growth of PCs and networking. In the United States, the ready availability of Microsoft's DOS operating system, used in IBM PCs, encouraged the growth of IBM-compatible PCs, which in turn encouraged networking. However, IBM did not make its Kanji version of DOS freely available in Japan. This made cloning more difficult and left room for the development of competing operating systems. NEC developed such a system and a superior sales network. By the late 1980s, NEC had captured roughly half of the Japanese market. This and Seiko Epson's NEC-compatible machines (an additional 8 percent of the market) inspired the writing of a large volume of software for the NEC operating system. At the end of the 1980s, IBM had less than 10 percent of the market, while Fujitsu, Toshiba, and others (with their own operating systems imperfectly compatible with IBM's) had the rest.[14] The multiplicity of PC operating systems discouraged the development of computer networking in Japan. In 1990 an estimated 2 percent of Japan's PCs were networked, as compared with 35 percent in the United States and 22 percent in Europe.[15]

Toward the end of the decade a shift in IBM's marketing strategies ultimately brought networking to Japan and stimulated the growth of the Japanese PC market. This new strategy centered on an effort to increase the desirability of its products by making its operating systems the industry standard in all sectors of the computer market. In 1989, the two competing Unix software groups, IBM-backed OSF and AT&T's UI, initiated a campaign to sign up Japanese makers of computers and peripherals.[16] Many Japanese firms ultimately acquired both.[17]

The initiatives of IBM and AT&T in basic operating system

software were followed by investments from independent U.S. network software companies in 1990. Novell, an innovative U.S.-based networking software company, formed a joint venture (holding 54 percent of its equity) with Canon, Fujitsu, NEC, Sony, and Toshiba, to develop Kanji-based networking software.[18] Microsoft followed in 1991, offering a Japanese version of its local area network (LAN) networking software, which was also acquired by most of Novell's partners.[19]

In 1991, hoping to break NEC's dominance of the PC market in Japan and expanding its own drive for product compatibility, IBM offered to license its new Kanji version of the DOS operating system for PCs. This version, known as DOS V in Japan, was the first operating system capable of using both English-language and Kanji applications software for DOS.[20] After some hesitation, rooted in fear of IBM domination, all Japanese computer makers except NEC and Seiko Epson accepted the IBM offer.[21] The widespread acceptance of DOS V set the stage for a competitive blitz of imports from the United States that sold at prices much lower than those then prevailing in Japan. Compaq started selling in Japan in late 1992, and Dell in early 1993.[22]

NEC was slow to meet the price cuts, apparently banking on the fact that there were far fewer Kanji software programs written for DOS than for the NEC operating system.[23] But in 1993 Microsoft (the creator of DOS) brought to Japan a new Kanji version of its user-friendly DOS-based Windows operating system. Microsoft's product was capable of running applications software written for the NEC operating system on both IBM-compatible computers and NEC computers.[24] By the end of the year, the share of DOS-based computers was rising sharply, as was the share enjoyed by Apple (whose notebook computer appealed to the cramped Japanese household). At the same time, the sales of all PCs were rising as the sales of mainframes fell. PC sales exceeded mainframe sales for the first time in Japan. This crossover occurred nearly a decade after a similar crossover in the United States.[25]

IBM was also diligent in drawing on Japanese companies'

manufacturing skills. This went well beyond the simple purchase of components. For example, although its own manufacturing skills were regarded as exemplary,[26] IBM turned to Matsushita in 1983 for help in manufacturing PCs for the U.S. market.[27] Matsushita had by then largely withdrawn from the computer business but was well known for its manufacturing skills in consumer electronics. Examples of IBM's seeking out Japanese process technology in the 1990s include (1) a joint manufacturing venture with Tokyo Electric to manufacture small computer printers; (2) an agreement with Hitachi Koki to jointly develop large printers;[28] and (3) cooperation with Canon in the development and production of a portable computer with a built-in printer.[29]

IBM also turned to Japan for useful developments in product technology. In 1989 it formed a joint venture with Toshiba to develop and mass produce liquid crystal displays (LCDs) for computer monitors, based on thin film transistors with a potential for quick response and sharp color image.[30] While LCDs were originally invented in the United States by George H. Heilmeier, working at RCA laboratories, the technology was developed by Japanese companies—first for pocket calculators and then for digital wristwatches. In the late 1980s, NEC, Sharp, and Toshiba were making progress in adapting the technology to making larger screens for computer monitors.[31] The joint venture with Toshiba allowed IBM to catch up with Japanese product developments as well as their methods of manufacturing LCDs.

DEC also drew on its exposure to Japanese manufacturing skills, adapting them to its operations in the United States. In the late 1980s, it adopted just-in-time inventory practices in its U.S. plants, programming its computers to transmit the company's forecasts of sales and production to its suppliers and to write checks to those suppliers as parts were delivered.[32]

Japanese Firms in the United States: Bringing Manufacturing Skills and Acquiring Workstation Technology[33]

Until the 1980s, Japanese companies' investments in the U.S.

Table 7.3

Employment in Japanese Firms: U.S. Affiliates of Computer and Office Equipment Manufacturing, 1990

SIC No.		Number of Plants	Employment
357	Computer and office equipment[a]	36	14,930
3571	Electronic computers	13	8,993
3572	Computer storage devices	8	1,640
3575	Computer terminals	2	C
3577	Printers and other peripherals	6	3,075
3578	Calculating and accounting equipment	1	A
3579	Other office machines[b]	6	G

Source: U.S. Department of Commerce (1993c).

Note: A = 0 to 19; C = 100 to 249; G = 1,000 to 2,499.

[a] Does not include Bull HN since Bull, a French company, was a larger shareholder than NEC.

[b] Includes portable electronic typewriters and parts, business forms–handling equipment, and time-recording/controlling equipment.

computer industry had been limited to the part interest in Amdahl acquired by Fujitsu, one of Japan's two leading computer companies, and Oki's early investment in printers. Even in the 1980s, Fujitsu's Amdahl holding remained the largest single Japanese investment and accounted for roughly one-third of employment in Japanese companies' U.S. affiliates in the industry.

In the 1980s many more Japanese companies entered the United States, manufacturing a wide variety of computers, components, and peripherals (see Table 7.3). These new investments fall into two groups. The first group consists of investments made by companies that were already producing similar products in Japan, often supplying U.S. companies. They entered the United States to improve their share of a rapidly growing market and to avoid retaliatory import restrictions applied in connection with the semiconductor dispute. The second, smaller group, consists of investments made by computer and other companies seeking new technology, mostly in workstations.

NEC, the other leading Japanese computer company and the largest investor in the first group, made a variety of investments. In 1987, it took a 15 percent interest in the newly formed joint venture Bull HN, with Compagnie des Machines Bull and Honeywell. (Since Bull was the larger foreign investor, employment in that venture, at one time approaching 4,000, is not reflected in Table 7.2.) For both NEC and Bull, the venture presented an opportunity to expand in the U.S. market, while for Honeywell it was the road to gradual pullout. NEC had gotten its start in the industry with Honeywell technology and, more recently, had supplied computers to both companies. NEC contributed its mainframe designs to the new joint venture.[34] After the withdrawal of Honeywell was completed in 1991,[35] Bull assumed full control of the by then somewhat troubled U.S. venture, and NEC traded its share in the U.S. venture for a 4.7 percent share in Bull itself.[36] This maintained NEC's entrée into European markets while permitting the company to operate independently in U.S. markets.

NEC's independent computer manufacturing operations in the United States were confined to personal computers, where its investments were the largest among those made by Japanese companies attracted to the growing U.S. market. Toward the end of the decade, NEC mounted a strong drive for market share. However, at least through 1992, NEC's products were judged unspectacular and overpriced by many U.S. market analysts.[37]

Investments in components and peripherals, accounting for another third of employment in those affiliates manufacturing computers and office equipment, were made by companies that had already become important suppliers to U.S. companies. Investments in storage devices included one in disk drives by Fujitsu (supplier to Amdahl) and one by Hitachi (a supplier to Unisys). Investors in printers included Seiko Epson (supplier to IBM) and Canon (supplier of engines to Hewlett-Packard). It is quite possible that these Japanese manufacturing operations were a competitive spur to U.S. producers.

The much smaller group of the investments made to acquire

new technology in workstations were more important than their size might suggest. Sony established a small wholly owned manufacturing company, presumably buying U.S. technology and hiring U.S. technical personnel. But the rest elected to learn by acquiring whole or part interest in new U.S. companies.

Matsushita, which had confined its computer operations to PCs and components during most of the 1980s, moved into higher technology realms in 1988 by acquiring a 52 percent interest in Solborne, a new U.S. company in Colorado. Solborne obtained a license from Sun Microsystems for that company's workstation architecture (based on AT&T's version of Unix) and SPARC, Sun's version of a powerful new RISC (reduced instruction set computing) semiconductor.[38] In the following year, Matsushita opened its own wholly owned plant in Illinois and, using the same licenses and drawing on Solborne designs and its own observations at Solborne, began to manufacture workstations there and in Japan. By 1990, Matsushita's relations with Sun Microsystems had ripened to the point of an agreement to market Sun products in Japan and to manufacture on an OEM (original equipment manufacturer) basis for sale under the Matsushita brand name.[39]

Fujitsu repeated the strategy used earlier with Amdahl, acquiring a part interest in a company headed by a former engineer at IBM. The company in this case, Hal, was headed by H. Andrew Heller, former leader of the team that developed IBM's engineering workstation. Hal was developing a new workstation and its own adaptation of the SPARC chip, which Fujitsu contracted to manufacture.[40]

In a cautious approach to computers, Canon, whose activities in the computer industry had been mainly in printers, acquired a 16.7 percent interest in NEXT Inc. in 1989. NEXT, founded by Steven P. Jobs, who had earlier founded Apple Computer, manufactured workstations and microcomputers. However, NEXT appears to have had trouble defining its market and abandoned manufacturing to concentrate on software in 1992.[41] Canon acquired NEXT's manufacturing arm and some of its expert staff, launching its own workstation manufacturing affiliate in the United States in 1993.[42]

Kubota, a producer of farm machinery seeking a new life in the high-tech end of the computer industry, acquired minority equity positions in three California firms between 1986 and 1989. They included Ardent and MIPS Computer Systems, two new firms making minisupercomputers and workstations, and Akashic Memories (superseded by Maxoptics), making hard disks. By 1988, Kubota was manufacturing in Japan to supply Ardent and to sell under its own name in the Far East.[43]

In 1989, Ardent merged with Stellar, a maker of similar but partly incompatible products in Massachusetts, to form Stardent. But in 1991, beset by problems of merging the products and personnel, Stardent went out of business after attracting $200 million in venture capital, mostly from Kubota. Kubota acquired worldwide marketing rights to the latest version of Stardent's Titan, which it was already manufacturing in Japan.[44] But it remains to be seen whether Kubota, a computer novice, can succeed in this highly competitive field. Kubota received some help from Oki Electric, an experienced Japanese computer maker to whom it had consigned some of its manufacturing of Ardent machines. Since Oki subsequently announced plans for manufacturing its own workstations in the United States,[45] that company appears to have been an important beneficiary of Kubota's investment.

Progress Report

The continuing U.S. lead in computer product technology, and the extent to which Japanese computer makers have managed to absorb that technology, is suggested by a *Datamation* tabulation of the shares of the top fifteen companies in world markets for major computer products in 1992 (see Table 7.4). In the oldest, weakening market sector, large-scale computer systems, the top fifteen companies in that market accounted for 94.1 percent of world sales, of which the Japanese share was 40 percent—nearly as large as the U.S. share, 47.5 percent. By contrast, in the rapidly growing world markets for workstations, the top 15 companies held 90 percent of the market, but U.S. companies held 61.2

Table 7.4

Share of Top Fifteen Companies in World Computer Markets in 1991, Six Major Products[a]

	U.S.	Japanese	Other	Top 15
Personal computers	50.7	21.3	5.6	77.6
Workstations	61.2	26.7	1.6	89.5
Midrange	54.7	30.6	8.0	93.3
Large-scale systems	47.5	40.0	6.6	94.1
Peripherals	51.9	15.7	10.4	78.0
Software				

Source: Datamation, June 15, 1992.
[a] Percent of revenues of top 100 companies for each product.

percent, more than double Japan's 26.7 percent. The top two Japanese companies in the list were Fujitsu and Matsushita, the two Japanese computer makers that had taken the learn-by-participation route. U.S. companies had a three-to-one advantage over Japanese companies in software and a more than two-to-one advantage in PCs.

Semiconductors

There are three main sorts of semiconductors: (1) discrete or individual devices; (2) integrated circuits (IC), which consist of many transistors on a single chip; and (3) optoelectronic devices, which respond to or emit light.[46] OECD has estimated that, in 1988, discrete devices, the oldest type, accounted for 15 percent of world production, integrated circuits for 81 percent, and optoelectronic devices, the newest sort, for 4 percent. Integrated circuits are further subdivided according to their functions—memory or logic (i.e., processing instructions according to rules of logic)—and whether or not they are built for a special purpose.

Computers absorb about 40 percent of the world's semiconductor production, while communications equipment (broadly defined to include household audio and TV) takes about 35 percent. Other important users include other consumer electronics, industrial electronics, the military, and transportation equipment.

Table 7.5

U.S. and Japanese Shares in World Semiconductor Markets, 1978–93[a]

	1978	1988	1993
United States	62	37	42
Japan	28	50	41
Other	10	13	17

Sources: Dataquest, as cited by Stevens (1992) p. 139; and *Nikkei Weekly*, December 20, 1993.

[a] Merchant semiconductor sales in current U.S. dollars, by nationality of firm headquarters. (Excludes "captive" production by firms for their own use.)

Technology, Changing Market Shares, and Policy Responses

The major product innovations of the 1980s and early 1990s centered on the creation of increasingly powerful and efficient computer microprocessors—the complex logic ICs that drive computer operations—and increasingly dense and versatile memory ICs. The new optoelectronic devices were also gaining importance. While U.S. companies had been global leaders in technology in the 1960s and 1970s, Japanese companies developed a lead in methods of mass producing high-quality memory chips in the 1980s. This superiority in process technology, together with aggressive pricing policy, pushed Japanese companies' share of the world's merchant markets to roughly that of U.S. companies by the mid-1980s. By 1988, it reached a peak of 50 percent, as compared to 37 percent for the United States (see Table 7.5). However, shares in merchant markets overstate the strength of Japan relative to the United States since they exclude "captive" production by companies for their own use, more prevalent in the United States than in Japan. In 1988, when the Japanese merchant market share peaked, shares of U.S. and Japanese companies in world production (including captive output) are estimated to have been about equal.[47] Moreover, even in the merchant market, Japanese strength was concentrated in dynamic random access memory (DRAM) chips, where Japanese skills in manufacturing and strength in clean rooms produced strikingly lower defect ratios. This contributed to a very strong market lead estimated by OECD to have been 72 percent in 1988 while the U.S. share dropped to an estimated 15 percent. In that decade, U.S. technological innovation was especially strong in microprocessors, the chips responsible for operating computing processes. In that market, U.S. producers developed and maintained a very strong market position—an estimated 70 percent of the merchant market as compared to 18 percent for Japan. In other products—other memory chips and custom circuits—U.S. producers maintained a reasonably comfortable lead.

Nevertheless, the relative importance of DRAMs pushed Japanese producers into the lead in the merchant market as a whole and provoked a strong U.S. response. The Japanese advance into the memory chip market in the United States had been accompanied by fierce price cutting, which had caused several U.S. producers to abandon the market. This led to complaints of dumping against Japanese vendors of two sorts of memory chips. To fend off U.S. retaliatory action, the Japanese agreed to cease predatory pricing and, in 1986, signed a vaguely worded five-year agreement to work for the expansion of the foreign share in Japanese semiconductor markets, then less than 9 percent.[48] This was renewed in 1991 for another five years, with the addition of a specific target ("expectations," in Japan's interpretation) of a 20 percent foreign share of the Japanese market to be achieved by the end of 1992.[49]

In 1987 the U.S. government moved to strengthen the manufacturing skills of the U.S. industry by organizing Sematech, a government-industry consortium. Much as the Japanese government's VLSI semiconductor program had done a decade earlier, Sematech concentrated increasingly on improving U.S. semiconductor manufacturing equipment (SME), described in chapter 8. In 1988, leading members of the U.S. semiconductor industry attempted to organize an industry consortium to manufacture memory chips, but this was abandoned in 1990.[50]

By the late 1980s, a number of Japanese companies (encouraged by their government) and U.S. companies (acting on their own) appear to have quietly decided that the best solution to the impasse was joint-venture investment. Those which ensued generated a fruitful two-way technology flow.

U.S. Investment in Japan and Joint Venture Technology Swaps

Until 1980, Texas Instruments had been the only U.S. semiconductor company manufacturing in Japan. Motorola and Analogue Devices started manufacturing early in the 1980s, and a third wave of investments, many of them joint ventures, developed late in the decade.[51] Since many in the third group did not start producing until 1991 or after, their presence is not fully reflected in Table 7.2, relating to 1990. The joint ventures were associated with three types of technology transfer: (1) an international exchange of technologies, reflecting the comparative technology advantages of the two countries in the semiconductor industry; (2) a broader dissemination of developing technologies within the semiconductor industry; and (3) a wider dissemination of existing technologies to Japanese companies outside the semiconductor industry and wishing to enter it. Beyond this, the old-timers among U.S. companies in Japan made the best of their presence there to absorb Japanese process technology.

An international exchange of technologies was generated by a joint venture of Motorola with Toshiba. Long frustrated in its attempts to manufacture in Japan, Motorola had finally succeeded in 1980.[52] Its later joint venture with Toshiba opened its first plant in 1988, producing DRAMs using Toshiba technology, and microprocessors using Motorola technology. Since Motorola had abandoned memory chips in the face of Japanese competition earlier in the 1980s, the joint venture gave Motorola access to Japan's superior process technology and allowed Motorola to resume its own manufacture of memory chips in the United States and in Japan in a new plant of its own, opened in 1991.

And because microprocessors were the weakest link in Japan's armory, the venture was very helpful for Toshiba as well.

In 1992, joint ventures helped along a lively international dissemination of technology in "flash" memory chips. Flash memory chips retain their memory when the power is turned off. Toshiba did exploratory work in flash chips in the early 1980s but put it aside to concentrate on DRAMs.[53] Toward the end of the 1980s, when the popularity of laptop and notebook PCs created a broad and growing market for such a device, Intel, Advanced Micro Devices, and Toshiba, working independently, hoped to establish their particular version of the flash chip as the industry standard. To this end, each of the three enlisted help from a company in the other country. Two involved joint ventures.

Intel turned to NMB, a new firm established by Minebea (a big manufacturer of ball bearings that was eager to enter the semiconductor industry). Intel placed OEM supply contracts with NMB and formed a joint marketing venture with NMB in the United States. While NMB had succeeded in producing simpler chips for Intel, it encountered difficulties producing Intel's new flash chips.[54] When NMB's failure to deliver in 1992 imperiled Intel's market lead, Intel stepped up its own production plans and turned to Sharp, an experienced Japanese semiconductor producer, for OEM supplies.[55]

At the same time, Toshiba intensified its efforts to regain leadership by enlisting U.S. industry support through technology agreements with IBM[56] and National Semiconductor.[57] In this competitive environment, Advanced Micro Devices (AMD) made a bold effort to come up from behind by forming a joint venture with Fujitsu to develop, manufacture, and sell flash chips. Product development was to remain at AMD headquarters in California, while new production was planned for Japan.[58] The two partners broke ground for a jointly financed plant in Japan in 1993, and expected to start producing in late 1994.[59]

U.S. semiconductor companies also formed joint manufacturing ventures with Japanese steel companies that were searching for growth opportunities. LSI Logic, a U.S. maker of ASICs (application specific integrated circuits), a product in which U.S. companies were strong, established a manufacturing joint venture with Kawasaki Steel, starting to produce in 1987. Texas Instruments, with a long history of production in Japan, decided to expand its sales by forming a joint venture with Kobe Steel. Kobe provided 75 percent of the capital which financed a new plant that opened in 1992. All of the plant's output—DRAMs and logic devices—was supplied to TI for sale under its own name in Japan or elsewhere.

Finally, longtime semiconductor producers in Japan—IBM and Texas Instruments—plus newcomer Motorola learned how to draw on Japanese university research in semiconductors. This was also true of Intel. (Largest U.S. producer of microprocessors, Intel had established a sales affiliate in Japan in 1976 and a design center in 1980, and supplied microprocessors to most Japanese PC producers. But it did not manufacture in Japan.) All four companies sent engineers to observe the laboratory of Tadahiro Ohmi, a professor at Tohoku University, who conducted research on ultraclean methods of semiconductor manufacturing. In 1987, Ohmi helped Intel design a chip fabrication line in California, which that company used to establish its 1992 lead in producing flash chips.[60]

Japanese Investment in the United States: Bringing Manufacturing Skills and Seeking Logic Chip Technology

Japanese investments in producing semiconductors in the United States accelerated in the late 1980s and continued to be strong in the early 1990s.[61] Like U.S. investments in Japan, they generated several types of technology transfers—in this case, (1) modest transfers of Japanese manufacturing skills to U.S. companies; (2) dissemination of existing semiconductor technology to Japanese companies in other industries seeking to enter the semiconductor industry; and (3) transfers of new semiconductor product technology from U.S. to Japanese companies.

The largest portion of Japanese investment came from the major Japanese semiconductor producers—NEC, Toshiba, Hitachi, Fujitsu, Mitsubishi, Matsushita, Oki, and Sony. Roughly two-thirds of their manufacturing capacity was established in 1986 and after, reflecting a desire to defuse trade tensions. Some of the plants were acquired from U.S. companies that were reducing the scale of their operations. Fujitsu offered to buy Fairchild Semiconductor (then owned by Schlumberger, a French company), but withdrew its offer when it became clear that the U.S. government had serious reservations on security grounds related to Fairchild's military contracts. Otherwise, Japanese investments proceeded smoothly, including Matsushita's later purchase of one plant, previously owned by Fairchild, from National Semiconductor (which had purchased Fairchild after Fujitsu withdrew).[62]

Output of the U.S. plants of Japanese semiconductor firms seems to have been concentrated on DRAMs, the field in which they excelled, with some attention to other memory chips and to custom chips, where they were competitive with U.S. companies. At least one producer, Mitsubishi, introduced an automated flexible manufacturing system, allowing it to shift its output back and forth between memory chips and ASICs (a custom logic chip) in response to fluctuating demand.[63]

While these investments brought Japanese manufacturing skills to their U.S. affiliate plants, the immediate effect on the process technology of U.S. companies may not have been very large. Because the affiliates were wholly owned, there were no U.S. partners to participate and learn. However, Sony's purchase of a Texas plant from Advanced Micro Devices in 1990 included an element of manufacturing technology transfer, which was publicized by both companies (and dismissed as hype by some market observers). The sale was accompanied by two special features: a five-year lease-back of part of the plant in which AMD continued to manufacture; and the proviso that AMD engineers would participate in retrofitting and operating the new Sony plant, thereby learning Sony's manufacturing methods.[64]

Japanese investments also included at least two of Japan's ever-present diversifiers from mature industries. In 1988 Nippon Mining acquired Gould, itself an extremely diversified company, which was then in the process of selling off assets. The remainder acquired by Nippon Mining was mainly focused on copper foil (used extensively in semiconductors) and electronic measuring equipment. Of its eleven plants, one produced integrated circuits, but this was subsequently sold. The second investor, NMB (whose supply relationships with Intel were described in the preceding section), purchased a 55 percent interest in Ramtron in 1990 as part of its drive to break into the semiconductor industry. Ramtron was a small U.S. company venturing into the forefront of memory chips by producing 16-megabit DRAMs of the sort used in workstations.

For technology transfers, the most important investments may have been those made by the big Japanese electronics companies to acquire the new RISC microprocessor technology through joint-venture investments in the United States. Their first investments were associated with acquiring part ownership in companies that made workstations—Matsushita in Solborne and Fujitsu in Hal—described in the preceding section. In 1993, Fujitsu strengthened its hand by acquiring Ross Technologies from Cypress. Ross was a small company manufacturing the SPARC chip for its creator, Sun Microsystems. When Sun turned to TI for its supplies, Cypress decided to sell Ross.[65] Fujitsu's subsequent purchase of Ross provided a SPARC chip supplier for Hal and added technology and expertise for Fujitsu.

The Scorecard in 1993

By 1993 the U.S. semiconductor industry was clearly feeling cheered by the progress that it had made since 1986. In Japan's semiconductor markets, U.S. investments in additional manufacturing in Japan, much of it in joint ventures, had helped to push the foreign share from less than 10 percent in 1986–88 to 20 percent in the fourth quarter of 1992. There was a slight slippage in the first three quarters of 1993, but a rebound to 20 percent in the fourth quarter.[66] In world merchant markets, U.S. companies' share of sales had risen to 42 percent in 1993, narrowly topping the 41 percent held by Japanese companies for the first time since the mid-1980s. This was a dramatic change from the 13 percentage point lead enjoyed by Japanese companies in 1988 (shown in Table 7.5). Continued and growing U.S. strength in microprocessors and the challenge to Japan mounted by South Korea and Taiwan in memory chips appear to have been responsible.

In related technology transfers, Japan's strong advances in process technology had been successfully transferred to U.S. companies in a number of ways: (1) the Motorola-Toshiba joint venture; (2) drawing on research in Japanese universities by U.S. companies manufacturing in Japan; and, more weakly, (3) the demonstration effect of Japanese companies manufacturing in the United States. U.S. innovations in processor chips were transferred to Japan by the Motorola-Toshiba joint venture and by Japanese investments in U.S. companies possessing the new RISC chip technology. In the new area of flash memory chips, the Advanced Micro Devices–Fujitsu joint venture, together with other U.S.-Japan technology collaborations, assured the swift international dissemination of that important contribution to laptop PCs and potentially larger PCs as well as other developing communications products.

Communications Equipment

Communications equipment, broadly defined, includes (1) telephone and telegraph apparatuses, ranging from central office switching and transmission lines to PBX systems, fax machines, and telephones; (2) radio and television communications equipment, including central office broadcasting equipment, satellites and satellite communications equipment, and cellular radiotelephone systems and the cellular phones themselves; and (3) consumer audio and video equipment.[67]

Innovations and Shifting Leadership Roles

During the 1980s and early 1990s, technological innovation burst forth in all sectors of this broad industry. Leadership roles in product innovation were more widely distributed among industrial countries than they were in computers and semiconductors. The basic technology underlying these innovations was widely available in view of AT&T's 1956 agreement to license its technology freely. But some companies moved more rapidly than others to develop important new products.

In the early 1980s, the United States was trailing France, Sweden, and Canada in the development and installation of digital central office switching systems. While AT&T had pioneered the development of electronic switching in the 1960s and early 1970s, it chose to develop an analog form, misjudging the speed of future semiconductor development. In order to protect its investment in analog switches, it delayed going digital until 1980, when liberalized telecom equipment markets and competition from Canada's Northern Telecom (by then manufacturing in the United States) forced the change.[68] With the final breakup of AT&T's monopoly in telecommunications and equipment in the early 1980s, U.S. companies played leading roles in developing cellular radiotelephone systems (analog in the 1980s and digital in the 1990s) and satellite communications equipment. But others were not far behind. In TV broadcasting and receiving equipment, Japanese companies realized their dream of being first to develop high-definition television (HDTV), putting an analog form into operation in 1992. They were soon surpassed by a group of mainly U.S. companies that developed a digital HDTV, expected to go into operation in the United States in the late 1990s. In the 1990s, U.S. companies also led in experimentation with multimedia communications services, such as interactive television and related equipment. Japanese companies were fully competitive in the development of asynchronous transfer mode (ATM) switches (capable of simultaneously transmitting high-resolution images, voice, and data), which were critical to multimedia systems.

Table 7.6

Indicators of the Dissemination of Communications Equipment in Major Industrial Countries

	Digital Switching (% of subscriber lines)		Cellular Radiotelephones (% of population)	
	1989	1994[a]	1990	1992
France	70.7	86.5	0.6	
Canada	51.4	87.5	2.2	
United States	42.5	68.2	2.0	4.3
Bell central offices	47.3	75.3		
Regional Bells	35.3	57.0		
12 major independents	75.0	87.0		
28 small independents	72.1	90.2		
United Kingdom	38.0	92.0	2.2	
Japan	31.0	76.0	0.7	1.7
Italy	16.1	b	0.7	
Germany	2.6	38.0	0.6	

Sources: U.S. Department of Commerce (1991); *Japan Economic Almanac* (1984 and 1985); Cellular Telecommunications Association (*New York Times*, March 3, 1993).

[a] Country forecasts.
[b] Data not available.

The diffused leadership in telecommunications product development in the 1980s is reflected in the differences between national telephone systems and cellular radiotelephone systems at the end of the decade, as shown in Table 7.6. Differences in the digitization of central office telephone switches at the end of the 1980s reflect differences between the times when telephone companies started to buy digital switches. The lead of both France and Canada over the United States is evident. The relatively low levels of digitization in the United States in 1989 and the forecast for 1994 both reflect the large volume of analog switches that AT&T and the regional Bell companies were still amortizing. However, the newer independent companies in the United States were fully as digitized as companies in France and Canada.

The greater penetration of cellular phones in the United States and the United Kingdom relative to other countries reflects the

United States' leadership role since the high usage of cellular phones in the United Kingdom was partly due to Motorola's strong presence there. The more than doubling of the still low penetration of cellular phones in the United States and Japan between 1990 and 1992 highlights the strong growth potential.

As noted earlier (Table 7.2), bilateral direct investment in the manufacture of communications equipment, broadly defined, was confined to Japanese investment in the United States. However, investments were not quite as lopsided as this suggests, since U.S. companies, capitalizing on their dual role in equipment manufacture and communications services, invested in Japanese communication service companies (mainly cellular radiotelephone systems) as a means of marketing equipment.

Japanese Companies in the United States: Suppliers and Learners

Japanese investment was attracted to the United States by the more rapid development of new communications systems and related technology there than in Japan, and by the openness of communications equipment markets. Japan's strategy seemed to have been to study developing markets closely, to apply its manufacturing skills to producing widely licensed equipment, and to apply available technologies to the development of new equipment crucial to the development of new communications systems.

Aside from expanding Japan's already substantial position in consumer audio and video equipment and its modest position in office PBX systems, Japanese investment in the 1980s[69] was focused on cellular mobile phones. Cellular radio telephone systems were developing much faster in the United States than in Japan. U.S. companies, the technology leaders, dominated the market for network infrastructure, but there was room for foreign (largely Asian) suppliers of subscriber equipment—the cellular telephone itself. In fact, Motorola was the only significant U.S. manufacturer.[70] The largest Japanese manufacturing operation in the United States was that of Oki, which had technology agreements with AT&T. As digitization of cellular systems approached in 1989, AT&T transferred its technology for digital cellular phones to Oki, and in 1991 the two companies announced that they would jointly develop and produce cellular telephones.[71] Other Japanese companies manufactured on a smaller scale, often in plants that assembled a variety of products.

In telephone switching equipment, Japanese companies expanded their investment in PBX systems, a maturing market in the United States in which Japanese and other foreign competitors were displacing U.S. producers.[72] But Japanese companies were unable to penetrate the market for digital central office switching. NEC, a major producer of digital central office switching equipment, stumbled badly in the early 1980s when it attempted to follow Northern Telecom's lead by manufacturing and selling in the United States. Its failure to deliver roughly half of the equipment ordered led to its being banned from the market for two years.[73]

With the appearance of a new switching technology, asynchronous transfer mode, in the early 1990s, strong U.S. interest in multimedia ventures made it likely that the U.S. market would develop earliest. Possibly remembering NEC's earlier fiasco in central office switching, both NEC and Fujitsu, Japan's two largest makers of central office switches, worked hard at product development in an all-out effort to make their mark in the U.S. market. Fujitsu received its first commercial order from a U.S. company, Bell South, in April 1993, and an NEC switch was scheduled to be delivered to Wiltel in 1993. But U.S. competitors were hot on their heels. AT&T, gearing up for an expected surge in demand in 1985, received an order from Warner Brothers to help it supply movies on demand to TV viewers, and Sprint installed an ATM switch produced by TRW.[74] Facing stiff U.S. competition, Fujitsu announced that it would start building ATM switches at one of its U.S. plants in 1995.[75] Competition between these formidable U.S. and Japanese adversaries is likely to improve the product.

In the 1990s, Japanese plans for future manufacturing in the

United States probably also included products related to the U.S. development of digital HDTV. While an analog form of HDTV was launched commercially in Japan in 1992,[76] the FCC's announcement late in the 1980s that it would be selecting a U.S. standard for HDTV in 1993 had already set off a race to develop a digital form. The deadline for submissions was the end of 1990. Early in 1990, General Instruments, a major maker of TV converters and satellite communications equipment, achieved a breakthrough. This galvanized others and ultimately, digital proposals were submitted by three groups: General Instruments and MIT; Zenith and AT&T; and NBC, David Sarnoff Labs, Philips, and Thomson. NHK, the Japanese broadcasting system, submitted its analog HDTV.[77] In 1993 the FCC found all the digital entries to have strong and weak points, and persuaded them to submit a joint proposal.[78] They did so in 1994.[79]

Early in the contest, Japanese companies moved to defend their turf as major suppliers of household TV sets and VCRs. In 1992 Toshiba formed a "consortium" with General Instruments and MIT. The agreement provided that Toshiba would be licensed to manufacture TV sets that incorporated a decoder produced by General Instruments.[80] Other Japanese companies and one Korean company approached the other competing groups with proposals for producing VCRs.[81]

When finally approved, it is likely that the new digital HDTV technology will be widely licensed. It may well supplant the analog system in Japan. And it seems very likely that Japanese companies will be major suppliers of digital HDTV receivers and VCRs.

U.S. Investment in Japanese Telecom Services and Technology Transfers

U.S.-based communications equipment had no manufacturing operations in Japan in 1990. However, three U.S. producers of communications equipment that were also active in communications services invested in the latter industry. These companies—Hughes Aircraft, AT&T, and Motorola—used their position in

Japanese communications services to sell their communications equipment products in two rapidly growing sectors of the industry: satellite communications and cellular phone systems. This process involved some transfers of technology to Japan.

The U.S. telecommunications equipment industry returned to full international competitiveness just a few years before the breakup of longstanding monopolies in Japan's telecommunications services created new opportunities for foreign entry into the Japanese telecommunications services and equipment industries. Until 1985, the government-owned NTT was the sole provider of telecommunications services within Japan and purchased its telecommunications equipment almost entirely from a small group of Japanese companies. Kokusai Denshin Denwa (KDD) was the sole provider of international communications services and followed similar equipment procurement policies. In 1985, NTT was "privatized" by sales of NTT shares to the public, although the government retained a majority position in the company. In addition, the new Japanese Telecommunications Business Law permitted privately owned companies to provide telecommunication services as Type I carriers that own and control their own transmission lines or as Type II carriers that lease lines from Type I carriers and provide value-added or other services. Foreign ownership was limited to one-third for Type I carriers but was unlimited for Type II carriers. Entry to and operations in these industries were regulated by the Ministry of Posts and Telecommunications (MPT). MPT also establishes standards and testing procedures for telecommunications equipment.[82]

By 1987, three new domestic telephone companies were in operation and were organizing cellular radio telephone subsidiaries; two new international telephone companies had been established; two new companies offering satellite communications services were about to open; and numerous companies providing paging and value-added services had been established.[83] There were further entries in succeeding years. Ultimately, U.S. producers of telecommunications equipment acquired an equity position in the new Japanese companies in most of these groups and managed to sell communications equipment to them.

The first U.S. investments were in the satellite communications industry. In 1983, the Japanese government had launched a program to develop its own satellite and associated launch service. To protect its own developing industry, it had prohibited imports of satellites when they interfered with that program. But in 1985, the U.S. government persuaded the Japanese government to permit the new privately owned satellite communications companies to purchase foreign satellites,[84] and Hughes Communications joined the Itoh and Mitsui trading companies to establish Japan Communications Satellite Company. Hughes Communications agreed to provide the entire satellite system and related technical and marketing advice.[85] (At the end of 1985 GM acquired Hughes Aircraft and all of its subsidiaries, including Hughes Communications, and established the GM-Hughes Electronics Corporation.)[86] Hughes also supplied satellites for Satellite Japan Corporation, one of the other two satellite communications in Japan, while another U.S. company, Space Systems/Loral (a subsidiary of Loral), provided the satellites for Space Communications Corporation.[87]

Hughes' investment in Japan no doubt transferred communication services technology to the Japanese communications services industry. But it is not clear that this investment was of much help to Japanese producers of communications equipment working to develop their own industry.

In the late 1980s, AT&T joined Kokusai Denshin Denwa, British Telecom, and France Telecom to install Transpacific Cable 3, linking the United States and Japan.[88] In 1990 AT&T established a wholly owned international value-added network (IVAN) affiliate in Japan to provide international transmission of fax messages. It became the leader among Japanese IVANs, which collect fax messages and transmit them internationally over dedicated telephone lines at rates some 50 percent cheaper than individual transmissions.[89] These investments may have helped AT&T develop closer relationships with NTT and the new communications companies. AT&T joined forces with NTT to develop a base station for NTT's digital cellular communications system, which commenced operations in 1993. It also collaborated with Nippon Idou Tsushin (IDO) in the development of its cellular phone system.[90] In 1991 AT&T and NEC submitted a joint bid for mutually compatible base station switching equipment for IDO; each won a contract to supply part of it.[91]

Motorola was slower than AT&T to invest in Japanese communications services. In the late 1980s, it concentrated on aggressive sales of its cellular phone to Japan's new cellular phone companies. It found a ready market for its analog cellular phone systems equipment with the first two Japanese firms to challenge NTT's analog cellular phone system. One, Daini Denden (DDI), a new long-distance phone company developing regional cellular phone systems, relied entirely on Motorola's equipment. The other, IDO, decided to develop one Motorola system and one using Japanese suppliers' equipment designed for the NTT system and not compatible with Motorola equipment. Since MPT allocated the one remaining frequency band in the Tokyo area to IDO, the U.S. government negotiated an agreement with the Japanese government in 1989 that was designed to assure that IDO would devote sufficient resources to Motorola stations to give Motorola access to the Tokyo market.[92] By 1994, when that did not seem to be happening, a new agreement was negotiated, which included a commitment by IDO to buy a specified number of Motorola base stations.[93]

By 1991, as the digital era dawned, Motorola had broadened its strategy by pushing for acceptance of some of its digital cellular phone technology as standard for the Japanese industry and by acquiring equity positions in cellular phone companies. By then, MPT was urging the industry to convert to digital systems, where more plentiful frequency bands would permit more competition, and for the establishment of national standards. Possibly helped by U.S. government support, the MPT accepted Motorola's digital voice encoder in 1991 as the standard for Japan —with the proviso that Motorola's technology be freely available to Japanese producers.[94] Shortly thereafter, Motorola made its first investment in Japanese communications services, taking an 8 percent interest in a joint venture with DDI and Nissan (who together held 52 percent), while an additional 12 percent was distributed among five other U.S. and foreign communications companies. The joint venture established two new cellular phone companies—Tu-Ka Cellular Tokyo and Tu-Ka Cellular Tokai (including Nagoya)—operated by the Japanese partners.[95] Motorola promptly received substantial orders for equipment from both companies. At the same time, Motorola, like AT&T, helped NTT with the design of its new digital cellular phone system and cooperated with NEC in developing an interface between Motorola base stations and NEC switching systems.[96] Motorola's efforts helped to assure the compatibility of all of Japan's competing digital cellular phone systems and promoted further assimilation of technologies originating in the United States. NTT Docomo started digital cellular phone service in 1993. The two Motorola-affiliated companies, plus four others operated by Japan Telecom in the four most densely populated areas of Japan, were expected to start service sometime in 1994.[97]

Motorola also signed up a DDI-sponsored consortium of eighteen Japanese companies to acquire a 15 percent interest in its ambitious Iridium.[98] This is a project for worldwide satellite transmission of voice and data signals between cellular instruments slightly larger and heavier than the 1993 Motorola phone. Other investors include communications companies in Canada, Italy, Thailand, and Venezuela, and two U.S. companies supplying equipment to Iridium—Lockheed and Raytheon.[99]

Conclusions

In the 1980s and the early 1990s, technology developments—computer networking, the digitization of a broad range of communications equipment, and semiconductor innovations essential to both—blurred the distinction between computers and communications equipment. This and the breakup of AT&T's monopolies in communications services and equipment encouraged the development of multi-industry giants in the United States, making industry structure in the United States and Japan a bit more similar than in the earlier postwar years. In these rapidly changing industries, bilateral direct investments speeded the transfer of U.S. product technology to Japan and Japanese process technology to the United States.

In computers, direct investments were instrumental in transmitting revolutionary U.S. product innovations to Japan in three ways: (1) by IBM-Japan's sales of its operating system technologies in Japan in an effort to establish them as industry standards; (2) by major U.S. software companies' joint ventures in Japan; and (3) by Japanese companies' technology-seeking investments in U.S. companies producing advanced workstations. In semiconductors, U.S. companies continued to lead in product innovations, but Japanese companies developed great strength in manufacturing one important type of semiconductor, the memory chip. After a period of confrontation, U.S. and Japanese firms settled down to an exchange of technologies in a series of joint ventures. Japanese companies also derived important product technology from participation in new and innovative U.S. companies. In both industries, Japanese companies in mature industries—steel, machinery, and mining—sought entry to the faster-growing computer and semiconductor industries by investing in or acquiring U.S. companies or by forming joint ventures with them. Results were mixed.

In communications equipment, technology leadership was more broadly distributed among industrial countries than it was in computers or semiconductors. In the very early 1980s, European and Canadian companies exploited a lead in digital central office switching for telephone systems by investing in U.S. manufacturing. But in the 1980s and early 1990s, U.S. companies gradually reasserted leadership, in mobile cellular phone systems, communications satellites, multimedia communications systems and related equipment, and in digital high-definition television. Japanese companies kept abreast of most of these developments through their investments in the United States, using their manufacturing expertise to supply needed equipment, especially cellular phones. In the 1990s they also proved adept at using existing technology to develop new products crucial to the development of multimedia communications.

The U.S. makers of communications equipment that had developed leading positions in new technologies did not attempt to manufacture in Japan, possibly because of the closed nature of the market when a government monopoly in communications services, NTT, favored domestic suppliers. But after 1985, when markets were open to private communications companies and to foreign investment in those companies, U.S. makers of communications equipment invested in the new Japanese service companies as a way of selling their equipment in Japan. In the case of digital cellular phone technology being developed and applied in the early 1990s, this led to cooperation with domestic suppliers and technology transfers to, or exchanges with, those Japanese producers.

Notes

1. This and the following paragraph draw on Faulhaber (1987) for AT&T policies and on U.S. International Trade Commission (1991a), pp. 2.5–2.8, for a useful summary of technological and regulatory developments.

2. Clausing, Allen, Berg, Dertouzos, Ferguson, Haavind, Moses, and Penfield (1989), p. 9.

3. U.S. International Trade Commission (1991a), pp. 2–4; and Wilkins (1974), p. 28.

4. For a fuller discussion of Japan's "intangible" barriers to imports and deregulation in telecommunications, see Christelow (1986).

5. MacKnight (1990) offers a useful analysis.

6. For a brief survey of the U.S. and Japanese computer industries from the late 1960s through the mid-1980s, see Clausing et al. (1989), pp. 21–35.

7. "New Supercomputers Signal Industry's Direction," *New York Times*, October 29, 1991.

8. "New Crusaders in Software's Holy War," *New York Times*, October 3, 1993.

9. "Nihon Unisys Pursues Two-Prong Strategy as Multivendor, Manufacturer," *Nikkei Weekly*, September 26, 1991; and "Burroughs-Sperry Merger Unlikely to Affect Japanese Subsidiaries," *Japan Economic Journal*, June 7, 1986.

10. "Foreign Computer Makers Face Self-Inflicted Troubles in Japan," *Japan Economic Journal*, January 22, 1985.

11. "Japan Will Be AT&T's Asian Base," *Japan Economic Journal*, January 21, 1991.

12. "Apple Moves to Third Place in Japan's PC Market," *Nikkei Weekly*, April 5, 1993.

13. "Big Three Computer Makers Ready to Tackle Big Blue," *Japan Economic Journal*, August 18, 1990.

14. "IBM Forms Alliances against NEC in Japan," *New York Times*, March 12, 1991.

15. "Preaching Love Thy Competitor: When in Japan," *New York Times*, March 24, 1992.

16. "U.S. Computer Industry Rides Fourth Wave with Unix System," *Japan Economic Journal*, August 12, 1989.

17. "Computer Makers Remain Divided on Unix," *Japan Economic Journal*, June 9, 1990.

18. See n. 15.

19. "LAN Market Beckons to U.S. Makers," *Japan Economic Journal* March 23, 1991.

20. "IBM Is Kept Waiting after Issuing RSVP," *Japan Economic Journal*, December 23, 1991.

21. "IBM Aims to Create PC Standards, Challenge NEC," *Japan Economic Journal*, March 23, 1991.

22. "U.S. Computer Firms Gain Ground with Low Price Strategy," *Nikkei Weekly*, December 28, 1992; and "New Battleground: Compaq and Other PC Makers Are Bringing U.S. Price War to Japanese Market," *Wall Street Journal*, March 31, 1993.

23. "Firms Hold Shares of Shrinking Market," *Nikkei Weekly*, August 2, 1993.

24. "Microsoft Opens Windows in Japan, Bringing Fresh Air to Market's PC War," *Wall Street Journal*, May 18, 1993.

25. *Japan Economic Almanac* (1994), pp. 80–81.

26. Clausing et al. (1989), p. 28.

27. "Matsushita and IBM Will Tie in Personal Computers," *Japan Economic Journal*, June 27, 1983.

28. "IBM, Hitachi to Team Up in Printer Development," *Nikkei Weekly*, July 11, 1992.

29. "IBM Seeks Canon Assistance to Bolster Flagging PC Division," *Nikkei Weekly*, September 12, 1992.

30. "Toshiba, IBM Set Up LCD Joint Venture," *Japan Economic Journal*, November 18, 1989.

31. "Invented in the U.S., Spurned in the U.S., a Technology Flourished in Japan," *New York Times*, December 16, 1990.

32. "Just in Time: The New Partnerships," *New York Times*, October 28, 1990.

33. Unless otherwise indicated, all of the statements regarding specific

Japanese companies investing in U.S. manufacturing, their date of establishment, affiliate employment, and products manufactured are drawn from MacKnight (1992a).

34. "Challenge for Honeywell-Bull," *New York Times*, May 19, 1987.

35. "Honeywell to Sell Bull Its Share in Venture," *New York Times*, April 17, 1991.

36. "France Lets NEC Buy 4.7% of Groupe Bull," *New York Times*, October 28, 1991.

37. "NEC Aims to Become Major U.S. Player, Too," *New York Times*, March 1, 1993.

38. "Matsushita Joins Rush to Market Workstations," *Wall Street Journal*, August 30, 1988.

39. "Matsushita Licensed to Produce Sun-Compatible Workstations," *Japan Economic Journal*, December 15, 1990.

40. "Fujitsu Buys Big Stake in U.S. Concern," *New York Times*, August 29, 1991; and "A Backer for a Renegade," *New York Times*, September 1, 1991.

41. "Behind NEXT's Sea Change, a Lesson about Market Niches," *New York Times*, February 21, 1992.

42. "Canon to Move into Workstations," *Nikkei Weekly*, May 17, 1993.

43. "U.S. Parts, Japanese Computer," *New York Times*, September 7, 1988.

44. "Stardent Computer to Close, Becoming One of Largest Venture-Capital Failures," *Wall Street Journal*, November 5, 1991.

45. "Oki to Make and Market Workstations in U.S.," *Nikkei Weekly*, June 22, 1991.

46. This and the following paragraph draw on Stevens (1992).

47. Ibid., p. 139.

48. For an interesting description of the U.S.-Japan semiconductor agreement and related negotiations and controversies, see MacKnight (1990).

49. "U.S.-Japan Accord in Semiconductors," *New York Times*, June 5, 1992.

50. "Computer Makers Halt a Challenge to Japanese Chips," *New York Times*, January 13, 1990.

51. MacKnight (1990) lists the manufacturing and sales affiliates of U.S. semiconductor companies established in Japan through 1990 and those then known to be planned for 1991 and 1992.

52. Mason (1992), pp. 220–31.

53. "Toshiba, National Semiconductor Are Flash Chip Team," *Wall Street Journal*, December 15, 1992.

54. "Intel's Delivery of New Flash Chips Delayed," *Wall Street Journal*, December 18, 1992.

55. "Flash Memory Pact May Ignite Industry," *Nikkei Weekly*, February 15, 1992.

56. "Toshiba Creates 16-Bit Flash Chips," *Nikkei Weekly*, October 26, 1992.

57. "National Semi, Toshiba Sign Deal," *Nikkei Weekly*, December 21, 1992.

58. "U.S. Maker of Chips in Alliance," *New York Times*, July 14, 1992.

59. "Chip Plant in Japan," *New York Times*, April 16, 1993.

60. "U.S. Chip Makers Awake to Call of Japanese Quality Control Guru," *Nikkei Weekly*, June 27, 1992.

61. See n. 33.

62. "Matsushita Set to Acquire Advanced Chip Plant in the United States," *New York Times*, November 22. 1990.

63. "FMS Planned for U.S. Plant," *Japan Economic Journal*, October 14, 1989.

64. "Sony to Share Data at U.S. Plant," *New York Times*, February 21, 1990; and "Advance Micro to Swap Factory for Sony Expertise," *Wall Street Journal*, February 21, 1990.

65. "Cypress Sells Chip Unit for $23 Million," *New York Times*, May 13, 1993.

66. *JEI Report*, No. 4B (January 28, 1994), p. 10.

67. These three groups are equivalent to the U.S. SIC groups 3661, 3662, and 3665 reported by the Bureau of the Census. The Bureau of Economic Analysis, Department of Commerce, in its reports on direct investment, lumps the three groups together in direct investment industrial classification (DIIC) 365.

68. Scherer (1992), pp. 86–91, describes the events summarized in this and the following paragraph.

69. See n. 33.

70. U.S. Department of Commerce (1990), p. 52.

71. "AT&T, Oki to Wed Mobile Phone Effort," *Japan Economic Journal*, July 20, 1991.

72. U.S. Department of Commerce (1990), p. 55.

73. U.S. Department of Commerce (1986b), p. 37.

74. "ATM Switches Catch First Wave Amid Carrier Bids," *Electronic News*, April 26, 1993; and "IBM Expected to Enter Market for ATM Gear," *Wall Street Journal*, July 13, 1993.

75. "Fujitsu Out Front among ATM Switch Providers," *Nikkei Weekly*, August 9, 1993.

76. "Producers Finally Say Roll 'Em for HDTV Programs," *Nikkei Weekly*, May 16, 1992.

77. "A Milestone in High-Definition TV," *New York Times*, December 3, 1991.

78. "Advanced TV Systems Are Called Flawed," *New York Times*, February 12, 1993.

79. "HDTV Panel Picks Zenith Signal System," *Wall Street Journal*, February 17, 1994.

80. "Toshiba Joins U.S. Consortium to Develop HDTV," *Nikkei Weekly*, May 23, 1992.

81. "VCRs Are Facing Two Revolutions," *New York Times*, March 7, 1993.

82. U.S. Department of Commerce (1990), pp. 135–39.

83. *Japan Economic Almanac*, 1988, pp. 112–13.

84. U.S. Department of Commerce (1990), pp. 137–38.

85. Dow Jones Wire Services, July 17, 1985.

86. *Moody's Industrial Manual* (1993), p. 1195.

87. "Telecom Satellites Soaring above Demand," *Nikkei Weekly*, June 20, 1992.

88. "AT&T Looks for Growth in Operations Abroad," *Japan Economic Journal*, September 30, 1989.

89. "Fax Services Provide Firms Telecoms Toeholds," *Japan Economic Journal*, May 18, 1991. Also *Japan Economic Almanac* (1988), p. 113.

90. "Growth of Cellular Phones Stirs Network Competition," *Nikkei Weekly*, April 25, 1992.

91. "AT&T, NEC Make Joint Bid in Japan on Cellular System," *Wall Street Journal*, July 3, 1991.

92. *JEI Report*, No. 8B (February 28, 1994), p. 11.

93. "Accord Will Allow U.S. Cellular Phones in Japan," *New York Times*, March 13, 1994.

94. "Motorola Digital Phone Format to Be Standard in Japan," *Japan Economic Journal*, April 13, p. 37.

95. "Foreign Firms Invest in Mobile Phone Services Venture," *Nikkei Weekly*, June 9, 1991; and *Japan Economic Almanac* (1993), p. 91.

96. "Digital Phone Market Beckons," *Nikkei Weekly*, October 19, 1992

97. *Japan Economic Almanac* (1994), p. 84.

98. Ibid.; and "Motorola Completes First Round of Funding for Satellite Phone Project," *Wall Street Journal*, August 2, 1993.

99. "Motorola Completes the First Round of Funding for Satellite Phone Project," *Wall Street Journal*, August 2, 1993; and "Motorola Identifies the Initial Members of Phone Consortium," *Wall Street Journal*, August 3, 1993.

8

More High-R&D Industries: Pharmaceuticals, Instruments, and Semiconductor Manufacturing Equipment

Bilateral direct investments also proved an important vehicle for two-way technology transfers in pharmaceuticals, the heterogeneous instrument industry, and semiconductor manufacturing equipment (SME). The latter is a small but important industry, whose segments are divided between the instrument and machinery industries in the standard industrial classification. In the 1980s, U.S. companies expanded their presence in those industries in Japan far more than Japanese companies expanded in the United States, as was shown in Table 2.4. The stronger U.S. advance at a time when financial incentives favored Japanese investment in the United States was largely due to strong U.S. technology. However, both governments' policies also contributed. Changes in Japanese patent law late in the 1970s encouraged investment by U.S. pharmaceutical companies in the 1980s. And in the United States, the Exon-Florio Amendment frustrated several Japanese attempts to acquire U.S. companies or parts of companies having especially strong technology and no doubt inhibited other Japanese companies from even trying.

However, related bilateral technology flows were probably more evenly balanced than the presence of U.S. and Japanese companies in each other's industries might suggest. U.S. companies continued to bring product technology to Japan. But in addition, U.S. companies long established in Japan and those newly investing there absorbed important Japanese process technology from joint ventures and from competition in Japanese markets. The experience of U.S. producers of SME demonstrated most vividly the critical importance of process technology to world competitiveness.

Technology Leads and Direct Investments

A look back at Table 2.4, which shows the relative importance of U.S. and Japanese companies in each other's industries in the early 1980s and in 1990, reveals that the pharmaceuticals and instruments industries stand out as the ones in which U.S. companies advanced most strongly in Japan, while the Japanese advance into the United States was modest. (The portion of the SME industry that was classified as industrial machinery was too small to affect the behavior of that large group of industries as a whole.) The stronger U.S. showing at a time when higher expected returns on investment in the United States and lower costs of capital in Japan favored stronger Japanese investment in the United States suggests a U.S. technology lead in those industries.

The relative strengths of Japan, the United States, and also the European countries strongest in these two industries is reflected in the position of the affiliates of Japanese and European countries in U.S. manufacturing. Table 8.1 compares employment in manufacturing establishments owned by Japanese companies with those owned by German, British, and Swiss companies. The latter group were technology leaders, highly competitive with U.S. companies, and the largest foreign investors in manufacturing pharmaceuticals and instruments in the United States. Since Japan's GDP in PPP U.S. dollars was roughly equal to that of the three European countries combined, it is useful to compare the position in the U.S. industries of Japan-based companies with the position of companies based in the three European countries. In pharmaceuticals, the position of the affiliates of Japanese companies was only one-tenth that of affiliates of companies based in the three European countries; in instruments it was one-eighth.

However, the instruments industry includes many diverse sectors. The three sectors in which Japanese investment was concentrated are also shown in Table 8.1. In one, photographic equipment, the position of Japanese companies' U.S. affiliates was stronger than that of the affiliates of the German, British, and Swiss companies combined. Available data do not permit similar comparisons for the small but strategically important SME industry.

The following three sections describe U.S.-Japanese bilateral investments and related technology transfers in the pharmaceuticals and instruments industries and the SME industry as a whole in the 1980s and early 1990s.

Pharmaceuticals

In pharmaceuticals, international differences in process technologies appear to have been small, while differences in product technology were large. In this industry, new products outmode old in rapid succession, and world markets are dominated by companies that offer new products protected by patent law in most industrial countries. The failure of Japanese companies to match U.S. and European companies in introducing new products was responsible for their continued competitive weakness.

Much of Japan's failure can be attributed to the unanticipated consequences of a series of Japanese government policies. Until the late 1970s, Japanese patent law, making new processes but not new products patentable, had encouraged Japanese companies to make "copycat" drugs and discouraged R&D to create new products. The revision of Japanese patent law in 1976, extending patent coverage to products, including the active ingredients in pharmaceutical compounds,[1] increased incentives to Japanese

Table 8.1

Employment in United States Manufacturing Establishments Owned by Companies Based in Japan, Germany, United Kingdom, and Switzerland: Pharmaceuticals and Instruments, 1990
(percentage of employment in all U.S. establishments)

SIC Code		Japan	Germany	United Kingdom	Switzerland	Three European Countries
283	Pharmaceuticals	2.3	7.7	9.8	6.9	24.4
38	Instruments	1.0	1.5	5.0	1.6	8.1
382	Measuring and controlling devices	1.6	1.9	7.7	2.9	12.5
384	Medical instruments and supplies	0.7	2.9	4.4	1.5	8.9
386	Photographic equipment and supplies	4.3	2.2[a]	0.5[a]	0.2	2.9
Memorandum						
	GDP at current prices and current PPPs (bil. U.S. $)	2,173.8	1,161.5	912.1	142.9	2,216.5
	(% of United States GDP)	39.8	21.3	16.7	2.6	40.6

Sources: U.S. Department of Commerce (1993c) Table 1.13; OECD, *National Accounts, Volume I: Main Aggregates, 1960–92,* p. 144.
[a] Midpoint of range given in U.S. Department of Commerce (1993b).

companies' R&D. But shortly thereafter, in 1980, a change in Japanese policy with respect to drug prices reduced them once again. As described earlier in chapter 3, doctors and hospitals had been given the franchise to dispense drugs when national medical insurance was adopted in 1961. By 1980 this powerful inducement to prescribe drugs had pushed expenditures for prescription and over-the-counter drugs to one-third of Japan's medical expenditures, as contrasted with 8 percent in the United States. To correct this unintended drain on the public purse, the authorities embarked on a series of reductions in price ceilings, beginning in 1980. By 1990, price reductions every other year had reduced drug prices by 70 percent, on average.

Successive price reductions eroded the ability of Japanese pharmaceutical companies to finance R&D. U.S. companies operating in Japan were also affected, but less seriously, since the cost of researching new drugs could be spread over a wider sales base, most of it in markets free of government price controls. The net result was to widen the gap between the R&D expenditures of U.S. and Japanese companies in the 1980s. In 1980, the U.S. pharmaceutical industry was spending 8.8 percent of its sales on R&D, nearly half again as large as the percentage spent by Japanese companies. By 1989, both groups had increased their expenditures, but the 14.6 percent of sales spent by U.S. companies was nearly twice the 7.5 percent spent by Japanese companies.

For U.S. pharmaceutical companies, the progressive liberalization of foreign direct investment and the new patent law provided new incentives to U.S. investment manufacturing in Japan. In 1979 Rorer acquired a majority share in Kyoritsu, adding Toho Laboratories in 1982. Merck acquired a 30 percent interest in Torii Yakuhin in 1981 and raised that equity position to 50 percent in 1983.[2] Merck also acquired 50 percent of Banyu, a company with which it had previously operated a joint venture.[3] These investments were estimated to give Merck a 4 to 5 percent share of the Japanese market.[4] Dow, long established in the Japanese chemicals industry, entered Japanese pharmaceuticals through its newly acquired U.S. pharmaceuticals affiliate, Merrell-Dow, forming joint manufacturing ventures with Otsuka and with Funai.[5] Smith Kline's did the same with Fujisawa.[6] During the decade, these and other U.S. and foreign drug companies expanded their operations in Japan, adding research laboratories and expanding their sales forces.[7]

The Japanese partners in these ventures received some of the profits generated by the sale of the new drugs. But they and other Japanese pharmaceutical companies recognized that to succeed in world markets, they would have to develop their own innovative skills. Faced with the steady lowering of price ceilings at home, some Japanese pharmaceutical companies sought a broader sales base by investment in the United States.[8] The three largest investments were acquisitions of existing companies. Very early, in 1976, Green Cross had bought Alpha Therapeutic Corporation, specializing in blood products. In 1985, Fujisawa acquired Lyphomed, maker of injectable drugs. In 1989, Otsuka acquired Pharmavite, maker of nutritional supplements. Fujisawa and Otsuka were already linked with U.S. companies in Japan and were supported by those companies in their U.S. ventures. But as already noted, Japanese investments were tiny relative to those made by European firms.

In 1992, apparently recognizing that across-the-board price reductions were discouraging Japanese drug companies' R&D, the Japanese government altered its policy. In that year, price ceilings on new drugs and others judged truly beneficial were left unchanged, while prices for older products and new variations on old products were severely cut.[9] This may well encourage Japanese innovation and thus narrow the technology gap between Japanese companies and their U.S. and European competitors.

Instruments

The instrument industries are a heterogeneous group with widely different technologies. Aside from semiconductor testing equipment, to be discussed later, bilateral investments have been concentrated in photographic equipment (copiers in particular), measuring and controlling devices, and medical instruments. In the first two groups, U.S. companies had made substantial investments in Japan in the 1960s and 1970s, bringing important new product technology with them, as described in previous chapters. In the 1980s, their Japanese affiliates maintained strong positions in their respective industries. Some of them generated a backflow of process technology to the U.S. parent companies. U.S. investment in medical instruments was new in the 1980s, and probably accounts for most of the doubling of the U.S. position in the instrument industries shown in Table 2.4. As already noted, Japanese companies invested in all of these industries in the United States. But given Japan's technology strength in photographic equipment, the position of Japanese companies' U.S. affiliates was strongest, relative to the U.S. industry and to other foreign-based competitors, in that sector.

Photographic Equipment: The United States' Absorption of Japanese Technology

In the photographic equipment industry, the lessons so successfully learned by Fuji-Xerox in its battles in Japan in the 1970s, noted in chapter 4, were put to good use by the Xerox parent company in the 1980s. Faced with serious market share losses from Japanese competitors from the mid-1970s onward, Xerox initiated a study of Fuji-Xerox in 1979 in an effort to understand the sources of that affiliate's strong competitive position in Japanese markets. Successive missions to Japan were impressed by the lower manufacturing costs, shorter product development schedules, and vastly superior quality in the sense of freedom from defects at Fuji-Xerox as compared with Xerox operations in the United States. By 1984, the parent company had adopted a total quality control approach, called CWQC (companywide quality control), that included reorganization of copier development and production, increased employee involvement, fewer suppliers and early supplier participation in the product design process, and greater emphasis on customer satisfaction.[10]

These efforts helped Xerox to hold and strengthen market share in the more sophisticated heavy end of the copier market and to improve integration of its operations with those of its affiliate in Japan. While drawing on Fuji-Xerox for lower-end products sold in the United States, Xerox concentrated on higher-end products, including new products exported to Japan. For example, in 1992 Xerox developed a high-speed copier with special features keyed to the needs of the Japanese market—lightweight oversized paper, and high contrast and high resolution useful for reproducing handwritten Japanese characters.[11]

Demonstrating Japanese strength in the lower end of the photocopier market, Canon and Ricoh expanded their earlier investments in photocopier manufacturing in the United States in the late 1980s, and Toshiba entered the field. Although employment in Japanese companies' U.S. affiliates producing all sorts of photographic equipment accounted for only 4 percent of employment in that more broadly defined U.S. industry, the proportion in copiers was undoubtedly higher.

Measurement and Control: Two-Way Technology Flows

In the measurement and control instruments industry, the largest U.S. companies manufacturing in Japan were Honeywell and Hewlett-Packard. In the early postwar years, both had established joint ventures; Honeywell with Yamatake and Hewlett-Packard with Yokogawa Electric. In the 1970s, Yamatake-Honeywell expanded into production of navigation instruments as well.[12] In the 1980s, both companies were leaders in their specialties: Yamatake-Honeywell in control systems,[13] and Yokogawa–Hewlett-Packard (YHP) in electronic measurement instruments.[14]

The ways in which these two U.S. companies used their Japanese affiliates in the 1980s was very different. Honeywell, preoccupied with problems of withdrawing from the computer industry, liquidated part of its investment in Yamatake-Honeywell, reducing its equity from 50 percent to 34 percent,[15] thus giving its affiliate more independence.

By contrast, Hewlett-Packard raised its equity share in YHP from 49 to 75 percent in 1983[16] and drew on its Japanese affiliate for process technology. In 1979, beset by problems of poor quality and high production costs in its U.S. operations, Hewlett-Packard embarked on a self-improvement program, sending engineers to YHP to gain insights into factors contributing to the affiliate's success in similar efforts in the 1970s. By 1988, Hewlett-Packard had substantially reduced its product defect rates. This allowed it to reduce the ratio of inventory to sales from 20.5 percent to 13.8 percent.[17] Since Hewlett-Packard operations in the United States include computer workstations and medical equipment, as well as electronic measurement instruments of the sorts produced by YHP in Japan, this infusion of process technology from Japan touched a number of U.S. industries.

During the 1980s, Japanese companies broke new ground by investing in those same industries in the United States. In at least one case these investments generated modest two-way technology flows. Yokogawa Electric, Hewlett-Packard's Japanese partner, decided to broaden its instruments expertise by forming a joint venture in the United States with Johnson Controls, a leading maker of air conditioning and other process controls. The joint venture opened one plant in 1980 (when Yokogawa also opened a plant of its own nearby in Georgia to manufacture flow meters) and a second in 1989. Johnson Controls, a diversified U.S. company, appears to have regarded joint ventures with Japanese companies as a way of learning their manufacturing technology, since it also formed two joint ventures with other Japanese companies to produce automobile seats. Yokogawa, after acquiring product technology and experience by working with Johnson Controls, purchased that company's Japanese subsidiary in 1989 and was expected to mount a strong challenge to Honeywell in Japan and in the United States.[18]

The most problematic Japanese investment in this group of instrument industries was that made by Nippon Mining in 1988, when it spent $1.1 billion to acquire the non–defense-related portions of Gould, a troubled U.S. diversifier with plants in the

United States, Canada, Mexico, Germany, and the United Kingdom.[19] Nippon Mining (which derived more revenue from petroleum refining than from mining) was originally attracted to Gould for its materials technologies and strong position in copper foil (used widely in electronic equipment), on which the two companies had already worked in a joint venture. But of the nine U.S. plants acquired, two produced electronic measuring equipment (analog recorders and oscilloscopes).[20] For Nippon Mining, its acquisitions in this and other unfamiliar industries proved to be mainly a source of problems and financial losses. In 1992, Nippon Mining merged with the Kyodo Oil Company to form Nikko Kyodo. Nikko Kyodo closed some of the Gould plants, including one of the two that produced instruments. The remaining one, and a plant in the United Kingdom, became a separate Nikko Kyodo subsidiary.[21] For the Japanese parents, their investments proved an expensive mode of entry into high-technology industries and should probably be judged an expensive diversion.

Medical: Competitive Development of Foreign Innovations

Bilateral investments in medical instruments were dominated by General Electric's major joint venture with Yokogawa Electric in Japan, initiated in 1982. But they also included a smaller Toshiba investment in the United States in 1989. Both investments reflect the competitive efforts of two powerful companies to develop path-breaking technology in diagnostic imaging equipment—computer-assisted tomography (CT, or CAT) and magnetic resonance imaging (MRI). Their competition differs from other U.S.-Japan competitive battles because neither group originated the technology. But the ability of both U.S. and Japanese companies to develop the product and their superior manufacturing skills drove the originator from the market.

The two related technologies were originally conceived and produced in the early 1970s by EMI, a British electronics and music-recording firm.[22] EMI recognized the potential of its initial breakthrough with the CAT scanner and that its specific product could be "invented around" by others, since much of the basic technology was in the public domain. Thus, it sought help in marketing from several companies active in medical instruments, including GE in 1971 and Toshiba in 1974. GE declined the 1971 offer, judging the device to be unpromising. But in 1974 it reversed its original judgment and embarked on a crash development program of its own, achieving technical leadership in 1978. Toshiba accepted EMI's original offer to assemble and market EMI scanners in Japan. But by 1979, it had developed its own machine and was followed by other Japanese companies, principally Hitachi.

EMI soldiered on independently in Europe and the United States, establishing a manufacturing plant near Chicago. But it encountered serious manufacturing difficulties, was buffeted by strong competition, and withdrew from the industry in 1979. GE acquired EMI's operations outside the United States in 1979, but antitrust constraints prevented GE from buying its U.S. business. Ultimately, a British company bought EMI, but Toshiba hired much of its technical staff.

In 1982, when GE entered Japan, it was the acknowledged world leader in CT and MRI technologies. But Toshiba—and to a lesser extent, Hitachi—proved well-prepared and strong competitors. This probably sharpened the skills of all concerned. By the end of the decade and the end of the boom years for this equipment, GE-Yokogawa seemed to have gained the largest single share of the Japanese market.[23]

As the market matured for CT and MRI scanners, a promising new type of medical diagnostic equipment, ultrasound systems, began to emerge. At the end of the decade in Japan, Toshiba and Aroca (a smaller Japanese specialist) led this market in Japan but were being challenged by Yokogawa–Hewlett-Packard, which was selling products produced by Hewlett-Packard in the United States.[24] In 1989 Toshiba moved to the attack in the United States, purchasing Diasonics, a specialist firm that had produced ultrasound systems since early in the decade but had run into manufacturing difficulties.[25]

Semiconductor Manufacturing Equipment

Semiconductor manufacturing equipment (SME) is a relatively small but important industry, with world sales of less than $9 billion at the end of the 1980s.[26] The industry is of special interest for its role in determining the capabilities of semiconductors and as a case study in international technology dissemination. U.S. companies created the industry and its technology in the 1960s and 1970s, and in 1980 they remained world leaders in product technology in most sectors. Most of the leading U.S. companies that started manufacturing in Japan when their lead was strong, often forming joint ventures, were far more successful in holding their lead than those that relied on exporting until their lead had vanished. The reason for the difference appears to have been that the early investors gained a better understanding of the needs of the Japanese market and absorbed Japanese process technology.

The Industry and Its Technology

SME's various segments serve stages of the semiconductor manufacturing process from silicon wafer manufacturing through repeated steps in wafer processing, assembly, and testing and measuring (see Table 8.2).

Wafer processing equipment, accounting for over half of industry sales at the end of the 1980s, includes several distinct types.[27] The largest is photolithographic equipment, which in turn includes photoresist processing equipment, which deposits a photosensitive layer (resist) on the wafer; equipment to make the masks on which each layer of circuitry is traced; and wafer exposure equipment, which shines light through the mask, tracing the circuit pattern onto the photosensitized wafer. Diffusion and oxidation equipment and ion implantation equipment offer alternative methods of applying dopants, insulators, and metals to create and insulate the circuitry. Etching and cleaning equipment removes unwanted bits of these layers. Deposition equipment applies a protective coating to each layer.

A second major type of SME, assembly equipment, includes machines to dice wafers into single semiconductor devices, bonding equipment to attach devices to lead frames, molding and sealing equipment to protect the devices from the environment, and finishing and marking equipment.

A third major type of SME, test equipment, accounts for about 35 percent of SME sales. The equipment is used throughout the many repetitions of wafer processing and to test packaged devices. It includes instruments such as optical bright-field microscopes and low-voltage scanning electron microscopes to test the accuracy of the circuitry being applied to the wafer, laser repair equipment, wafer probing equipment, and process monitoring equipment.

Perhaps because SME is a relatively new and small industry, there are no regularly published official trade or output statistics describing the behavior of the industry as a whole. Both wafer processing and assembly equipment fall into SIC classification 3559, along with other machinery, and labeled specialized industrial machinery and equipment not elsewhere classified. OECD classifies the SIC 35 group as a whole as a medium-R&D industry. But wafer processing equipment, considered by itself, would probably be classified as high-R&D. Test equipment is classified, along with other non-SME items, as instruments to measure electricity (SIC 3825), and thus is classified as high-R&D by OECD.

Like the semiconductor industry that it serves, SME and basic SME technology originated in the United States. In its early days, the companies making semiconductors devised their own SME, adapting standard machinery or creating entirely new machinery to perform required tasks. In fact, until the mid-1970s, major product innovations in SME came from the semiconductor producers. These included chemical vapor deposition, ion implantation, and direct bonding in the late 1960s, and polysilicon deposition, plasma etching, and the use of electron beams in mask making in the 1970s.[28] Manufacturing of the new equipment was generally taken over by large firms making other industrial machinery, such as Thermco, Varian, Eaton, and Perkin Elmer in

Table 8.2

World Sales of Semiconductor Manufacturing Equipment, 1989

	World Sales ($ millions)	Share of Total (%)
Silicon wafer manufacturing	54	0.6
Wafer processing	4,516	53.4
Photolithographic	1,647	19.5
Photoresist processing	382	4.5
Wafer exposure	1,207	14.3
Mask-making	59	0.7
Diffusion and oxidation	343	4.1
Ion implantation	471	5.6
Deposition	1,135	13.4
Etching and cleaning	920	10.9
Assembly[a]	911	10.8
Test and measuring	2,975	35.2
Test	1,235	14.6
Automated test	1,190	14.1
Wafer measuring and inspection	438	5.2
Burn-in	65	0.8
Other[b]	1,237	14.6
Total	8,456	100.0

Source: U.S. International Trade Commission (1991b).

[a] Includes equipment for dicing, die bonding, wire bonding, molding and sealing, and finishing and marking.

[b] Includes equipment for mask and reticule inspection, laser repair, wafer probing, materials handling, process monitoring, and materials monitoring.

wafer processing equipment, and Teradyne in test equipment. The growing industry also prompted the creation of new firms specializing in SME, such as Applied Materials and Materials Research (in deposition, etching, and cleaning), and a host of small firms (there were 850 SME producers in 1989).[29]

In the mid-1970s, some SME producers began to generate their own innovations. Of these, the most important were in photolithography (also known as microlithography), which permitted semiconductor makers to put more and more circuits on a single semiconductor, thereby increasing its memory or microprocessor capabilities. In 1973, Perkin Elmer introduced a scanning projection aligner, a new method of wafer exposure that used ultraviolet light. The scanning projection aligner was designed for use with a mask containing all of the duplicative patterns of a single semiconductor device, or chip, to be printed on a single wafer. The scanner moved the mask and the wafer in exact synchronism through the path of light. This was the most used equipment in the rest of the 1970s. In 1976, the Geophysical Corporation of America (GCA) developed the stepping aligner, which increased the fineness of the circuitry that could be traced on a single chip by using a demagnifying lens. However, the mask used with the stepping aligner could not accommodate all of the duplicative patterns of that chip to be printed on a single wafer. Thus the mask was held fixed in an optical path and the wafer was stepped across that path to create the desired number of chip images on the wafer. Although the stepper was much slower than the scanner, its finer circuitry capabilities made it the equipment of choice during most of the 1980s.[30]

Perkin Elmer responded by concentrating on new technology, spending close to $100 million, to top the stepper with a step-and-scanner, which it called the Micrascan.[31] Looking ahead to the time when future semiconductors would outrun the capabilities of optical lithography, Perkin Elmer and a few smaller companies worked to develop a technology that used the electron beam (E-beam)—already in use to trace circuit patterns on masks —to "print" computer-programmed circuit designs directly on the wafer. This not only eliminated the mask-making step in wafer processing but also permitted finer circuitry. IBM devoted considerable attention to even more advanced X-ray lithography.[32]

As the Japanese semiconductor industry began to develop in the late 1960s and 1970s, it initially depended very heavily on the manufacturing equipment of U.S. companies. In the late 1970s, a substantial portion of the Japanese government's efforts to foster the growth of the Japanese semiconductor industry was devoted to encouraging and subsidizing the development of a Japanese SME industry, as noted in chapter 4. As in the United

States, some of the companies in the new industry specialized in SME; for example, Tokyo Electron (TEL), currently one of the world's largest SME companies, which produces both processing and test equipment; and Advantest, a leader in test equipment. Nikon and Canon came to photolithography equipment with a strong background in related industries, such as cameras and photocopiers, in which they continued to operate. Though dominated by these and a few other large firms, the Japanese industry also included numerous small firms, for a total of about 100 at the end of the 1980s.

Early innovations in automated assembly equipment came from Japan, where government insistence on assembly in Japan created a demand for labor-saving devices. U.S. semiconductor producers tended to assemble in low-wage countries. However, the savings in labor and other costs made possible by Shinkawa's automated wire bonder and Disco's dicing saws encouraged U.S. semiconductor makers to assemble at home and made Japanese equipment producers the world market leaders in the 1970s. By the 1980s, U.S. assembly equipment producers had responded, introducing improvements such as digitally controlled wire bonding, thus stemming further market share losses.[33]

But in the late 1970s and through the 1980s, most of Japan's R&D efforts were devoted to absorbing the United States' SME product technology, adapting this technology to the needs of Japanese semiconductor producers, whose product lines differed from those of U.S. companies, and making substantial improvements in process technology. The latter was especially notable for the development of clean rooms, which greatly reduced quality defects in semiconductors.

Direct Investment and Two-Way Technology Flows

In the 1980s, the Japanese semiconductor industry expanded explosively, as described in chapter 7, and with it the Japanese SME industry. The Japanese market for semiconductor manufacturing equipment rose from 23 percent of the world total in 1979

Table 8.3

Shares of U.S. and Japanese Companies in Major Semiconductor Manufacturing Equipment Markets, 1979, 1985, and 1990[a] (%)

	1979	1985	1990[b]
In world markets			
U.S.-based	76	61	45
Japan-based	16	30	44
U.S.-Japan joint ventures[c]		5	3
Other	8	4	9
In U.S. market			
U.S.-based		80	75
Japan-based		17	22
Other		3	3
In Japanese market			
U.S.-based		36	17
Japan-based		48	76
U.S.-Japan joint ventures[c]		14	6
Other		2	1
In other markets			
U.S.-based		59	47
Japan-based		29	22
Other		12	31
Memorandum:			
Relative importance of U.S., Japanese, and other markets			
United States	67	48	37
Japan	23	33	40
Other	10	18	23

Sources: U.S. International Trade Commission (1991b), p. 4-2, based on data from VLSI Research; U.S. Department of Commerce (1985c), p. 35.

[a] Based on sales in current dollars and current exchange rates.

[b] Joint ventures in Japan.

[c] Estimated by USITC.

to 40 percent in 1990 (see Table 8.3). The table also shows that most of Japan's gains and the United States' losses in world markets for SME during the 1980s were due to the increased importance of U.S. losses in the Japanese market, which were roughly similar to Japanese gains in the U.S. market.

However, as Table 8.4 makes clear, U.S. and Japanese gains and losses were by no means evenly distributed among the various sectors of SME. In most types of wafer processing—diffusion

Table 8.4

World Market Shares of U.S.- and Japan-Based Companies in Semiconductor Manufacturing Equipment, 1979, 1982, and 1989 (%)

	1979[a]		1982		1989	
	U.S.-based	Japan-based	U.S.-based	Japan-based	U.S.-based	Japan-based
Silicon wafer manufacturing					42	6
Wafer processing	76	15	60[b]	28[b]	43	47
Photolithographic					26	63
Photoresist processing					33	57
Wafer exposure			58	35	18	71
Mask-making					96	4
Diffusion and oxidation			50	37	41	55
Ion implantation			72	28	62	37
Deposition			55	19	48	31
Etching and cleaning			70	24	55	31
Assembly[c]	39	44	39	26	36	47
Test and measuring	90	7	78[a]	20[a]	d	d
Test						
Automated test			53	24	44	45
Wafer measuring and inspection					67	20
Burn-in					88	12
Other[e]					d	d

Sources: U.S. International Trade Commission (1991b), pp. 4-7 to 4-14; U.S. Department of Commerce (1985c), Table 16.

[a] From U.S. Department of Commerce (1985c). Coverage is not entirely consistent with USITC data for 1982 and 1989.

[b] Based on weighted average of subcategories for which information is given in the table.

[c] Includes equipment for: dicing, die bonding, wire bonding, molding and sealing, and finishing and marking.

[d] Data not available.

[e] Includes equipment for: mask and reticle inspection, laser repair, wafer probing, materials handling, process monitoring, and materials monitoring.

and oxidation, ion implantation, deposition, and etching and cleaning—in assembly equipment, and in automated test equipment, losses of U.S.-based companies in world markets were very moderate. But in photolithographic equipment, and in wafer exposure equipment in particular, U.S. losses were devastating.

One important reason for this striking difference in the United States' competitive performance was that in those SME sectors where the U.S. remained strong, leading U.S. companies had invested in manufacturing or extensive R&D in Japan early in the 1980s or before, at a time when their product technology was strong and sought-after by Japanese semiconductor makers. Major U.S. investments are listed in Table 8.5.

Most U.S. companies investing in Japan in the 1980s and before took the joint venture route and, in so doing, transferred much needed product technology to Japanese companies. Some early U.S. investors had unhappy experiences and withdrew. But the strong U.S. companies that persevered, operating independently or in joint ventures, generally prospered as they learned to meet the needs of Japanese semiconductor companies and absorbed Japanese process technologies. In fact, in all SME sectors except photolithography, the U.S. industry's losses of the world market share between 1982 and 1989 were modest.

Some of the U.S. companies that invested in Japan in the 1980s actually gained world market share in that decade—notably BTU in diffusion and oxidation equipment and Applied Meterials in deposition equipment and etching and cleaning equipment. Teradyne held its own in automated testing equipment, and Eaton came close to doing so in ion implantation equipment. It is true that a few large U.S. investors encountered difficulties. On the other hand, Thermco, which had operated a joint venture in Japan since 1968, became a victim of the U.S. merger and acquisitions wave of the 1980s, and its new U.S. owners dissolved its joint venture in Japan.[34] And Materials Research, which had formed a joint venture with a small Japanese electronics company, ran into difficulties; the entire U.S. company was acquired by Sony in 1988. (These and other Japanese investments in the United States are shown in Table 8.6.) But all in all, these U.S. industries came through the 1980s in strong form.

The generally favorable experience of many United States SME producers investing in Japan in the 1980s seems to have encouraged further investments in the 1990s. Kulicke and Soffa, a large U.S. firm which had introduced digitally controlled wire bonding, established a Japanese manufacturing plant in 1990, probably hoping to reverse its losses in world market share during the 1980s. Teradyne, the largest U.S. maker of test equipment, enlarged the scope of its Japanese operations, adding manufacturing to its existing R&D facilities in 1992. At about the same time KLA, a U.S. company that excelled in imaging technology, started manufacturing in Japan and also formed a joint venture with Nippon Mining (the indefatigable diversifier) to produce equipment for testing liquid crystal displays.[35]

By contrast, the two U.S. leaders in photolithography, GCA and Perkin Elmer, relied on exporting, using Japanese sales agents, until late in the day, when they were already overwhelmed by Japanese competition. The delay gave strong Japanese companies time to reverse engineer GCA's stepper, and the U.S. companies' absence from Japan may have led them to underestimate the importance of Japanese process technology. By 1990, the U.S. share of world markets for wafer exposure equipment had fallen to 18 percent.

Nikon and Canon, the major Japanese players, were already strong in optical systems and precision manufacturing when they entered the industry in the 1970s. They acquired the basic technology that they needed entirely through reverse engineering, first some very early Perkin Elmer technology, then the GCA stepper. In 1981, after five years of R&D and many trials and errors in its own labs and on the production lines of its customers, Nikon produced a stepper judged superior to GCA's. Canon followed a few years later.[36] By the mid-1980s, the superiority of the Japanese product came to be recognized by U.S. semiconductor producers as well as those in Japan. In 1986 the Japanese share in world markets for wafer exposure equipment moved ahead of the U.S. share for the first time; in the balance of the decade, it soared.

Relative to the timing of Japanese companies' successful challenge in microlithography, U.S. companies' investments in Japan were too little and too late. GCA never manufactured in

Table 8.5

Manufacturing Investments in Japan by Leading U.S. SME Producers and Their World Market Shares

Industry Sector and U.S. Company	Japanese Partner	Opened or Acquired	Liquidated	World Market Share[a]					
				U.S. Company		United States		Japan	
				1982	1989	1982	1989	1982	1989
Wafer processing									
Photolithography									
Perkin Elmer	Citizen Watch	1986	1990	32.6	b	58.3	17.6	34.5	70.7
Diffusion and oxidation									
Thermco	TEL	1968	1988	21.5		50.2	41.0	36.6	54.9
BTU[c]	Ulvac	1984		b	8.8				
Ion implantation									
Varian	TEL	1982		40.7	24.1	72.3	61.5	27.7	36.6
				12.9[d]	16.2[d]				
Eaton	Sumitomo Heavy Industry	1984		24.9	21.8				
					8.5[d]				
Deposition									
Materials Research	Small electronics company	1983		7.4	(6.3)[f]	54.5	48.0	19.2	31.4
Applied Materials[e]	None	1984		13.0	14.9				

Segment / Company	Acquisition	Year						
Etching and cleaning		1984	1986					
Applied Materials[e]	None	1984 8	12.7[b]	20.8	69.9	55.3	24.4	31.3
Lam Research	TEL	1986		9.8				44.3
Assembly								
Kulicke and Soffa	None	1990	13.7	9.1	38.9	33.7	26.3	44.3
Automated test								
Teradyne	None	1984[g,h]	16.8[b]	16.8[b]	52.6	43.9	23.9	44.5
KLA	None	1992						
KLA	Nippon Mining	1990						

Sources: U.S. Department of Commerce (1985c), p. 43; U.S. International Trade Commission (1991b), pp. 4-7–4-14; MacKnight (1991, p. 11); *Japan Economic Journal*, December 22, 1990; January 19, 1991; *Moody's Industrial Manual*, 1990, p. 4173 and 1991, p. 4156.

[a] USITC (1991b) apparently allocated joint ventures by location.
[b] USITC (1991b) reports only shares of top 5 companies in each world market.
[c] Acquired part of Thermco from Allegheny International, 1988.
[d] Joint venture share. Parent companies shares also included in U.S. and Japanese companies' shares in world markets.
[e] R&D, final assembly, and testing.
[f] Materials Research was acquired by Sony in 1988.
[g] No information.
[h] R&D since 1984; manufacturing in 1992.

Japan. In the late 1970s and early 1980s, their Japanese customers complained about the unreliability of GCA products and the company's failure to respond to requests for changes in equipment to meet their special needs.[37] Yet it was not until 1983 that GCA announced the formation of a joint venture with Sumitomo to "retrofit" faulty products in Japan, but it is not clear when the facility actually went into operation.[38] In 1988, GCA succumbed to Japanese competition, selling its stepper operation to General Signal (a producer of control instruments, telecom, and power transmission equipment as well as other sorts of SME).[39] General Signal was unable to salvage GCA, ultimately liquidating it in 1993.[40]

Waking late to the need for a presence in Japan, Perkin Elmer established a manufacturing joint venture with the Citizen Watch Company in 1986.[41] At that time however, Perkin Elmer did not have ready for marketing a product that was fully competitive with the Japanese stepper. And, since Citizen was not an experienced SME producer, both partners probably needed a breaking-in period. Only a few years later, in 1989, weak sales of its wafer exposure equipment and expected high costs of completing development work on its Micrascan led Perkin Elmer to put all of its SME operations up for sale.[42]

In 1990 the Micrascan operations were sold to Silicon Valley Group (SVG) and E-beam operations were sold to a new company, Etec, whose equity was shared by IBM (a long-time supporter of Perkin Elmer's research) and four other large companies with some interest in the technology. However, Perkin Elmer retained a small minority interest in each of these ventures.[43]

Japanese direct investments in the United States' SME industry, shown in Table 8.6, were modest and of two sorts. In the 1980s, investments designed to exploit technology strengths predominated. In the 1990s, investments or attempted investments were focused on obtaining access to innovative research under way in U.S. companies.

In the largest of the first kind of investments, Advantest, the largest Japanese test equipment company, established a manufac-

Table 8.6

Investments of Japanese Companies in U.S. Production of Semiconductor Manufacturing Equipment

Industry Sector	U.S. Company	Japanese Company	Japanese Share (%)	New or Acquired	Employees	Number of Plants	Year Plant Opened or Acquired
Wafer processing equipment							
Photolithography							
Electron-beam	Lepton Inc.	Canon	10	A	22	1	1990
Photoresist striping	Mattson Technology	Marubeni Hytech	20	A	[a]	1	1991
Diffusion and oxidation	AG Associates	Canon Sales	30	A	85	1	1989
Ion implantation	Varian-TEL	TEL[b, c]	50	N	12	1	1990
Deposition	Ulvac North America	Ulvac[b]	100	A	50	1	1980
	Materials Research[b, d]	Sony	100	A	300	1	1989
Test equipment	Siscan	Mitsubishi	25	A	60	1	1985
	Advantest America	Advantest[b]	100	N	235	1	1987
	LTX[b]	Sumitomo Metal[e]	15	A	940	2	1990
Assembly equipment	YKC Technologies	YKC	100	N	15	1	1986
Unspecified	Disco Hi-Tec America	Disco	100	N	40	1	1984
	Samco-March	Samco International	50	N	12	1	1986

Source: MacKnight (1991, 1992a); U.S. International Trade Commission (1991b).

[a] Data not available.

[b] Denotes company having one of 5 largest shares in world market for equipment group in 1989.

[c] Varian, the U.S. partner, is also one of the world's five largest producers.

[d] Materials Research also produces semiconductor materials in two other plants.

[e] Reduced share to 9.2% in July 1993.

turing plant in Illinois in 1987. This venture probably gave the company a better understanding of the special needs of U.S. makers of logic chips and no doubt contributed to Advantest's dramatic gain in world market share, from 12.1 percent in 1983 to 26.5 percent in 1989. It probably also prodded U.S. test equipment companies. (Only one of them, Teradyne, was then operating in Japan.) Other investments designed to expand in U.S. markets included: an early investment by Ulvac, a large producer of deposition equipment; investments by YKC and Disco, producers of assembly equipment already enjoying strong exports to the United States; and a more recent investment by TEL-Varian, the U.S.-Japan joint venture which had long manufactured ion implantation equipment in Japan. The small number of employees in all of the plants except Advantest suggests that those plants were confined to final assembly and distribution.

Japanese investments designed to acquire new technology included two by companies interested in expanding the scope of their operations to encompass a new industry. Sony, already a giant in electronics and related industries, added still another when it acquired Materials Research, a major producer of deposition equipment and also an important producer of semiconductor materials. Sumitomo Metals, another diversifier from a low-R&D industry, acquired a 15 percent interest in LTX, the second largest U.S. producer of test equipment in 1990, but later reduced it to less than 10 percent.

However, the prime focus of Japanese interest in U.S. technology was photolithography. Even as Nikon and Canon were driving their main U.S. competitors out of the industry, the Japanese companies were exhausting the possibilities of incremental improvements in stepper technology. Thus, there was a need for new product technology. Japanese companies had great respect for U.S. product technology and did their best to acquire it. In 1988, Nikon and Canon made a small joint investment in Cymer Laser Technologies. In 1990, Canon acquired a 10 percent interest in Lepton, a small U.S. company that produced E-beam equipment used in mask-making, with aspirations to sell equipment for direct writing onto wafers.[43] In 1989, when Perkin-Elmer put its microlithography operations up for sale, Nikon expressed an interest in buying this treasure trove of technology. But the resulting furor in U.S. government circles and among some U.S. semiconductor producers (and no doubt the Exon-Florio threat) led Nikon to withdraw.[44]

In the early 1990s, SVG Lithography (SVGL), ensconced in Perkin Elmer's old facilities in Connecticut, continued to develop Micrascan. They managed to sell a number of Micrascan II systems—to IBM, a committed supporter, and also to Toshiba and Sony. But the volume of sales was disappointing,[45] and development of an improved Micrascan system was going slowly. In 1973 SVGL's problems and Canon's financial strength and interest in Micrascan technology led the two companies to discuss the possibility of a technology agreement.[46] Canon sought the right to manufacture the Micrascan (including a new version then under development with MIT–Lincoln Laboratory) and to sell it in Japan and in the rest of Asia (except Korea). However, negotiations collapsed in 1994. In the meantime SVG revenues and profits had improved. Semitech pledged additional funding with a proviso limiting outright sales, but not swap of Micrascan technology. And the two companies were unable to agree on terms including such a swap.[47]

Sematech and the Warming Trend
in U.S.–Japan Relations

Sematech, the government-industry consortium established in 1987 to strengthen the U.S. semiconductor industry, contributed to some warming in U.S.–Japan relations in the SME industry. The fiascoes at GCA and Perkin Elmer focused the attention of Sematech on the SME (especially microlithography) part of the problem. Whereas only 20 percent of Sematech's first budget was allocated to SME producers, this allocation had risen to about half, or $100 million, by 1991.[48] Most of this went to Allied Signal's ultimately unsuccessful efforts and to SVGL.

Sematech not only financed R&D but also pressured U.S. semiconductor producers to test prototypes, putting them on their production lines.

Sematech's initial attitude toward possible membership of Japanese companies operating in the United States seems to have been exclusionary, apparently based on the view that U.S. technology should be protected from Japanese predators. But as U.S. semiconductor companies persisted in buying their steppers from Nikon and Canon—on the grounds that they needed the best equipment available to compete in world markets[49]—Sematech's views changed. Acknowledging that the best technology was not all in the United States, it became more cooperative and outreaching. One example was its informal agreement in 1992 to work with the Ultra Clean Society, a group of Japanese scientists headed by Tohoku University's Professor Ohmi (who had previously designed a semiconductor plant for Intel). The society's research focuses on contamination controls, semiconductor materials, and SME technologies.[50] A second example of Sematech's changed thinking was its support for SVG's contemplated technology agreement to Canon.[51] It seemed to welcome the financial (and process technology) support that Canon could bring to SVGL.

Whether this change in the policies at Sematech is enough to assure the viability and strength of this sector of the U.S. SME industry remains to be seen. Much will depend on the degree of cooperation forthcoming from both sides of the Pacific.

Conclusions

In the high-tech pharmaceuticals, instruments, and semiconductor manufacturing equipment industries, bilateral direct investments were accompanied by vigorous two-way technology flows. This contributed to and reflected the convergence of industrial country technologies.

In pharmaceuticals, new product technology counts for far more than process technology. Enactment of a new Japanese law making product innovations patentable, which was designed to spur Japanese innovation, roughly coincided with other measures liberalizing foreign investment in Japan and a series of reductions in price ceilings for drugs. The net result was to encourage strong U.S. investment in Japan and to constrain Japanese innovation. But by the early 1990s, adjustments in Japanese policy and Japanese investment in the United States were helping to ease those problems.

In the heterogeneous instrument industries, two veteran U.S. investors in Japan, Xerox and Hewlett-Packard, drew lessons in manufacturing technology from their seasoned Japanese affiliates. The largest new investment of the 1980s was GE's joint venture in Japan with Yokogawa Electric in electronic medical diagnostic equipment, such as CAT scanners and MRI equipment. Both GE and Toshiba had devoted great effort to developing the revolutionary innovations of the British company, EMI (which was ultimately driven from the industry by U.S. and Japanese competition). GE's outstanding success in Japan demonstrated that U.S. as well as Japanese companies can play the adapt-and-improve game. Competition between the two giants was probably useful to both, and seems to have encouraged Toshiba to make a small investment in the U.S. industry.

As for the crucially important but small and multifaceted SME industry, U.S. firms had been its creators. They were still the technology leaders, holding roughly three-fourths of world markets at the end of the 1970s. But during the 1980s, Japanese companies acquired U.S. technology through joint ventures and strenuous reverse engineering. Then, applying their own process technology skills, they emerged in the late 1980s as strong challengers in most industries and as clear market leaders in microlithography (about 20 percent of the SME industry). The difference in outcome seems to have been heavily influenced by the strategies of the original U.S. leaders. Many companies that invested early in Japan, while their leadership position was still strong, seem to have absorbed Japanese process technology and managed to maintain a strong position in world markets. But in the photolithography sector, the two U.S. leaders relied on exports to penetrate Japanese markets until too late, when superior Japanese products were already driving them out of the market. In the early 1990s, joint ventures and competitive cross investment continued in SME sectors. In photolithography, U.S. and Japanese companies and the U.S. government-industry consortium, Sematech, experimented with new methods of acquiring one another's technologies.

Notes

1. This and the following paragraph draw heavily on MacKnight (1992b), p. 3.
2. *Moody's Industrial Manual* (1987).
3. "Merck Pushes Deeper into Japanese Market," *Chemical Week*, April 10, 1983.
4. "Weak Enough to Work Together," *The Economist*, August 13, 1983.
5. *Moody's Industrial Manual* (1989).
6. "Japanese Joint Ventures: Soft Pill to Swallow," *The Economist*, November 28, 1991.
7. *Japan Economic Almanac* (1988), p. 162.
8. In this chapter, as in others, names of Japanese companies investing in manufacturing in the United States in the 1980s, names of their U.S. affiliates, and products are from MacKnight (1992a), unless otherwise indicated.
9. "Prescription for Drugmakers: More R&D," *Nikkei Weekly*, May 23, 1992.
10. Clausing, Allen, Berg, Dertouzos, Ferguson, Haavind, Moses, and Penfield (1989), pp. 39–40, describe the restructuring of Xerox.
11. "Japan Is Tough but Xerox Prevails," *New York Times*, September 3, 1992.
12. "Yamatake-Honeywell Is Going to Make Maritime Devices," *Japan Economic Journal*, January 1, 1974.
13. "Yamatake-Honeywell Obtains Large Orders," *Japan Economic Journal*, July 23, 1988.
14. "Supertek Finds Yokogawa's Outlook Irresistible," *Japan Economic Journal*, July 29, 1989.
15. "Honeywell Sells 16% of Yamatake," *New York Times*, October 26, 1989.
16. *Moody's Industrial Manual* (1987).
17. Young (1988), p. 315.
18. See n. 14.
19. "Gould Being Acquired by Nippon Mining," *New York Times*, August 31, 1988.
20. See n. 8.
21. "Nikko Kyodo Draws Flak for Decision to Dissolve Gould," *Nikkei*

Weekly, September 13, 1993; "Gould Parent Breaks Out T and M Unit," *Electronic News*, September 13, 1993.

22. This and the following paragraph draw heavily on Scherer (1992), pp. 78–86.

23. *Japan Economic Almanac* (1988), p. 123.

24. Ibid.

25. Scherer (1992), p. 85.

26. U.S. International Trade Commission (1991), pp. 4–7.

27. Ibid. Appendix E provides a useful description of SME products and the semiconductor manufacturing process.

28. U.S. Department of Commerce (1985), pp. 1–3, 1–9.

29. The structure of the U.S. and Japanese SME industries is described in U.S. Department of Commerce (1985a), pp. 40–47, and in U.S. International Trade Commission (1991), pp. 1-3–1-9.

30. U.S. International Trade Commission (1991), pp. E-3, E-4.

31. Ibid., p. E-4.

32. "Etching the Chips of the Future," *New York Times*, June 20, 1991.

33. U.S. Department of Commerce (1985b), p. 61, and U.S. International Trade Commission (1991), p. 4–14.

34. *Moody's Industrial Manual*, for relevant years, indicates that, from 1968 to 1982, Thermco was owned by Sunbeam Corporation, maker of household consumer durables. In 1982, Sunbeam was acquired by Allegheny International. The latter sold part of the Thermco operation to the Silicon Valley Group and part to BTU in 1988. The Thermco-TEL joint venture was terminated.

35. "KLA Plans Production in Japan," *Japan Economic Journal*, December 22, 1990.

36. U.S. International Trade Commission (1991), pp. 4–10 and p. 4-14.

37. Ibid, pp. 4–9 and 4–11.

38. *Moody's Industrial Manual* (1983, 1986).

39. *Moody's Industrial Manual* (1991).

40. "GCA Takes Its Last Step with 'Very Successful' Liquidation," *Electronic News*, December 13, 1993.

41. *Moody's Industrial Manual* (1991).

42. MacKnight (1991), pp. 5, 6.

43. "Etching the Chips of the Future," *New York Times*, June 20, 1990.

44. MacKnight (1991), p. 5.

45. "Canon, SVG Litho Know-How May Create Stir," *Electronic News*, May 10, 1993.

46. "Litho Question: To Be or Not to Be," *Electronic News*, May 17, 1993.

47. "Silicon Valley Group, Canon Calls off Partnership in Chipmaking Technology," *Wall Street Journal*, November 28, 1994.

48. MacKnight (1991), p. 8.

49. Ibid.

50. "Sematech Turns to Japan for Chip Insight," *Nikkei Weekly*, January 25, 1992.

51. See n. 48.

9

Conclusions

This book has traced the story of bilateral direct investments between the United States and Japan from the end of World War II through the early 1990s. It has focused on the dramatically changing contributions of those investments and related two-way technology flows to the growth of the two economies and to the convergence of their technologies. It has also considered the effect of these changes on the two countries' positions in the convergence of all industrial countries' technologies. Detailed analysis of bilateral investments and associated technology transfers has been limited to those in manufacturing and closely related service industries. These investments accounted for most bilateral technology transfers. They constituted about 60 percent of U.S. direct investments in Japan but only about 20 percent of Japan's direct investments in the United States.

The Changing Direct Investment Relationship

In the early postwar years, total direct investments flowing between the two countries were entirely one-way—from the United States to Japan. In Japan even more than elsewhere, U.S. direct investments were focused primarily on exploiting superior technology. Those investments were much smaller than U.S. direct investments elsewhere and they played a negligible role in financing Japan's modest current account deficit. The technology transfers associated with U.S. direct investments in Japan made a very large contribution to Japan's efforts to catch up with other industrial countries. Technologies transferred included some process technologies (such as new and more efficient methods of shipbuilding) and a flood of important product technologies for numerous industries, including computers, semiconductors, instruments, and pharmaceuticals—all high-technology industries.

In the mid-1970s the bilateral relationship began to change dramatically. And by the second half of the 1980s net direct investment flows from Japan to the United States were seventeen times as large as the flow from the United States to Japan. Further, net direct investment flows from Japan to the United States were financing a substantial portion of the very large U.S. current account deficit with the rest of the world. This deficit reflected a level of domestic savings insufficient to finance the investments of U.S. firms.

A change in financial incentives probably contributed to this dramatic reversal in bilateral direct investment flows. The dollar depreciated irregularly relative to the yen throughout the period, moving from strong overvaluation, in PPP terms in 1970, to undervaluation in the latter half of the 1980s and the early 1990s. Moreover, during much of the period, the real cost of capital to business borrowers in domestic markets and the related expected returns on business investment were significantly higher in the United States than in Japan and many other industrial countries. It is true that U.S. multinationals could and did finance much of their affiliates' operations in Japan by borrowing in Japan. Nevertheless, the higher expected returns on business investments in the United States encouraged liquidation of some U.S. investments in Japan and encouraged direct Japanese investment in the United States. The high proportion of finance-intensive industries in Japan's direct investments in the United States attests to the strength of financial influences.

At the same time technology flows associated with past and current direct investments between the two countries became vigorously two-way as Japanese firms developed their own technology strengths. These two-way transfers were generated by U.S. firms long established in Japan and those newly investing there, and by Japanese firms newly investing or previously established in the United States. Despite the disparity between the direct investment flows between the two countries in the 1980s and early 1990s, the presence of the manufacturing affiliates of U.S. firms in Japan (as measured by their share of the Japanese industry employment) in 1990 was slightly larger than the Japanese presence in U.S. manufacturing.

By 1990, companies based in both countries had significant positions in most of the other country's industries where technology transfers were important. But their relative strengths differed. In the high-technology industries, the U.S. position in Japan was stronger than Japan's in the United States in computers, pharmaceuticals, and instruments, while Japan's position in the United States was stronger in semiconductors and communications equipment. In other industries, Japan's position in the United States was stronger in steel and rubber tires; the U.S. position in Japan was stronger in oil refining and chemicals; and the two countries' positions were probably roughly equal in auto assembly and industrial machinery.

A Look at Technology Transfers

The technology transfers generated by both groups of firms included those made to exploit the investing firms' own superiority in that technology and those made to acquire needed technology. In the case of technology transfers made to exploit the investor's superior technology, that technology was further disseminated in the host country in three ways: (1) to host-country partners in the numerous joint ventures in both countries; (2) by the competitive challenge posed by demonstration effects, and (3) by efforts by the investing companies to establish their new technology as the industry standard in the host country. This last strategy was developed by IBM-Japan in the late 1980s and was later adopted by others.

The U.S. technology transferred to Japan by U.S. or Japanese investors was mainly new product technology, while the Japanese technology transferred to the United States was mainly process technology. Since process technology involves new methods of manufacturing new or existing products—at lower cost and of higher quality—the two technologies are clearly complementary.

The complementarity of the two countries' technology strengths has meant that many direct investments by U.S. or Japanese companies in one another's countries have generated two-way technology flows. Some investments, especially recent ones, were designed to generate technology exchanges. Examples are Motorola's joint venture with Toshiba in Japan to manufacture semiconductors, or Advanced Micro Devices' joint venture with Fujitsu to manufacture flash chips in Japan using Fujitsu's manufacturing skills and product technology generated in AMD. Fujitsu's early investment in Amdahl to acquire computer technology may also have conveyed some of Fujitsu's process technology to Amdahl.

But often a two-way flow of complementary technologies has proved to be a longer-term consequence of an investment initially made with simpler objectives. In the case of U.S. investments in Japan, most were initially made to exploit superior product technology. But those affiliates of U.S. companies that prospered in Japan generally absorbed Japanese process technology as they competed in the Japanese market place. These process technologies were ultimately transferred to the parent company in the United States. Outstanding examples are investments in Japan by IBM in computers, Texas Instruments in semiconductors, Hewlett-Packard in measuring and control instruments, and Varian in semiconductor manufacturing equipment.

There are fewer instances of long-term backflow of complementary technology in Japan's investments in the United States. This is at least partly because most of those investments have only recently been made. However, there are some signs that early Japanese investments in manufacturing communications equipment in the United States may be having that effect. Those early investments exploited skills in manufacturing products previously developed by others, notably PBX equipment. In the late 1980s and early 1990s, multimedia communications and supporting communications equipment were developing much faster in the United States than in Japan. Japanese companies used their position manufacturing simpler sorts of communication equipment in the United States as observation posts. By close observation they were able to discern the new product technologies most likely to be in demand and devote their R&D efforts to them. In the case of one new product essential to multimedia communications, asynchronous transfer mode (ATM) switches, they seem to have succeeded in bringing them to market at roughly the same time as their U.S. competitors.

In general, however, Japanese companies seem to have found it quite difficult to acquire the basic expertise needed to develop new product technology. By contrast, many U.S. companies appear to have succeeded in absorbing the basic principles underlying Japanese process technology, applicable to a wide range of industries. Possibly this is because these basic ideas originated in the United States, but were neglected there until they were revived by the challenge of Japanese competition. However, U.S. companies' applications of the basic quality control principles have not yet been as extensive and widespread as those of Japanese companies.

Bilateral Investment and Converging Technologies

Both bilateral direct investments and associated technology flows had important consequences for convergence of industrial country technologies and the relative positions of the United States and Japan. Recent estimates of manufacturing technology levels in industrial countries suggest that most of the convergence between them occurred in the early postwar period and tapered off to minor proportions sometime in the 1970s. But some of them also suggest that Japan continued to improve its ranking in the 1980s. Clearly, the improvement of Japan's relative technology ranking throughout the postwar period owes much to the product technology transfers to Japan that were associated with the two countries' bilateral direct investments.

Further, the cessation or severe slowing of convergence of

industrial countries' manufacturing technologies in the 1980s implies a faster rate of U.S. technology growth relative to that in other industrial countries than was evident in the earlier postwar period. Japanese direct investment contributed to this faster growth by adding to the pool of capital required to finance ongoing R&D by U.S. companies developing new product technology when domestic savings in the United States proved inadequate. In addition, U.S. and Japanese direct investments generated a flow of badly needed process technology from Japan to the United States, thus accelerating the growth of U.S. technology.

Changing Government Policies

The policies of the United States and Japanese governments toward direct investments and technology flowing between their two countries changed considerably during the postwar period. These changes reflect changes in the two countries' perceptions of their financial and technology strengths relative to one another. In the early postwar years, the Japanese felt threatened by U.S. multinationals, especially those based in the United States. Taking a defensive stance, the Japanese authorities limited foreign investment to the minimum required to obtain foreign technology not available on any other terms. They also did their best to prevent majority foreign ownership of any Japanese company. In this respect they failed in two important cases, IBM and Texas Instruments, whose technology was of crucial importance. As Japan prospered and became more competitive with the United States and other industrial countries, most early restrictions on direct investment per se were gradually eliminated, although some barriers in domestic markets remain.

By the late 1980s, it was the United States' turn to feel threatened. U.S. policies, previously laissez-faire, turned increasingly defensive at home and aggressive in Japan. The Exon-Florio Amendment of 1988 was enacted to prevent foreigners' acquisition of U.S. companies whose technologies were determined to be of strategic importance to the United States. This deterred several Japanese acquisitions of U.S. companies in high-technology industries. U.S. efforts to force open Japanese markets were focused on sales of goods produced by U.S.-based companies, imported into or produced in Japan, rather than on direct investment itself. Nevertheless, the Japanese government's reluctant agreement to actively promote increases in the foreign share of the Japanese market for semiconductors tended to make U.S. joint venture investments in Japan especially welcome.

In the early 1990s, as the complementarity of U.S. product technology and Japanese process technology became more widely recognized in the United States, U.S. government policies began to assume a somewhat less confrontational stance. New attitudes were most evident in Sematech, the government-business consortium organized in the late 1980s to help the U.S. semiconductor industry to overtake Japanese competition. In its early days, it had discouraged Japanese companies' interest in joining the consortium for fear that they might gain U.S. technology in semiconductor manufacturing equipment. But in the early 1990s Sematech sought advice from a group of Japanese experts in semiconductor manufacturing processes. It also supported the sale of new product technology to Canon by SVGL, a financially pressed U.S. company seeking to perfect and promote an important innovation in chip making. The success of the new Sematech policies could well influence the future course of government policies regarding direct investments and technology transfers in other industries as well.

Bibliography

Allen, G. C. 1958. *Japan's Economic Recovery*, Oxford: Oxford University Press.

Anchordoguy, Marie. 1988. "Mastering the Market: Japanese Targeting of the Computer Industry." *International Organization* (Summer).

Arrison, Thomas S.; Bergsten, C. Fred; Graham, Edward M.; and Harris, Martha Caldwell, eds. 1992. *Japan's Growing Technology Capability*. Washington, DC: National Academy Press.

Barnett, Donald F., and Crandall, Robert W. 1986. *Up from the Ashes: The Rise of the Steel Minimill in the United States*. Washington, DC: Brookings Institution.

Baumol, W. J. 1986. "Productivity, Growth, Convergence, and Welfare." *American Economic Review* (December).

Blumenthal, Tuvia. 1976. "The Japanese Shipbuilding Industry." In Patrick (1976).

Borrus, Michael; Millstein, James E.; and Zysman, John. 1983. "Trade and Development in the Semiconductor Industry." In Zysman and Tyson (1983).

Cantwell, John. 1989. *Technological Innovation and Multinational Corporations*. Cambridge, MA: Basil Blackwell.

Caves, Richard E. 1982. *Multinational Enterprise and Economic Analysis*. Cambridge: Cambridge University Press.

Caves, Richard E., with Uekusa, Masu. 1976. "Industrial Organization." In Patrick and Rosovsky (1976).

Chang, C. S. 1981. *The Japanese Auto Industry and the U.S. Market*. Praeger.

Choy, John. 1991. "Research and Development in Japan, 1991 Update." *JEI Report*, No. 36A (September 27).

———. 1993a. "An Update on Research and Development: The Party Is Over." *JEI Report*, No. 38A (October 15).

———. 1993b. "Foreign Direct Investment Down in Japan." *JEI Report*, No. 27B (July 23).

———. 1994. "Corporate Restructuring Hits Japanese Research Spending." *JEI Report*, No. 33A.

Christelow, Dorothy B. 1980. "National Policies toward Foreign Direct Investment." *Federal Reserve Bank of New York Quarterly Review* (Winter).

241

————. 1985–86. "Japan's Intangible Barriers to Trade in Manufactures." *Federal Reserve Bank of New York Quarterly Review* (Winter).

Clausing, Don P.; Allen, Jonathan; Berg, John A.; Dertouzos, Michael; Ferguson, Charles H.; Haavind, Robert; Moses, Joel; and Penfield, Paul L., Jr. 1989. "The U.S. Semiconductor, Computer, and Copier Industries." In MIT Commission on Industrial Productivity (1989).

Cusumano, Michael A. 1985. *The Japanese Automobile Industry: Technology and Management at Nissan and Toyota.* Cambridge, MA: Council on East Asian Studies, Harvard University, and Harvard University Press.

Dalton, Donald H. 1992. *JEI Database* (diskette) (based on MacKnight [1992] but including some revisions to include other information).

Dalton, Donald H., and Yoshida, Phyllis Genther. 1992. "Japanese Direct Investment in U.S. Manufacturing." In Negandhi and Serapio (1992).

Denison, Edward F. 1962. *The Sources of Economic Growth in the United States and the Alternatives Before Us.* CED Supplementary Paper 13. Committee for Economic Development.

————. 1967. *Why Growth Rates Differ: Postwar Experience in Nine Western Countries.* Washington, DC: Brookings Institution.

Denison, Edward F., and Chung, William K. 1976. "Economic Growth and Its Sources." In Patrick and Rosovsky (1976).

Dollar, David, and Wolff, Edward N. 1993. *Competitiveness, Convergence, and International Specialization.* Cambridge, MA: MIT Press.

Fabricant, Solomon. 1954. *Economic Progress and Economic Change.* New York: National Bureau of Economic Research.

Faulhaber, Gerald R. 1987. *Telecommunications in Turmoil. Technology and Public Policy.* Cambridge, MA: Ballinger.

Fikré, Ted. 1990–91. "Equity Carve-outs in Tokyo." *Federal Reserve Bank of New York Quarterly Review* (Fall–Winter).

Flemings, Merton; Clark, Joel; Cohen, Morris; Eager, Thomas; Elliott, John; Gutowski, Timothy; Thurow, Lester; and Tuller, Harry. 1989. "The Future of the U.S. Steel Industry in the International Market Place." *Working Papers of the MIT Commission on Industrial Productivity.* Vol. 2.

Froot, Kenneth A., and Stein, Jeremy. 1991. "Exchange Rates and Foreign Direct Investment: An Imperfect Capital Markets Approach." *Quarterly Journal of Economics* (November), pp. 1191–1217.

Gilbert, Milton, and Kravis, Irving B. 1954. *An International Comparison of National Products and the Purchasing Power of Currencies.* Paris: OECD.

Graham, Edward M., and Krugman, Paul R. 1989. *Foreign Direct Investment in the United States.* Washington, DC: Institute for International Economics.

Griliches, Zvi. 1994. "Productivity, R&D, and the Data Constraint." *American Economic Review* (March).

Grossman, Gene M. 1994. "Endogenous Innovation in the Theory of Growth." *Journal of Economic Perspectives* (Winter), p. 23.

Grossman, Gene M., and Helpman, Elhanan. 1991. *Innovation and Growth in the Global Economy.* Cambridge MA: MIT Press.

Hadley, Eleanor M. 1970. *Antitrust in Japan*. Princeton, NJ: Princeton University Press.

Hyun, Jun Taik, and Whitmore, Katherine. 1989. *Japanese Direct Foreign Investment: Patterns and Implications for Developing Countries*. Washington, DC: World Bank.

International Monetary Fund (IMF). Database for balance of payments statistics. (On line at Federal Reserve Bank of New York, August 1994.)

Japan Economic Institute (JEI). 1993. "Statistical Profile: Japan's Economy and International Transactions of Japan and the United States in 1992." *JEI Report*, No. 34A.

Jorgenson, Dale W., and Kuroda, Masahiro. 1992. "Technology, Productivity, and Competitiveness of U.S. and Japanese Industries." In Arrison, Bergsten, Graham, and Harris (1992).

Krause, Lawrence, and Sekiguchi, Sueo. 1976. "Japan in the World Economy." In Patrick and Rosovsky (1976b).

Kravis, Irving B., and Lipsey, Robert E. 1989. "Technological Characteristics of Industries and the Competitiveness of the U.S. and its Multinational Firms." Working Paper No. 2933. Washington, DC: National Bureau of Economic Research.

Lockwood, William M. 1955. *The Economic Development of Japan: Growth and Structural Change, 1868–1938*. Oxford: Oxford University Press.

MacKnight, Susan B. 1981. *Japan's Expanding Presence in the United States: A Profile*. Washington, DC: Japan Economic Institute.

————. 1990. "U.S. Access to Japan's Semiconductor Market." *JEI Report*, No. 44A (November 16).

————. 1991. "U.S.-Japan Competition in Semiconductor Manufacturing Equipment." *JEI Report*, No. 21A (June 7).

————. 1992a. *Japan's Expanding Manufacturing Presence: 1990 Update*. Washington, DC: JEI.

————. 1992b. "U.S.-Japan Competition in Pharmaceuticals: No Contest?" *JEI Report*, No. 13A (April 3).

————. 1992c. "Politics Complicate MITI's Car Quota Decision." *JEI Report*, No. 5B (February 7).

————. 1993. "Car and Truck Production in the United States and Canada, 1985–1992." (Table.) *JEI Report*, No. 15A (April 23).

————. 1994. "Struggling Japanese Car Makers Finally Get Some Good News." *JEI Report*, No. 16B (April 22).

March, Artemis. 1989. "The U.S. Machine Tool Industry and Its Foreign Competitors." In MIT Commision on Industrial Productivity (1989). Vol. 2.

Mason, Mark. 1992. *American Multinationals and Japan. The Political Economy of Japanese Capital Controls*. Cambridge, MA: Council on East Asian Studies, Harvard University, and Harvard University Press.

McCauley, Robert N., and Zimmer, Stephen A. 1989. "Explaining International Differences in the Costs of Capital." *Federal Reserve Bank of New York Quarterly Review* (Summer).

———— 1992. "Exchange Rates and International Differences in the Cost of

Capital." Paper presented at the Conference on Exchange Rate Effects on Corporate Financial Performance and Strategies, New York University Solomon Center, Leonard N. Stern School of Business (May 1).

McManus, George J. 1993. "The Direct Approach to Making Iron." *Iron Age* (July), pp. 20–24.

Massachusetts Institute of Technology (MIT) Commission on Industrial Productivity. 1989. *The Working Papers of the MIT Commission on Industrial Productivity.* Cambridge, MA: MIT Press. 2 vols.

Nanto, Dick K. 1990. "Japan's Industrial Groups, the Keiretsu." In U.S. Congress (1990).

National Science Foundation. 1988. *Science and Technology Resources of Japan: A Comparison with the United States* (NSF 88–318). Washington, DC: National Science Foundation.

Negandhi, Anant R., and Serapio, Manuel G., JR. 1992. *Research in International Business and International Relations: Vol. 5. Japanese Direct Investment in the United States: Trends, Developments, and Issues.* Greenwich, CT: JAI Press.

Office of Management and Budget. 1988. *Standard Industrial Classification Manual, 1987.* Washington, DC: Office of Management and Budget.

Ohkawa, Kazushi, and Rosovsky, Henry. 1973. *Japanese Economic Growth: Trend Acceleration in the Twentieth Century.* Stanford, CA: Stanford University Press.

Organization for Economic Cooperation and Development (OECD). 1986. "R&D, Invention, and Competitiveness." *OECD Science and Technology Indicators*, No. 2. Paris: OECD.

————. 1994. *OECD Economic Outlook* (June).

Pack, Howard. 1994. "Endogenous Growth Theory: Intellectual Appeal and Empirical Shortcomings." *Journal of Economic Perspectives* (Winter).

Patrick, Hugh, ed. 1976. *Japanese Industrialization and Its Social Consequences.* Berkeley and Los Angeles: University of California Press.

Patrick, Hugh, and Rosovsky, Henry. 1976a. "Japan's Economic Performance: An Overview." In Patrick and Rosovsky (1976b).

————, eds. 1976b. *Asia's New Giant: How the Japanese Economy Works.* Washington, DC: Brookings Institution.

Petroleum Industry Law. Japan. 1962 (Summary and explanatory notes in English. Full text in Japanese.) Tokyo: K. K. Central Tsushin Sha.

Poterba, James M. 1991. "Comparing the Cost of Capital in the United States and Japan: A Survey of Methods." *Federal Reserve Bank of New York Quarterly Review* (Winter), pp. 20–32.

Reich, Robert B., and Mankin, Erich D. 1986. "Joint Ventures with Japan Give Away Our Future." *Harvard Business Review* (March–April).

Romer, Paul M. 1994. "The Origins of Endogenous Growth." *Journal of Economic Perspectives* (Winter), pp. 3–22.

Scherer, F. M. 1992. *International High Technology Competition.* Cambridge, MA: Harvard University Press.

Shields, Jerry. 1986. *The Invisible Billionaire.* Boston, MA: Houghton Mifflin.

Smitka, Michael J. 1991. *Competitive Ties: Subcontracting in the Japanese Automotive Industry*. Studies of the East Asian Institute, Columbia University. New York: Columbia University Press.

Solow, Robert M. 1956. "Perspectives on Growth Theory." *Journal of Economic Perspectives* (Winter), pp. 45–54.

Staelin, David H.; Bozdogan, Kirkor; Cusumano, Michael A.; Ferguson, Charles H.; Filippone, Stephen F.; Reintjes, J. Francis; Rosenbloom, Richard S.; Solow, Robert M.; and Ward, John E. 1989. "The Decline of U.S. Consumer Electronics Manufacturing: History, Hypothesis, and Remedies." In MIT Commission on Industrial Productivity (1989), Vol. 1.

Stevens, Candice. 1992. *Globalization of Industrial Activities: Four Case Studies. Auto Parts, Chemicals, Construction, and Semiconductors*. Paris: OECD.

Teece, David T. 1976. *The Multinational Corporation and the Resource Cost of Technology Transfer*. Cambridge, MA: Ballinger.

Tilton, John E. 1971. *International Diffusion of Technology: The Case of Semiconductors*. Washington, DC: Brookings Institution.

Toa Nenryo Kogyo. 1964. *25 Years of Tonen*. Tokyo: Tonen.

Tsurumi, Y. 1976. *The Japanese Are Coming: A Multinational Spread of Japanese Firms*. Cambridge, MA: Ballinger.

U.S. Congress. 1990. Joint Economic Committee. *Japan's Economic Challenge*. Study papers submitted to the Joint Economic Committee. Washington, DC: U.S. Government Printing Office.

U.S. Department of Commerce. 1960. Bureau of Economic Analysis. *U.S. Business Investment in Foreign Countries*. Washington, DC: U.S. Government Printing Office.

————. 1975. Bureau of Economic Analysis. *U.S. Direct Investment Abroad, 1966: Final Data*. Washington, DC: U.S. Government Printing Office.

————. 1981a. Bureau of Economic Analysis. *Selected Data on U.S. Direct Investment Abroad, 1950–1976*. Washington, DC: U.S. Government Printing Office.

————. 1981b. Bureau of Economic Analysis. *U.S. Direct Investment Abroad, 1977*. Washington, DC: U.S. Government Printing Office.

————. 1982. Bureau of the Census. *Annual Survey of Manufactures: Industry Statistics*. Washington, DC: U.S. Government Printing Office.

————. 1983. Bureau of Economic Analysis. *Foreign Direct Investment in the United States, 1980*. Washington, DC: U.S. Government Printing Office.

————. 1984. International Trade Administration. *International Direct Investment. Global Trends and U.S. Role*. Washington, DC: U.S. Government Printing Office.

————. 1985a. Bureau of Economic Analysis. *U.S. Direct Investment Abroad, 1982: Benchmark Survey Data*. Washington, DC: U.S. Government Printing Office.

————. 1985b. International Trade Administration. *A Competitive Assessment of the U.S. Construction Machinery Industry*. Washington, DC: U.S. Government Printing Office.

————. 1985c. International Trade Administration, Office of Microelectronics and Instrumentation. *A Competitive Assessment of the U.S. Semiconductor Manufacturing Industry.* NTIA Special Publication No. 91–267. Washington, DC: U.S. Government Printing Office.

————. 1986a. Bureau of Economic Analysis. *U.S. Direct Investment Abroad. Balance of Payments and Direct Investment Position Estimates. 1977–81.* Washington, DC: U.S. Government Printing Office.

_____. 1986b. Office of Telecommunications. *A Competitive Assessment of the U.S. Digital Central Office Switch Industry.* Washington, DC: U.S. Government Printing Office.

_____. 1990. International Trade Administration and National Telecommunications and Information Administration. *U.S. Telecommunications in a Global Economy: Competitiveness at a Crossroads.* Washington, DC: U.S. Government Printing Office. Mimeo.

————. 1991a, 1992a, 1993a. Bureau of Economic Analysis. *Foreign Direct Investment in the United States. Operations of U.S. Affiliates of Foreign Companies, Revised 1988 Estimates.* Same for 1989 and 1990. Washington, DC: U.S. Government Printing Office.

_____. 1991b. National Telecommunications and Information Administration. *The NTIA Infrastructure Report: Telecommunications in the Age of Information.* Washington, DC: U.S. Government Printing Office. Mimeo.

————. 1992b. Bureau of Economic Analysis and Bureau of the Census. *Foreign Direct Investment in the United States: Establishment Data for 1987.* Washington, DC: U.S. Government Printing Office.

_____. 1993b. Bureau of Economic Analysis. *U.S. Direct Investment Abroad: Operations of U.S. Parent Companies and Their Foreign Affiliates. Revised 1990 Estimates.* Washington, DC: U.S. Government Printing Office.

_____. 1993c. Bureau of Economic Analysis and Bureau of the Census. *Foreign Direct Investment in the United States: Establishment Data for Manufacturing, 1990.* Washington, DC: U.S. Government Printing Office.

————. 1993d. Bureau of Economic Analysis. *Foreign Direct Investment in the United States. Operations of U.S. Affiliates of Foreign Companies. Preliminary 1991 Estimates.* Washington, DC: U.S. Government Printing Office.

U.S. International Trade Commission (USITC). 1991a. *Global Competitiveness of U.S. Advanced-Technology Manufacturing Industries: Communications Technology and Equipment.* Report to the Committee on Finance, United States Senate. Washington, DC: U.S. Government Printing Office.

————. 1991b. *Global Competitiveness of U.S. Advanced-Technology Manufacturing Industries: Semiconductor Manufacturing Equipment.* USITC Publication No. 2434. Washington, DC: U.S. Government Printing Office.

van Ark, Bart, and Pilat, Dirk. 1993. "Productivity Levels in Germany, Japan, and the United States: Differences and Causes." *Brookings Papers on Economic Activity. Microeconomics*, 2. Washington, DC: Brookings Institution, pp. 1–69.

Vernon, Raymond. 1966. "International Investment and International Trade in the Product Cycle." *Quarterly Journal of Economics* (May), pp. 190–207.

Weiss, Stephen E. 1987. "The Formation of Corporate Linkages—Negotiation Processes." *Columbia Journal of World Business* (Summer).

Wilkins, Mira. 1974. *American Business Abroad from 1914 to 1970.* Cambridge, MA: Harvard University Press.

Wolff, Edward N. 1991. "Capital Formation and Productivity Convergence Over the Long Term." *American Economic Review* (June).

Womack, James P. 1989. "The U.S. Automobile Industry in an Era of International Competition: Performance and Prospects." In MIT (1989).

Womack, James P.; Jones, Daniel T.; and Roos, Daniel. 1990. *The Machine that Changed the World.* Rawson Associates (Macmillan). Paperback edition, Harper Perennial, New York (1991).

Yashiro, Masamoto. 1984. "Government and Business in Japan: Exxon's Experiences." *Business Luncheon Notes.* Japan Society, New York, March 16.

Young, John A. 1988. "Technology and Competitiveness: A Key to the Economic Future of the United States." *Science,* Vol. 241, pp. 313–316.

Zysman, John, and Tyson, Laura, eds. 1983. *American Industry in International Competition.* Ithaca, NY: Cornell University Press.

Annuals, Periodicals, and Newspapers

American Machinist
Automotive News
Business Japan
Business Week
Chemical Week
Consumer Reports (CR)
Datamation
The Economist
Electronic News
Forbes
Iron Age
JEI Report
Japan Economic Almanac
Japan Economic Journal
Manufacturing Week
Monthly Finance Review (Japan)
New York Times
Nikkei Weekly
Survey of Current Business
Wall Street Journal
Ward's Auto World
Ward's Automotive Yearbook.

Statistical Reference Books

AMT. The Association for Manufacturing Technology. *The Economic Handbook of the Machine Tool Industry*. (Annual.)

Bank of Japan. *Balance of Payments Monthly*. (Appendices in June issues, 1965–90 and April issues, 1991–94.) Tokyo.

International Monetary Fund (IMF). *Balance of Payments Statistics Yearbook*.

————. *International Financial Statistics Yearbook*.

Ministry of Finance (Japan). Institute of Fiscal and Monetary Policy. *Financial Statistics of Japan*.

————. *Monthly Finance Review*. Appendix in June issues.

Moody's Industrial Manual (annual).

Organization for Economic Cooperation and Development (OECD). *Foreign Trade by Commodities*. Series C (annual).

————. *Industrial Structure Statistics* (annual).

————. *Main Science and Technology Indicators* (quarterly)

————. *National Accounts, Volume I: Main Aggregates* (annual).

Prime Minister's Office, Statistics Bureau. *Japan Statistical Yearbook*.

U.S. Department of Commerce, Bureau of the Census, *Annual Survey of Manufactures*.

————. Bureau of the Census. *Census of Manufactures*. (Quinquennial).

————. Bureau of Economic Analysis. *Business Statistics. 1963–91*.

Index

About the Author

Dorothy Christelow is a former research economist with the Federal Reserve Bank of New York. She is now retired but continues to write on international trade and finance.